UNDOCUMENTED FEARS

JAMIE LONGAZEL

UNDOCUMENTED FEARS

Immigration and the Politics of Divide and Conquer in Hazleton, Pennsylvania

TEMPLE UNIVERSITY PRESS
Philadelphia • *Rome* • *Tokyo*

TEMPLE UNIVERSITY PRESS
Philadelphia, Pennsylvania 19122
www.temple.edu/tempress

Library of Congress Cataloging-in-Publication Data

Names: Longazel, Jamie.
Title: Undocumented fears : immigration and the politics of divide and
conquer in Hazleton, Pennsylvania / Jamie Longazel.
Description: Philadelphia : Temple University Press, 2016. | Includes
bibliographical references and index.
Identifiers: LCCN 2015019049 | ISBN 9781439912676 (cloth : alkaline paper) |
ISBN 9781439912683 (paper : alkaline paper) | ISBN 9781439912690 (e-book)
Subjects: LCSH: Latin Americans—Pennsylvania—Hazleton—Social conditions—
21st century. | Immigrants—Pennsylvania—Hazleton—Social conditions—21st
century. | Illegal aliens—Pennsylvania—Hazleton—Social conditions—21st
century. | Hazleton (Pa.). Illegal Immigration Relief Act. | Illegal aliens—Legal
status, laws, etc.—Pennsylvania—Hazleton—History—21st century. | Language
policy—Pennsylvania—Hazleton—History—21st century. | Ethnic conflict—
Pennsylvania—Hazleton—History—21st century. | Hazleton (Pa.)—Ethnic
relations—History—21st century. | Hazleton (Pa.)—Politics and government—
21st century. | Hazleton (Pa.)—Emigration and immigration—Political
aspects—History—21st century. | BISAC: SOCIAL SCIENCE / Emigration &
Immigration. | POLITICAL SCIENCE / Public Policy / General. | SOCIAL
SCIENCE / Ethnic Studies / Hispanic American Studies.
Classification: LCC F159.H45 L66 2016 | DDC 305.8009748/32—dc23
LC record available at http://lccn.loc.gov/2015019049

Printed in the United States of America

9 8 7 6 5 4 3 2

For Becky and Conrad

And for the people of Hazleton

Contents

Author's Comment on the Notes Section

This book has a somewhat unconventional balance between the text and the notes. The chapters are relatively short; the Notes section is extensive. I intentionally employed this structure to maximize accessibility to a wide range of audiences. Cognizant that readers' interests and familiarity with topics and ideas are likely to vary, for example, I detail some basic ideas and theoretical nuances throughout the notes. Following conventions used in history and legal scholarship, the notes also contain evidence pulled from many sources to bolster my arguments, contribute to the historical record, and help readers with a particular focus on this case.

In short, there is more than one way to read this book. Readers can grasp the full story by using the notes on an as-needed basis, while those who seek deeper exploration of theory, evaluation of local data, or a primer on related issues will find the notes to be a valuable steady companion to the text.

Preface

This book is about the politics surrounding the passage of the Illegal Immigration Relief Act (IIRA) in Hazleton, Pennsylvania, a local ordinance that set penalties for renting to or hiring undocumented immigrants and declared English the city's official language. (See Appendix B for the full text of the ordinance.) I decided to write this book in part because of the IIRA's national prominence. When it passed in 2006, the controversial ordinance put this northeastern Pennsylvania city, located some two thousand miles from the U.S.-Mexican border, at the epicenter of the immigration debate in the United States. The national media swarmed:[1] Several major television networks and print outlets ran in-depth pieces on the IIRA, including one by CNN's Lou Dobbs, who broadcast a special segment of *Lou Dobbs Tonight* titled "Broken Borders" live from Hazleton. It was there that he tellingly declared, "Hazleton, the community, is leading the battle against illegal immigration."[2]

The media frenzy captures only a small piece of the IIRA's notoriety. Hazleton was also instrumental in helping to kick off a parade of similar measures. After the IIRA, as the immigration scholar Monica Varsanyi put it, what was a "trickle of state and local immigration policy activism soon turned into a flood."[3] Although there had been prior subnational attempts to regulate immigration—notably, California's 1994 ballot initiative, Proposition 187[4]—Hazleton's legislative action came while the immigration debate was hot. That year, Congress had tried and failed to pass comprehensive immigration reform, vigilante groups had staked out the U.S.-Mexican border, and hundreds of thousands of immigrants and their allies rallied in cities across the country.[5] All of these events took place amid changing immigration patterns. Across the United States in recent decades, economic factors have pushed many immigrants, mostly from Latin America, away from traditional "gateway" destinations and into small, interior cities and towns.[6] "New faces in new places,"[7] the absence of federal legislation, and strong swirling sentiments thus set off a perfect storm in which Hazleton wound up squarely in the middle. After Hazleton took action, many other cities and towns across the United States followed its lead by passing similar measures. Some even copied the IIRA's language verbatim. More than one hundred cities and counties and several states—including Arizona, which issued the highly controversial SB 1070 in 2010—have since passed or considered immigration-related measures.[8]

By looking closely at how the local debate unfolded in the city that set off the broader trend, this book contributes to an understanding of U.S. immigration politics in this tumultuous first decade and a half of the twenty-first century. Indeed, the politics surrounding the Hazleton case have much in common with national (and to a considerable extent, international) debates with respect not only to immigration but also to issues of race, social class, and law more generally. At the same time, a "thick description" of the local-level politics in Hazleton is useful in its own right.[9] As the sociologist Gary Alan Fine puts it, because "the local is a stage on which social order gets produced," it offers us "a lens for understanding how particular forms of action are selected."[10] The following in-depth, on-the-ground account of familiar politics playing out in a small interior city, in short, not only has broader implications but also offers a glimpse of how uniquely local considerations shape the trajectory of the immigration debate.

This project also holds personal meaning for me. Hazleton is where I was born and raised. I spent my childhood roaming the scarred landscape of this former coal mining town. Although I have since moved away, Hazleton remains the place I call home, and I continue to be deeply committed to its betterment.

This connection has undeniably shaped my approach to this book. I have always been fascinated by the history of my hometown, particularly the experience of the European immigrants who arrived in the late nineteenth century seeking work in the region's anthracite coal mines. Many of these early immigrants confronted a combination of ruthless exploitation and virulent ethnic animosity—the latter enabling the former, as mine bosses notoriously pitted ethnic groups against one another to quell labor strife (see the Conclusion). Contrary to the platitude that today's situation is entirely distinct,[11] fueled by myths that "our" ancestors "followed the proper procedures,"[12] worked harder, and were more committed to learning English, the more I learned about Hazleton's present, the more I realized we were in many respects reliving our past.

As a result, what follows differs from much of the current commentary on immigration. I do not provide a policy analysis, and my focus does not concern jurisdiction or how we can best "deal with" undocumented immigration. From my perspective, the more pressing issue at the root of this debate is how dominant ideologies relating to race and social class embedded in immigration politics continue to divide and conquer ordinary people today. Instead of advocating a particular "top-down technocratic policy [solution],"[13] my approach thus aligns with what the sociologists Joe Feagin and Hernán Vera refer to as *liberation sociology*, "concerned with alleviating or eliminating various social oppressions and with creating societies that are more just and egalitarian."[14]

This perspective, Feagin and Vera note, "not only seeks sound scientific knowledge but often takes sides with, and takes the outlook of, the oppressed and envisions an end to that oppression."[15] Although some may question the validity of such an approach, it is important to acknowledge that *all* social science research chooses its topic of inquiry with a "*subjective* choice . . . not made in social isolation but according to personal and collective tastes."[16] In my case, I have chosen to use established methodological standards to study how dominant ideologies re-create inequalities in a region that I know and love. (For more on this study's data and methods, see Appendix A.) Although research that caters to the status quo is more likely to claim impartiality than not, Feagin and Vera emphasize that it is just as politicized as research that challenges it.[17]

I make this point to disclose my politics at the onset; however, this idea also foreshadows one of the book's key arguments: Those at the top of economic and racial hierarchies often mask their own assertions of power while vilifying those who seek to subvert that power. The result is a blurring of society's actual structure (see Chapter 1),[18] a misattribution of existing social problems (see Chapter 2), and, in many cases, a dismissal of human suffering (see Chapter 3). I therefore expect some to be hesitant about or even resistant to an approach that is deliberate and straightforward in its mission to challenge the status quo. However, I would remind those who feel such hesitance that, although it may run counter to what we often hear, I take this approach because I have the best interests of poor and dispossessed people of all colors in mind.

I get inspiration in this regard from people like the author and activist Parker Palmer. Speaking about patriotism, Palmer notes that if you allow voids within yourself to be filled by an uncritical embrace of the way things are, "then you can't do what a true patriot needs to do, which is to have a *lover's quarrel* with your own country . . . something [you] love too much to let it sink to its lowest life form."[19] For me, asking difficult questions about my city rather than simply accepting its "essential goodness"[20] has inspired an even greater appreciation for it, a better understanding of it, and a desire to think about social action and democratic participation much more than I did when the project began. Although most readers will, of course, identify less strongly than I do with the case at hand, I hope they will find in what follows the opportunity to draw parallels to other contexts and experiences. In other words, the ultimate goal of this book is to contribute to the broader project of offering new ways to see the familiar—an opportunity to interrupt "business as usual," as the social justice educators Rita Hardiman and Bailey Jackson put it, by "[calling] into question the truth of what we have learned about the power relationships among different social groups and our own position vis-à-vis these dynamics."[21]

Acknowledgments

This project has traveled with me for nearly a decade, and I have received much help along the way (though I alone am responsible for any errors). It began as a doctoral dissertation in the Department of Sociology and Criminal Justice at the University of Delaware, and I am grateful for all the support I received there. Most notably, I owe a huge debt of gratitude to my mentor and friend Ben Fleury-Steiner. He was instrumental in helping to get this project off the ground, and he has continued to offer support with his characteristic selflessness, brilliance, and passion. Without years of Ben's advice and thorough critical feedback on countless drafts, this book would not have come to fruition. Yet what will stick with me the most are the valuable life lessons he has taught me along the way.

In 2009, I received the Law and Social Science Dissertation Fellowship, generously co-sponsored by the American Bar Foundation (ABF), the Law and Society Association (LSA), and the National Science Foundation (NSF Grant No. 0 719 602). I am most grateful to these organizations for giving me this opportunity. The fellowship allowed me to work exclusively on this project for two years, in residency at the ABF in Chicago. I could not imagine a more stimulating place to research and write. I owe a thank-you to the entire intellectual community of the ABF, for it is there that the project really began to take shape. I offer special thanks to Jordan Gans-Morse, Terry Halliday, Bonnie Honig, Bob Nelson, Laura Beth Nielsen, Shaun Ossei-Owusu, Susan Shapiro, Rashmee Singh, and Kim Welch for mentoring, supporting, and sharing ideas with me during those years.

The project wrapped up while I was an assistant professor at my current institution, the University of Dayton. It has been a pleasure to work in an environment that embraces scholarship with a social justice orientation. I owe many thanks to my colleagues in the Department of Sociology, Anthropology, and Social Work for their camaraderie. I particularly thank Simanti Dasgupta for reading a draft of the manuscript and offering insightful comments; Leslie Picca, our department chair, for her patience while the book occupied so much of my time; and Ruth Thompson-Miller for offering very helpful advice, ideas, and feedback on parts of the manuscript. I write these acknowledgments in fond remembrance of our colleague Linda Majka. Thanks also to Paul Becker, Shawn Cassiman, Jenny Davis-Berman, Jeremy Forbis, Lance Gibbs, Jeanne Holcomb, Art Jipson, Laura Leming, Stephanie Litka, Theo Majka, Dan Miller, and, especially, Nancy Terrell, our administrative assistant, for all of the work that she does. My students deserve acknowledgment, as well, for the inspiration they continually offer. Special thanks go to Jake Berman, who did some transcribing for me, and to Bridget Shane, who helped put together the Bibliography.

I am also grateful to Joel Best and Kitty Calavita for their incredibly sharp advice on previous drafts and to Brian Chad Starks, a great friend who not only provided feedback on this project but also, more importantly, strategized with me so much over the years about navigating academia and creating social change. The Citizenship and Immigration Collaborative Research Network (CRN) of the LSA has also provided me with a supportive scholarly community for many years. Because of the CRN, I have had the great pleasure of working with such distinguished immigration scholars as Marie Provine, Maartje van der Woude, and Marjorie Zatz, each of whom also provided useful comments on a paper that was the basis for a chapter in this book.

I am grateful for the permissions granted to include previously published material in altered form herein. Some of the chapters in this book draw from the following articles: Jamie Longazel and Benjamin Fleury-Steiner, "Exploiting Borders: The Political Economy of Local Backlash against Undocumented Immigrants," *Chicana/o-Latina/o Law Review* 30

(2011): 43–64 (Chapter 1); Jamie Longazel, "Moral Panic as Racial Degradation Ceremony: Racial Stratification and the Local-Level Backlash against Latina/o Immigrants," *Punishment and Society* 15 (2013): 96–119, doi: 10.1177/1462474512466200 (Chapter 2); Jamie Longazel, "Rhetorical Barriers to Mobilizing for Immigrant Rights: White Innocence and Latina/o Abstraction," *Law and Social Inquiry* 39, no. 3 (2014): 580–600, copyright © 2014 American Bar Foundation (Chapters 3 and 4); and Jamie Longazel, "Subordinating Myth: Latino/a Immigration, Crime, and Exclusion," *Sociology Compass* 7, no. 2 (2013): 87–96, doi: 10.1111/soc4.12018. I am grateful to those who granted me permission to access various archival sources.

Temple University Press deserves a very big thank-you, as well. I am indebted to everyone there who had a hand in bringing this manuscript to publication. I especially thank my editor, Aaron Javsicas. He saw promise in this project, helped me stay on schedule while remaining patient when I veered off, and provided fantastic suggestions as I refined the manuscript down the stretch. Susan Deeks's meticulous copyediting improved the manuscript drastically, and for that I am extremely thankful. Susan Thomas's work on the index is likewise much appreciated. I also thank the two anonymous reviewers for their useful comments and suggestions.

To those who graciously agreed to participate in my research, devoting their time and telling their stories, I offer my utmost appreciation.

And last but far from least, I thank my family members. I am forever grateful for the goodwill and unending love I have always received from my mom and dad, Bernadine and Greg. Thanks also go to Josh, my brother and dear friend, for his companionship. And above all, I thank my closest friend and spouse, Becky, and our son, Conrad, who have been incredibly patient, compassionate, and loving throughout this voyage. I dedicate this book to them.

UNDOCUMENTED FEARS

Introduction

Immigration and the Politics of Divide and Conquer

"Nestled deep in the Pocono Mountains," began a segment of CBS's *60 Minutes*, "Hazleton, Pennsylvania, has the look and feel of an all-American town."[1] The first visual of the telecast is a glimpse of the city's landscape. The screen then switches to images of smiling high school cheerleaders wearing red-and-white uniforms, walking down the street waving their pom-poms in unison. The viewer can hear the drumbeat of a marching band. The narrator continues, "Most of the people who turned out for the town's annual end-of-summer parade are descendants of immigrants, including the mayor, Lou Barletta."

"The Barlettas came from Italy," the voice specifies, "and ended up with a street named after them." We then see the mayor sitting atop the backseat of an antique convertible that parades him down the road. He waves to his constituents, who are all cheering him on. "Good job mayor! Way to go!" shouts one of his fans.

The narrator then chimes in with the story's hook. "Now the mayor is making a name for himself by going after a different kind of immigrant." Above the still audible cheers from the crowd, you can hear another shout from a vocal onlooker: "Keep the illegals out!" The camera zooms in on the mayor, whose bright white shirt and red tie stand out against the empty maroon-painted brick storefront in the background. He smiles, nods, and waves again.

The scene then briefly shifts away from the parade to show a snippet from an interview with Lou Barletta—"I'm going to eliminate illegal aliens from the city of Hazleton," he says—and just like that, we return to the jovial celebration. Now there is a tuba blaring, the crowd continues to cheer, and there is another picture of the mayor smiling and giving a thumbs-up.

That portion plays on for a few more seconds before the celebratory sounds abruptly go silent. The visual changes over to a close-up of a clear glass door, presumably to a small grocery store. Hanging from the door is an advertisement handwritten in black marker on white poster board: "PLATANO Verdes 8 x 1.00." Someone wearing a dark red flannel shirt and blue jeans opens the door and walks inside. We cannot see a face; we see only a rear view of the person, from shoulder to calf. Over this image the narrator explains in more detail what motivated Hazleton's passage of the Illegal Immigration Relief Act (IIRA): "Barletta believes what's been going on in Hazleton is a microcosm of what's been going on all over the country: that illegal immigrants are overwhelming his city, draining its resources, and ruining the quality of life."

The *Local* Latino Threat Narrative

This book has two primary aims. The first is to problematize how misconceptions about Latina/o immigrants coupled with nostalgic collective imaginings of "Small Town, America," contribute to the construction of a racialized community identity that embraces exclusionary immigration policy. The powerful juxtaposition in the *60 Minutes* telecast introduces this argument quite well. Celebratory music, imagery of cheerleaders and marching bands, allusions to tradition, and references to European immigrants who "made it" bolster the description of Hazleton as a place with the "look and feel of an all-American town." In sharp contrast, the broadcast speaks only briefly of a "different kind of immigrant"[2] depicted as a shadowy—indeed, *faceless*[3]—figure that confronts unquestioned accusations of ruining what we are led to assume is an idyllic quality of life.[4]

The anthropologist Leo Chavez has examined the pervasive nature of such representations around Latina/o immigration, which coalesce into what he calls the Latino Threat Narrative. The taken-for-granted "truths" that this narrative comprises, he writes, are that "Latinos are not like previous immigrant groups, who ultimately became part of the nation."[5] "Rather, they are part of an invading force from south of the border that is bent on reconquering land that was formerly theirs (the U.S. Southwest) and destroying the American way of life."[6]

As locales across the United States take action against undocumented immigration,[7] we see an extension of this familiar script. Thousands of Latina/o migrants arrived in Hazleton in the years leading up to the IIRA, and, as we will see, the story of what led them there is quite complex (see Chapter 1) and their experience is rich. The *60 Minutes* report, along with other, similar descriptions, however, narrowly depicts an unlikely "hero" emerging to "stem the tide" as the so-called "problem" of undocumented immigration "seeps" into the interior and afflicts an "All-American town."[8] It will become even clearer as I trace the politics surrounding Hazleton's IIRA over several stages how tales of a harmonious small town in peril represent a local-level iteration of the nationalistic threat of reconquest that Chavez describes. Regardless of the geographic space it imparts to protect, the narrative remains characterized by strong assertions that "they" have arrived with the intent to harm "us."

Part of my objective is to show how race permeates this narrative. I use two concepts to accomplish this: *Latina/o degradation* and *White affirmation*.[9] By Latina/o degradation, I mean the subordination that accompanies the (often subtle, but nonetheless consequential) symbolic linking of negative traits to Latina/os. Although this debate begins as a backlash against so-called "illegal aliens," cloaked race-neutrally as a defense for the rule of law, it will become apparent that exclusionary rhetoric about legal status is often simply an entry point for a discussion about larger racialized fears. Indeed, there are examples throughout the book of how this narrative extends its reach to encompass Latinas/os who are not undocumented immigrants.[10] There are also examples of how it is used to vilify pro-immigrant activists who resist.[11] The narrative holds strong to the notion that traits such as criminality, fiscal burdensomeness, and a penchant for seeking "special privileges" *characterize* "outsiders," even though these assumptions are grossly inaccurate,[12] problematically narrow,[13] and drawn from a long history of racism and nativism.[14] Quoting Lisa Marie Cacho, rhetoric that appears throughout this debate therefore constructs the undocumented and others by racialized association as *"ineligible for personhood."*[15] What becomes taken-for-granted conventional wisdom is that "they" are *perpetu-*

ally incapable of following the law, *always* undeserving of public services, and *never* entitled to legal recourse. Put another way, Chavez explains how degradation amounts to *virtualization*. Epitomized by the facelessness of the figure in the *60 Minutes* report, "The virtual lives of 'Mexicans,' 'Chicanos,' 'illegal aliens,' and 'immigrants' become abstractions and representations that stand in the place of real lives. . . . They are no longer flesh-and-blood people; they exist as images."[16] It is in this context that it troublingly becomes acceptable to discuss "eliminating" a group of people.

By White affirmation, I refer to the parallel process—that is, (again, non-explicitly) associating positive characteristics with Whiteness while asserting whom in particular the alleged "immigrant invasion" has harmed. Importantly, White affirmation works *through* Latina/o degradation. Because "whiteness is a relational concept, unintelligible without reference to nonwhiteness,"[17] the defining of Latinas/os as inferior becomes a necessary step in the construction of White superiority.[18] Idyllic depictions of who "we" are—the cheerful parade, and so on—become more comprehensible when placed alongside assertions of who "we" *are not*.[19] Racialized binaries are apparent at each stage of Hazleton's immigration debate I explore: law-breakers and law abiders; fiscal drains and hardworking people; separatists and egalitarians; neighbors who are noisy, messy, and careless and neighbors who are quiet, kempt, and careful.[20]

Beyond reinforcing difference and belonging, these binaries amplify the perception of the Latino Threat by *specifying who is threatened*. Representations of "invaders," in other words, are used to construct the identity of the "invaded." Encapsulated in the notion of White affirmation is thus what Cacho has elsewhere referred to as the *ideology of white injury*.[21] Even though it is Latinas/os and other people of color who endure degradation and confront institutional barriers because of their race, in this narrative Whites are continually constructed as *victims* of undocumented immigrants' criminality, as *suffering* because of "their" burdensomeness, and as *treated unfairly* by "efforts to remedy racial discrimination."[22]

The Politics of Divide and Conquer

The second aim of this book is to highlight how this narrative contributes to the perpetuation of social inequality at the intersection of race and social class. My thesis here is that, on one hand, Latina/o degradation enhances the exploitability of immigrant laborers and imposes limits on meaningful resistance. On the other hand, White affirmation prompts an embrace of a White collective identity that not only degrades but also misdirects animosity and stunts the formation of class-based coalitions that could pursue economic justice.[23]

The history of U.S. immigration policy is largely an intertwining of economic exploitation and nativism.[24] In the particular case of immigrants from Latin America, U.S. officials have had a long history of calling on migrants when they needed them—during wartime labor shortages, for example—and forcibly removing them when labor demands subsided and anti-immigrant hostilities intensified.[25] In the contemporary political economic context, near-record numbers of immigrants are arriving in the United States.[26] However, the vacancies they fill this time around are the result not of labor shortages but, rather, of *"structural transformations."*[27] Amid globalization and rapid technological change, jobs in sectors such as manufacturing are leaving the United States, and immigrants are filling the often temporary, low-wage employment opportunities that crop up in their place. Companies competing in the global economy doing all they can to cut costs have grown increasingly reliant on "inexpensive" immigrant laborers—many of whom have been uprooted from their home countries by the same processes, including especially the so-called free-trade agreements that leverage U.S. control over other national economies.[28]

In contrast to the American dream narrative, which suggests that newcomers who start at the bottom can work their way up, the reality of a system that requires so much low-wage work is that it thrives on the labor of the marginalized.[29] When we realize that "exploitation can be more easily justified if the exploited are placed within a fixed hierarchy,"[30] Latina/o degradation emerges as an ideological tool that caters to such arrangements in the current historical moment.[31] While many reap the economic benefits of exploited immigrant labor, virtualization makes it harder to realize immigrants' place in the social structure and it belittles the various social harms that many who live their lives on the social, economic, and legal margins confront. From this perspective, we can delink the presence of undocumented immigrants from the notion of "unsecure borders." As Nicholas De Genova puts it, capitalists in a cutthroat global economy prefer "the continued presence of migrants whose undocumented legal status has long been equated with the disposable (deportable), ultimately "temporary" character of the commodity that is their labor power."[32] Because citizenship is often "visibly inscribed on bodies"[33] and, as Kitty Calavita writes, "immigrants' position in the economy inevitably *reproduces* the visible markers of poverty, and further generates . . . material and social exclusion," many migrants who do have authorization also find themselves caught up in this web of marginality and exploitability.[34]

For poor and working-class U.S.-born Whites such as those who make up the bulk of Hazleton's population, economic uncertainty also abounds under these conditions. The structural patterns that have attracted immigrants to places like Hazleton have also enhanced insecurity for many people accustomed to stable, decent-paying work.[35] For example, Hazleton's Luzerne County has lost more than half of its manufacturing jobs since the late 1970s, with low-wage industries filling that void; temporary employment agencies seem to be popping up on every corner; and the city struggles with budget issues at the same time that many recently arrived firms are enjoying lavish tax breaks (see Chapter 1).[36] In short, de-manufacturing, demographic shifts, and austerity are all of a piece. However, just as few openly or accurately discuss the role of immigrant labor in the economy, I show how what some have called "depoliticized neoliberalism" (see Chapter 1) has helped conceal the relationship between these patterns, effectively removing them from the public debate. Individualistic assessments of economic circumstances predominate,[37] for example, and acknowledgments of job quality rarely accompany boasts of job creation.

This context provides fertile soil for the Latino Threat Narrative.[38] It plays simultaneously to the powerful sentiments of those experiencing insecurity and mourning the economic decline of their hometowns and to negative assumptions about people of color that are so deeply embedded that many accept them even in the face of clear contradictory evidence.[39] For this reason, part of this story is about pure political ambition. As an extension of the "Southern Strategy" launched by the Republican Party in the 1960s to attract racially aggrieved poor and working-class White voters,[40] many politicians have begun deploying racially coded rhetoric as they "[search] for electoral gold in warning about the Hispanic threat."[41] Electoral success accordingly follows the politician who can best depict himself or herself as tough on "illegal immigration," willing to "take a stand," "stem the tide," or "take back" "our" city or country.

When the *Washington Post* interviewed Mayor Barletta about the IIRA in the summer of 2006, he commented, "I lay in bed and thought, I've lost my city. I love the new immigrants; they want their kids to be safe just like I do. I had to declare war on the illegals."[42] These words concede that things are not going well in Hazleton. The city is *lost*. Yet rather than providing commentary on how Hazleton should weather the economic storm, I argue in this book that this kind of rhetoric shifts the blame. Resembling what the legal scholar Ian Haney López refers to as "dog whistle politics,"[43] statements such as this are at the heart of the Latino Threat Narrative, portraying people without documentation narrowly and inaccurately as posing a profound (i.e., requiring a declaration of "war") and urgent (i.e., "I had to") problem and drawing attention to the politician who is accordingly prepared to lead the "fight." What makes this rhetoric especially powerful is that it is capable of withstanding any charges of racism that may arise—note here how race is never mentioned explicitly and how an expression of "love" for immigrants is sandwiched between the realization of loss and the declaration of war.

Ultimately, however, this is not a story about individual politicians.[44] *Undocumented Fears* connects the proliferation of the Latino Threat Narrative to a broader ideological project designed to divide and conquer poor and working people. While degradation assures the existence of exploitable immigrant laborers, *affirmation* encourages poor and working-class Whites to embrace their racialized rather than class-based identities. Akin to what some scholars refer to as a "racial bribe,"[45] the Latino Threat Narrative in this way promises a symbolic uplift to those White workers who choose to ally with White political and economic elites instead of conspiring with their fellow workers of color to protest their shared economic plight. Although it does little to improve their socioeconomic standing, the bribe is, and long has been, enticing for many, particularly at these moments of uncertainty, because it grants "public deference" and a "psychological wage."[46] Thus to paraphrase W.E.B. Du Bois, members of the White working class often become content with their class position once they come to see themselves, in this case, as "not Latina/o."[47]

The ideology of White injury factors in here, as well. More than simply evoking race *instead of class*, the rigid "us" and "them" binaries in this narrative *reinforce particular understandings of socioeconomic relations*. The politics I describe in this book use race to promote an individualistic worldview that attributes, quoting Katherine Beckett, "the plight of the average American" to people said to be "looking for the easy way out":[48] "'cheats,' 'thieves,' 'freeloaders[,]'"[49] and, in this case, "illegals." That is to say, my argument in this book is that the Latino Threat Narrative is embraced, at least in part, for its "*capacity to explain* the declining social and economic position of working people."[50] As opposed to concern about financial burdens imposed on *workers*, the understanding that has prevailed suggests that the behavior of racialized outsiders is *economically injurious to Whites* (e.g., "'Our' community is destitute because 'they' commit crime and milk the system").

In short, the Latino Threat Narrative reconstitutes the terms of the debate, controlling what we see and what we do not in a way that allows existing hierarchies to remain intact. Degradation reasserts the subordinate social and economic position of many Latina/os. Yet its color-blind rhetoric masks racism, its virtualizing of real people "blunts the empathetic response,"[51] and its scapegoating makes exclusionary policies appear justified. Mobilizing for immigrants' rights and racial justice in this context is therefore not surprisingly an uphill battle (see Chapters 3 and 4). Existing economic arrangements that concentrate wealth in the hands of just a small number of people also avoid contestation by remaining invisible to many. Working-class politics are drowned out along with the potential for class-based, cross-racial/ethnic solidarity as the prevailing narrative depicts immigrants not as workers but as fiscal burdens and encourages working-class Whites to see themselves *in contrast to* such racialized representations. The "harm" that the Latino Threat Narrative suggests Whites experience *as Whites* in this way becomes the harm around which activists in favor of laws like the IIRA can successfully mobilize. Consequently, it is this problematic conception of harm that garners the lion's share of attention. What we end up with, I argue, are counterproductive, *de-democratizing* local-level mobilizations:[52] calls for additional state power and control over racially marginalized populations and collective efforts that reinforce the market ideology responsible for perpetuating global and local economic inequality.

Plan of the Book

The book begins with an examination of how the structural arrangements I have just described filter down to the local level. In many nations striving to enhance their economic standing in the increasingly competitive world of global capitalism, immigrants are attracted for their inexpensive labor and subsequently demonized.[53] Domestically in the United States, many small cities and rural towns are also struggling to remain economically viable as their industrial base withers and they compete with other locales to attract industry. Many communities in this situation are settling for exploitative firms and, as a result, are attracting large numbers of immigrant laborers who, in turn, are subject to backlash.[54]

In Chapter 1, I provide an account of this by studying the history of Hazleton's primary community economic development group, CAN DO. This organization provides a window through which we can see how broader political economic forces have affected Hazleton. By tracing CAN DO's evolution from its founding in the 1950s, through the introduction of a market-centric ideology in the 1980s, and into the present, we become aware of the structural shifts that both created economic uncertainty among local residents and prompted Latina/o immigration to Hazleton. My analysis also suggests that CAN DO has responded to recent economic shifts and demographic changes with a depoliticized approach that is characteristic of the current political economic order. In short, Chapter 1 documents the setting of the structural and ideological stage for the politics that ensue.

Chapter 2 begins with a comparative analysis of the media coverage of two homicides committed in Hazleton. The first is a Latino-on-Latino murder that prompted calls for calm. The second is the killing of a White Hazleton resident, for which two undocumented Latino immigrants were initially charged. The second homicide prompted a moral panic and catalyzed passage of the IIRA. This analysis introduces us to how politicians and other city officials draw from the broader Latino Threat Narrative and mold it to fit the local context. In the reaction to the Latino-on-White homicide, the notion that "they" have harmed "us" and that we therefore must "get tough" is very apparent. That is not so in the case featuring a Latino victim.

I follow the moral panic over the murder of the White resident into City Council debates, where it became the impetus for the introduction of the IIRA. Here, I suggest clear instances of Latina/o degradation and White affirmation are on display. Officials extend the implications of this single criminal incident with blanket constructions of undocumented immigrants as "crime-prone" and Hazletonians as potential innocent victims of their criminality. I show how officials also bring other issues in at this juncture—claiming, for example, that immigrants are a drain on city resources—as they construct what I interpret as an alternative explanation for Hazleton's economic decline.

Chapters 3 and 4 explore how members of the community majority respond to various pro-immigrant efforts put forth by local Latina/o community leaders and their allies. The first of these chapters focuses on how the majority used a particular strand of the Latino Threat Narrative to fend off pro-immigrant mobilizations that directly contested the IIRA. In this version of Latino Threat, which is similar to what scholars have documented in other local contexts and emblematic of national immigration debates,[55] we see Latina/o activists' efforts to claim discrimination and assert their rights dismissed by the majority as "inappropriate" evocations of race and "excessive" demands for "special rights." At the same time, the majority constructs its own rights claims and legal mobilizations as acceptable, even necessary, to ensure continued community harmony.[56] Thus, the backlash to the initial protests by Latina/o community leaders quelled pro-immigrant mobilizations and added "self-interested," "reverse racist" activists to the list of those who supposedly pose a threat to a previously "harmonious" Hazleton.

I also explore in Chapter 3 how these activists had a similar experience when they later turned to litigation, challenging the ordinance in the high-profile case *Pedro Lozano et al. v. City of Hazleton* (hereafter, *Lozano v. Hazleton*). Although pro-immigrant groups were ultimately victorious in court, the lawsuit and subsequent decision prompted some of the most vitriolic politics of the entire debate. Even in the shadow of the IIRA's defeat, we see how the conception of local Latino Threat further intensifies as "powerful litigators" and "activist judges" face accusations that they, too, have undermined this "innocent small town."

In Chapter 4, I examine subsequent pro-immigrant efforts—specifically, a volunteer coalition of Latina/o and White residents who mobilized with the goal of building a bridge between recent immigrants and established residents and institutions. As an adaptation to the backlash the initial pro-immigrant mobilization faced, this group was able to make important progress by avoiding contentious issues. For example, some infrastructure is emerging to support immigrants, the issue of integration has gained visibility and positive press, and there has even been cooperation from some who previously championed backlash politics. In this respect, what we see is a pattern that mirrors a common refrain in national immigration debates: Things will get better as time goes on, and conflicting groups are able to compromise. Remaining cognizant of how meaningful these gains have been, but also questioning this uncritical assessment, I argue that here, too, the Latino Threat Narrative still looms large and that the debate remains on the ideological turf of those who sit atop racial and economic hierarchies. Specifically, I point to several key political limitations that activists continue to confront, including an ability to bring attention to the specific harms and burdens Latina/o immigrants endure, to directly contest the ideology of White injury, and to introduce class-based politics into the debate.

I conclude by recounting an example from Hazleton's history that I think takes on particular significance in light of these contemporary events. Back when it was a coal mining town, Hazleton was riddled by ethnic strife and labor-capital disputes. I argue that collective engagement with this history is but one tactic that has the potential to foster new community identities capable of resisting the politics of divide and conquer in Hazleton and beyond. As immigration law and politics localize, in other words, it becomes vitally important that we contest top-down constructions of community identity that have their basis in racialized myths and economic distortions and replace them with engaged, bottom-up activity that authentically and democratically confronts racial and economic inequality.

1

The Political Economy
of Local Backlash

By 1955, Hazleton's coal industry had bottomed out. Oil was now the nation's primary energy source, making work in the anthracite coal mines scarce. The city's unemployment rate hovered around 25 percent, and "gone to Jersey" became a popular local slogan as scores of families began seeking work elsewhere.[1] Hazleton was "swiftly becoming a ghost town."[2]

It was at this point, the story goes, that "a small corps of merchants and professional men [who] had faith that . . . they could turn the tide" decided to create a community economic development organization.[3] Dr. Edgar Dessen, a local radiologist and president of the Greater Hazleton Chamber of Commerce led the way. He recalled the challenge of creating such a group "in the face of the inherent disillusionment . . . and the prevalent atmosphere of depression over the entire community":

> One very prominent local banker in town from one of the larger banks just was extremely pessimistic about this whole concept. He just said flatly, "You can't do it. You can't do it." And, of course, those words rang in my ears. That night I couldn't sleep because

those words were there: "You can't do it." So that was the night that I decided to name the organization CAN DO.[4]

Hazleton's new community economic development group was thus born out of a spirit suggested by its name. It was not until weeks later that Dessen arranged the words Community Area New Development Organization to fit the acronym. CAN DO's founding occurred as similar groups were cropping up across the United States. Initially in urban areas where people of color were denied employment and later in rural areas where job opportunities were scarce, community development corporations (CDCs) "from the beginning . . . were to accomplish bottom-up, comprehensive development."[5]

To get started, CAN DO orchestrated a fund drive, encouraging residents to donate a "dime-a-week" that they would put toward their effort to replace coal with new industries. Publications from the organization recall how this helped "revive community spirit" and suggest that it was quite a remarkable feat:

Hundreds of bright red lunch pails were placed in restaurants, stores, public buildings, plants, and other places where people congregated. The slogan "Operation Jobs" was painted on the lunch pails. . . . A windup phase of the drive was a "Miles of Dimes." People were asked to place a mile of dimes, end to end, on tape glued to Broad Street between Laurel and Wyoming Streets. The long lines of tape were quite impressive. Starting early one Saturday morning, men, women, and children came to place their dimes on the tape. It was heartening to watch the money line grow.[6]

After the initial drive generated funds and revived community morale, other efforts followed. Parades, bond sales, and media campaigns continued to excite Hazleton's downtrodden public. "The more they became involved, the more enthusiastic they became."[7] One fund drive apparently generated such a stir that social clubs were practically "fighting in the streets" over who could sell the most bonds.[8] Ministers, priests, and rabbis supported CAN DO, giving sermons about the importance of the drive.[9] Local media outlets offered extensive coverage and rewarded donors by publishing their photos. "Being a part of the CAN DO movement [was] the THING to do in Hazleton."[10]

These efforts raised more than $2 million, which was enough at the time to purchase a large swath of land on which to develop an industrial park.[11] With that, the replacing of Hazleton's coal industry with a manufacturing base became a reality as dozens of factories that provided many with relatively stable employment opened in the 1960s and 1970s.

CAN DO retained its position as Hazleton's primary economic driver in the following decades. Subsequent shifts in the global economy, however, have made it difficult for them to stay true to their grassroots origins. More specifically, as I contend in this chapter through an analysis of the organization's archives, the rise of neoliberalism in the 1980s—a market-centric approach to structuring society and solving social problems[12]— prompted CAN DO to rethink its community economic development strategy. In response to increased competitiveness, I suggest that CAN DO, like other CDCs affected by these political economic shifts, has taken on a far more businesslike approach. I see this as especially evident in the organization's support of policies that offer huge incentives to corporations, often at the expense of the community. Characteristic of neoliberalism's depoliticized nature, I also contend that CAN DO in recent years has limited the extent to which it engages meaningfully with the community regarding the important social, political, and economic circumstances it confronts. The story of CAN DO in this way provides important background for my larger inquiry into the immigration politics that ensued. It uncovers the political economic factors that both prompted immigration to Hazleton and increased economic uncertainty among local, native-born residents. We also see here how neoliberal ideology helped remove important economic considerations from the debate, making way for the racial politics that would follow.

"Chang[ing] Its Way of Thinking in Order to Compete"

The 1980s put CAN DO and other CDCs around the country to the test. With blatant hostility toward government and an unbridled commitment to the market, the Reagan administration ushered in a wave of deregulation and cuts in government programs.[13] To give just one example, during President Ronald Reagan's first term, "nonprofits that relied on federal community development funding faced 70% cuts."[14] In theory, these "roll-back" policies would lessen the role of government, thereby providing locales with more "economic freedom."[15] But in practice, as Jason Hackworth observes, "The choices available to cities are highly constrained even for the most powerful municipalities."[16] Another way to say this is that Regan-era neoliberal policies have exerted what community development scholars have called "economic discipline" on locales while disillusioning them with a "myth of community control."[17]

In this climate, rather than occurring *within* locales, competition occurs *across* them. The result is what Arthur Rolnick and Melvin Burstein have called an "economic war."[18] To attract industry and jobs, municipalities do whatever it takes to lure corporations before they set up shop elsewhere.[19] It is here that neoliberal ideology has exerted its discipline: Many economic development groups, facing increased competition but left to their own devices without government support, have rethought their strategies, often feeling as though they confront just two options: abandon their grassroots origins to become more businesslike or fail.[20]

These changes began to affect CAN DO in the mid-1980s, when the group was involved in a bidding war to have Saturn, a new division of General Motors, locate its plant in the Hazleton area. Having successfully attracted industry to the city for nearly thirty years by this point, CAN DO was accustomed to some competition, but the battle for Saturn was like nothing it had previously seen. CAN DO officials admitted publicly that "competition for attracting industry to an area . . . [is] tougher than it was years ago" and that community economic development was now characterized by "frantic one-upmanship."[21] The appropriate response to "stiffened" competition, as they saw it, was to become "more tenacious in their pursuit of prospective industries."[22]

Although CAN DO failed to land Saturn—the company ultimately chose Spring Hill, Tennessee—this recruitment effort marked an important turning point. Realizing the need to "change its way of thinking in order to compete in today's fight to attract industry,"[23] CAN DO embarked on a project of organizational remodeling that it hoped would lay "the foundation for coordinated and more professional marketing efforts to attract industry."[24] Within a period of six months, CAN DO made "sharp deviation[s] with past . . . policy" by "sprucing up its approach to luring industry."[25] It announced plans to hire a public relations firm, began a new campaign featuring magazine advertisements, developed a new brochure, and merged with other local development groups "to get more aggressive"—efforts that one CAN DO executive called "a new path for the nonprofit organization."[26] The message was clear: By "reshaping" its image and "redesign[ing] its marketing tools," CAN DO was doing its best to give Hazleton a leg up on the competition.[27]

Perhaps clinging to its original community-based, government-supported model, however, CAN DO appears to have done this with some reluctance. In 1986, just over a year after Saturn announced its decision not to locate in Hazleton, Representative Paul Kanjorski asked local development officials to comment on the Reagan administration's cuts in community development funding at a U.S. congressional field hearing he hosted in Hazleton. All expressed clear-cut opposition. Howard Grossman, who was the executive director of the Economic Development Council of Northeastern Pennsylvania, called the elimination of federal programs "deleterious," adding, "The absence of federal support ... would be a great handicap[,] in many respects a great tragedy."[28] A county-level developer told Congress that there was "no question" that such cuts would cause local projects to "suffer."[29] W. Kevin O'Donnell, CAN DO's current president, testified, "Cutting back [on federal funding] is like taking our toolbox away, or like taking tools out of our toolbox."[30]

Unfortunately for CAN DO, these pleas fell on deaf ears. Perhaps feeling it had no other options, the organization went on reshaping its approach in ways that cater to industry. In 1990, CAN DO opened a $3 million business facility in the heart of downtown Hazleton that it hoped would serve as the "focal point when important people visit the area."[31] More recently, it was reported that when representatives of potential firms visit Hazleton, they are strategically routed through scenic parts of the community to avoid the "eyesores" that are Hazleton's abandoned coalfields.[32] A recent iteration of CAN DO's website was filled with what appear to be stock photos that scream corporatization.[33] Perhaps most reflective of these changing objectives is the group's current mission statement, "to improve the quality of life in the Greater Hazleton Area through the creation of employment opportunities."[34] This is a profound departure from its original mission to "involve the entire community, to raise money, to represent all facets of the public on the board of directors."[35]

The Race to the Bottom

One of the hard truths about neoliberalism is that it creates an environment in which even highly entrepreneurial locales struggle.[36] In the 1990s, with job prospects in the Hazleton area continuing to decline, even though its primary economic development group was adhering to neoliberal demands, CAN DO sought to lure a warehouse for the multinational company Target. Complementing its spruced-up image, CAN DO at the time had a county-level tax incentive at its disposal that would make it rather inexpensive for Target to do business in the Hazleton area.[37] Without the incentive, CAN DO officials admitted they "would be out of the game," as Target was "receiving tax breaks from everyone."[38] Reminiscent of the failure to woo Saturn, CAN DO was nevertheless let down again as Target chose to open its warehouse in New York, the state that, not coincidentally, was reportedly leading the nation in reducing business taxes at the time.[39]

By this point engrossed in what is commonly termed neoliberalism's "race to the bottom," Hazleton, led by CAN DO, responded to the setback by doing what many locales in similar circumstances do: making huge sacrifices of which they otherwise probably would not have dreamed. In 1998, about six months after receiving the news that Target had chosen New York, CAN DO announced it would be launching an effort to have certain local sites designated "tax-free zones" through participation in Pennsylvania's new Keystone Opportunity Zone (KOZ) initiative.[40] Modeled on similar "enterprise zone" legislation designed to "remove as much government as possible" with the hope of stimulating economic growth in struggling areas, laws like KOZ were promoted heavily across the United States by the Reagan administration.[41] Republican Governor Tom Ridge and Republican State Representative Joseph Gladeck pioneered Pennsylvania's version. Comments from these two politicians expose the bill's neoliberal roots. According to Ridge, KOZ represents "the most powerful market based incentive: no taxation"; Gladeck finds KOZ desirable because "rather than pumping millions of state funds into various state and local run programs . . . [KOZ] gets the government out of the way."[42]

After KOZ became law, the state gave municipalities the chance to compete for the right to have certain properties designated "opportunity zones." They were required to demonstrate the magnitude of their economic need and the presence of blight within their borders. The government would then permit successful applicants to offer tax breaks to businesses using such zones, which in many cases amount to a moratorium on all taxes for a dozen years.[43]

CAN DO submitted its application to the state without a local hitch. It had backing from community leaders and minimal pushback from the public. Desperate for jobs and perhaps unable to envision an alternative, the school board and other affected entities that needed to sign off before the application could go through gave CAN DO their blessing.[44] Mayor Lou Barletta also supported the implementation of KOZ in Hazleton, providing the state with a letter of "support and endorsement" for the initiative.[45] CAN DO's application suggested that with its abundance of mine-scarred land and above-average unemployment rates, Hazleton fit the KOZ criteria "very well."[46] Evaluators agreed, granting Hazleton's Luzerne County the most KOZ acreage in Pennsylvania.[47]

There is no denying, as we will see, that KOZ quickly became a powerful force for luring industry. Yet it is important to recognize that such incentives also pull a significant amount of money away from the local tax base. As Rolnick points out, tax breaks like these make it a "struggle to provide such public goods as schools and libraries, police and fire protection, and the roads, bridges and parks that are critical to the success of any community."[48] An especially illustrative example of this is a Hazleton Area School District official's estimate that the implementation of KOZ cost the district approximately $979,000 in one year.[49]

Latina/o Immigrants' Arrival

Armed with a surplus of corporate-friendly tax-free land, CAN DO finally achieved the results that had evaded the group when it was recruiting industrial heavyweights such as Saturn and Target. As O'Donnell told me in an interview, "KOZ proved to be the equalizer, the leveling plane to make us at or above other communities." Except now, rather than attracting the decent-paying, permanent manufacturing jobs that have kept Hazleton on its feet in recent decades, KOZ has served as a magnet for "big box" warehouses, distribution centers, and, most prominently, a Cargill meatpacking plant.[50] In other words, while using KOZ to recruit firms, CAN DO began attracting the type of industries that offer temporary employment, pay lower wages, and expose workers to poor, if not outright dangerous, working conditions.[51] Many such firms also have reputations for exploiting immigrant labor.[52]

At the time, Cargill representatives admitted that they "would not be building [in the Hazleton area] if not for Gov. Tom Ridge's Keystone Opportunity Zone program."[53] The plant opened in 2001, one year after the census calculated that 95 percent of Hazleton's approximately twenty-four thousand residents identified as White.[54] A 2005 estimate from city officials suggested that the plant employed almost one thousand workers—which would make Cargill by far the largest employer operating in a CAN DO industrial park—an estimated 70 percent of whom are Latina/o.[55] Migrants—mostly from the Dominican Republic, Mexico, and Peru,[56] and many of whom originally settled in New York or New Jersey—make up the bulk of Hazleton's new labor force. Many talk about how the availability of jobs and low cost of living made Hazleton an appealing place to resettle.[57] Thus, rather suddenly, Hazleton's population began to grow, and its demographics began to change. By 2006, officials were estimating the city's population at thirty-one thousand, with 30 percent of residents identifying as Latina/o.[58] In 2009, Hazleton's Luzerne County ranked number one in the nation in terms of Latina/o population growth.[59] By the time the 2010 census was taken, the number of people who identify as Latina/o in Hazleton had grown to 37.3 percent, a 670 percent increase in Latina/o residents since 2000.[60] The rise of neoliberalism, CAN DO's adaptation to it, and the subsequent arrival of a meatpacking plant and other low-wage industries in this way can be interpreted as having contributed to the attraction of a Latina/o immigrant labor force that would become the subject of backlash.

CAN DO Today: Depoliticized Neoliberalism

All told, the rise of neoliberalism has left many Hazleton residents with grim economic prospects. In the years before 1980, the number of manufacturing jobs in Luzerne County was consistently higher than forty thousand; by 1990, that number had dropped below thirty thousand. In 2000, it had further fallen to about twenty-five thousand, and recent figures suggest that fewer than twenty thousand Luzerne County residents currently work in the manufacturing sector.[61]

Despite this, structural shifts were not the subject of the debates that ensued. Through the course of my research, I found that very few people in Hazleton publicly connected political economic shifts, CAN DO, KOZ, new industries, and the arrival of immigrants. "Gee, I never thought of KOZ like *that*," one local official who had voted in favor of the initiative tellingly remarked after hearing me explain the interconnections described in this chapter.[62] One way we can account for this is by exploring how neoliberal ideology shapes the public conversation. A defining feature of neoliberalism is that it ignores complex social circumstances that surround policy initiatives, replacing them with sanitized and *depoliticized* versions of reality.[63] High-stakes decisions likewise are rarely, in practice, put out for public debate. Instead, neoliberalism works under the assumption that *there is no alternative*. Henry Giroux explains this quite well:

> Within the discourse of neoliberalism that has taken hold of the public imagination, there is no way of talking about what is fundamental to civic life, critical citizenship, and a substantive democracy. Neoliberalism offers no critical vocabulary for speaking about political or social transformation as a democratic project. Nor is there a language for either the ideal of public commitment or the notions of a social agency capable of challenging basic assumptions of corporate ideology as well as its social consequences. In its dubious appeals to universal laws, neutrality, and selective scientific research, neoliberalism "eliminates the very possibility of critical thinking, without which democratic debate becomes impossible." This shift makes it possible for advocates of neoliberalism to implement the most ruthless economic and political policies without having to open up such actions to public debate and dialogue.[64]

Consider, as an example, how CAN DO pitched the KOZ initiative to local boards. Offering essentially a zero-sum proposition—adopt the initiative or blight prevails—they called KOZ the "brass ring" for attracting industry and warned that without it "community development and job growth in Hazleton would grind to a halt."[65] The underlying message seemed to be that this is about making "the community as attractive as possible *to business and industry*."[66]

I point this out not to argue that CAN DO has naively embraced KOZ or that the organization is unconcerned with de-manufacturing. To the contrary, as they have in the past, CAN DO officials continue to express reluctance even as they use these policies. O'Donnell remarked to a local board while pitching KOZ that "it's kind of scary to think [that using tax incentives is] where we're headed, but that's what's happening."[67] When I spoke with him, he was similarly careful to preface our discussion of KOZ by saying, "I don't think there's an economic developer in the United States today that likes these giveaway incentives. However, having said that, if you don't use them you're out of the game."[68]

One interpretation of such statements is that they offer a realistic appraisal of current circumstances. Given the cutthroat climate of cross-locale competition, it is not hard to see why such conclusions might be drawn. Yet it is also important to consider how the ideological power of neoliberalism is reflected in these remarks. Notice how in each statement acknowledgments of *undesirability* are accompanied by a nod to *inevitability*. Again, the now accepted narrative is that even if we do not like it, *there is no alternative.*[69] Troublingly, a robust discussion around economic issues remains absent. The consideration of other approaches was not part of CAN DO's pitch; nor did there appear to be meaningful hesitance rooted in the incentive's potential to hurt the local tax base or attract low-quality jobs.[70] Without these challenging concerns and under the veneer of inevitability, the decision to adopt KOZ seems obvious. Both boards that heard the pitch turned out to be "easy sells" and each unanimously approved the initiative. As one approving board member revealingly commented, "I'm all for it. . . . I think it's great. At least you'll be putting people to work."[71]

Similar examples abound. A review of the materials CAN DO distributes to the public reveals an almost exclusive focus on organizational competence and success, with minimal commentary on social complexities.[72] Themes I noticed while analyzing brochures and other recent public relations materials include a fetishizing of the organization's fabled founding and depictions of ribbon-cutting ceremonies and the like used as evidence that the "can do" spirit lives on. Again, especially given the circumstances, it is understandable why the organization would want to present itself and its community in a positive light. In the end, however, low wages, poor working conditions, higher-than-average unemployment rates, attendant poverty, and increases in contingent labor are all absent from this narrative. Even as the number of Hazleton residents living below the poverty line reached its highest level in twenty years in the wake of the Great Recession,[73] the materials distributed by the city's primary economic development group convey that Hazleton, under their guidance, is "meeting the challenge,"[74] with "steady growth and expansion."[75]

When Cargill announced the opening of its meatpacking plant in the Hazleton area, as another example, the press responded with hyperbolic announcements: "Meat Plant Eyes up to Seven Hundred Jobs for Hazleton," "New Jobs for Area . . . 'Excel-lent,'" "EXCELerated into Production: Meat-Processing Plant in Humboldt to Employ 500 in 6 to 8 Months."[76] These headlines frame the issue narrowly as "jobs" versus "no jobs," making such celebration seem unquestionably worthy. A deeper inquiry might have noted the quality of such jobs, Cargill's reputation, or the changes Hazleton predictably would experience with the arrival of a meatpacking plant of this size.[77] A more thorough public discussion might have also put the issue of fairness at the forefront: Should a multinational company be able to forgo taxes for a dozen years while residents of an economically struggling city foot the bill?[78]

To be sure, a handful of area residents did warn of the KOZ program's "hidden costs."[79] There is also a history of residents working to make people aware of environmental and public health harms that factories operating on CAN DO properties may be causing. How developers, with what appears to be an increasingly narrow focus on "growth," have received such dissent, however, provides yet another example of neoliberal ideology in action. When a group of grassroots protestors assembled in the 1990s to oppose a CAN DO plan to rezone and industrialize previously protected land, a CAN DO attorney publicly tarred them as "anti-growth, anti-[industrial] park, anti-progress people."[80] One local activist similarly complained that his resistance to CAN DO's practices has not gained traction because "[CAN DO officials] say I'm against everything."[81] When I informally asked O'Donnell about such activists, he jokingly referred to them as "BANANAs"—a play on the acronym NIMBY (Not in My Back Yard)—which stands for "Build Absolutely Nothing Anywhere Near Anything."[82]

Responding to Immigrants' Arrival

After Hazleton's demographics shifted, CAN DO distanced itself from any associated political ramifications. Their sentiment was that the organization "shouldn't take the credit or the blame for something like that."[83] CAN DO similarly refused to take a position after the city proposed the Illegal Immigration Relief Act (IIRA), despite pleas for support from Hazleton's Latina/o business community, whose members struggled as they watched many of their customers leave town because of the ordinance.[84] "We're rather apolitical," O'Donnell said. "We've got our job to do, and we try to stay focused on what we're doing, and we didn't really see the need to take sides on something that was either going to happen or not with us or without us."[85]

I draw attention to this not to question the decision making of a single organization but to highlight a crucial characteristic of the broader neoliberal order. This distancing is indicative of what Lisa Duggan refers to as the "most successful ruse of neoliberal dominance . . . the definition of economic policy as primarily a matter of neutral, technical expertise." Decisions with real social implications, she argues, echoing Giroux, are "presented as separate from politics and culture, and not properly subject to specifically political accountability or critique."[86]

In an interesting twist of fate, the demise of manufacturing brought a host of unexpected benefits to Hazleton. The arrival of Latinas/os engendered new life in what was a dying city. Hazleton's population had been declining and aging, with its educated youth moving away in droves because of the lack of opportunity for professional employment.[87] After 2001, Hazleton experienced its first population increase in decades, fueled by a younger demographic.[88] A report by the Joint Urban Studies Center explains how migration revitalized local institutions, improved the housing market, and spurred the growth of Latina/o-owned small businesses.[89] There is now at least some vitality in a downtown area that had become a line of empty storefronts.

According to one Latino business owner I spoke with, however, CAN DO has done little to embrace these developments. "CAN DO and the [Greater Hazleton] Chamber of Commerce are more receptive to chain stores," he said, "which leaves Latino small-business owners forced to go their own way." Without the help of the most powerful economic entities in the community, he continued, "it makes no sense . . . to open a business when you can make more money working in a factory."

Although not taking a position on contentious issues may seem like the safe approach, posturing as apolitical is, indeed, *a political stance*. The business owner's comment, like the previous examples, exemplifies how, by separating economic policy from social realities, neoliberal discourse, in Duggan's words, "disguises the upwardly redistributing goals of neoliberalism—its concerted efforts to concentrate power and resources in the hands of tiny elites."[90] A depoliticized stance, in this respect, quells public debate about economic issues, in this case further enabling corporations to enjoy the benefits of tax breaks with minimal pushback. And just as Reagan's cuts exerted "economic discipline" on community development groups, when the same ideologies filter down to the local level, residents such as the business owner I spoke with are told they can do as they please but nevertheless find themselves being funneled into low-wage work.

Conclusion

I contend here that CAN DO's shift from grassroots organization to neo-liberal developer has played a crucial role in altering Hazleton's social landscape. Yet paradoxically, the basis for the ideology I argue the organization has embraced in the process is a *mystification of the social.* The result is a very different city with minimal explanation offered for why changes have occurred. As the next chapter shows, this is fertile ground for the Latino Threat Narrative to take root. As Kitty Calavita writes, "It may be precisely because material uncertainty remains a reality that the racialized face of immigration is so scary."[91] Rather than de-manufacturing, corporate tax breaks, and the like, warnings about the social and economic ills that accompany "illegal immigration"—despite having a basis in myth rather than reality—emerge to fill this explanatory void. Once officials mold this already familiar narrative to fit the local context and to account for particular local conditions and events, the story becomes one of "greedy," "crime-prone" "outsiders" coming in uninvited to disrupt an otherwise "tranquil" "small-town" lifestyle.

2

"The Straw That Broke the Camel's Back"

Derek Kichline, a White Hazleton resident, was working on his truck on East Chestnut Street the evening of May 10, 2006, when two men allegedly shot him at point-blank range. He died hours later from the gunshot wound. Police charged Pedro Cabrera and Joan Romero, two twenty-three-year-old undocumented Latino immigrants, with the murder, although prosecutors later dropped the case for lack of evidence.[1] A crucifix and the words "RIP Derek Gone but not Forgotten 1976–2006" were scrawled in black on the concrete foundation of his home.[2] Several items rested nearby in remembrance of the twenty-nine-year-old homicide victim. "This should not have happened to Derek," his grieving fiancée told reporters a week after the murder as she added artifacts to the memorial. "He would give you the shirt off his back if you asked for it."[3]

Just a few blocks away on Green Street were the remnants of another memorial. "Flaco Que Descanze en paz. . . . En mi corazon siempre estarás" ("Flaco, Rest in peace. . . . You will forever be in my heart") read a note left by a mourner. The note clung to a vase filled with green leaves and roses, surrounded by candles.[4] A little more than six months before the Kichline homicide in October 2005, another Hazleton resident, Antonio Castro Sanchez, killed his thirty-two-year-old acquaintance, Julio Angel Mojica

Calderon, called "Flaco" by his friends. According to news reports citing police affidavits, the two Latino men had been in a dispute that began with an argument over a borrowed vehicle and escalated into Sanchez striking Calderon's wife. Fearing retaliation, Sanchez—later convicted of the murder—shot a fleeing Calderon three times in the back, leaving him for dead in broad daylight in downtown Hazleton.[5]

Factually, these two tragic cases are very similar. The homicide victims were close in age, as were the (alleged) offenders; all the actors were men; and the crimes occurred just six months apart in the same section of town. Each also garnered several local headlines, which is understandable, considering the relative infrequency of violent crime in the small city. The Uniform Crime Reports list only four homicides, including these cases, from January 2000 to May 2006. Hazleton's primary local newspaper, the *Standard-Speaker*, named the Calderon homicide the top news story of 2005 and the Kichline homicide the top news story of 2006. Other crimes involving firearms were also committed in Hazleton in temporal proximity to each murder.[6]

While we might expect two very similar reactions to two very similar crimes, I contend in this chapter that what unfolded was a call for calm in one case and panic in the other. Whereas officials dismissed the Calderon homicide as an unfortunate incident, the Kichline murder became the catalyst for the Illegal Immigration Relief Act (IIRA). Mayor Lou Barletta often refers to it as "the straw that broke the camel's back."[7] I use a content analysis of local newspaper reports on each homicide to explore this differential response in more detail. News reports are useful in this regard, as they tend to rely almost exclusively on public officials, who have the ability to "use their news-making power to channel the coverage of social problems into a definitive direction."[8] I argue that officials commenting on the Kichline case drew from the Latino Threat Narrative and molded it to fit the local context, depicting crime-prone "outsiders" as a threat to Hazleton. The corresponding response was a call for a law-and-order approach and ultimately the passage of punitive legislation targeting undocumented immigrants. In the Calderon case, where the victim was Latino, similar notions of what constitutes a threat seemingly led officials to conclude that the crime was not part of a broader, concerning trend. Placed alongside the response to Kichline's murder, my analysis associates the conception that "we" were not "under attack" with the official decision to deem further action unnecessary.

In the second part of the chapter, I follow the panic over the Kichline homicide into City Council debates over the IIRA. My analysis of officials' justifications for the ordinance in these debates, as well as in subsequent public commentary, suggests that they expanded the implications of this single criminal incident, using racialized conceptions of "them" to articulate an oppositional conception of "us." I conclude by reflecting on the implications of these politics, in terms of both how they affect lived experiences and how they altered the trajectory of the debate.

A Tale of Two Homicides: The Initial Reaction

When police initially identified Antonio Sanchez as the assailant in the Calderon homicide, the *Standard-Speaker* ran two front-page articles about the crime. The first line of the lead article set a nonjudgmental tone: "Hazleton city police identified the man suspected of shooting another man to death at a busy intersection one block away from Broad Street Thursday afternoon."[9] Reporters and their sources went on to declare that drugs and gangs were not involved and, therefore, that the event was a random incident rather than an emerging local problem. It was not *that* type of crime, officials consoled the people of Hazleton in their comments to the press: "[Hazleton Police Chief Robert] Ferdinand emphasized that the shooting was not drug- or gang-related and that it could have happened in any city, town or borough. He called [the murder] a deliberate act, not a random shooting, and said it was over a minor incident that led to a violent confrontation between the suspect and the victim."[10] "Residents should not feel unsafe because of the shooting," the article went on, paraphrasing Chief Ferdinand. Mayor Barletta added, "The public should not take this as a reason to fear for their own safety."[11] In reacting to the crime, officials did call for increased law enforcement, but these calls were vague and unfocused.[12]

Twice as many articles (four) appeared on the front page of the *Standard-Speaker* the day after Kichline's alleged killers had been charged. The lead article—titled "Cops: Men in Country Illegally, Dealt Drugs"— began by announcing, "A pair of 23-year-old men who are illegal immigrants were charged Tuesday with the murder of a Hazleton resident that occurred six days earlier."[13] Unlike the generic opening line in the article about the prior case, here coded juxtapositions imply distinctions between "us" and "them" (i.e., "a Hazleton resident," "illegal immigrants"). The next sentence further emphasizes the alleged offenders' citizenship status and connects it to their criminal history—specifically, their prior involvement with drugs—thereby pulling from a larger cultural repertoire about the social ills allegedly associated with undocumented immigrants.[14] "Joan Romero and Pedro Cabrera lived together [and] *came to the United States illegally* from the Dominican Republic," the paper reports, "and were *heavily involved in drug dealing* before their arrests."[15] Whereas officials were silent about other local crimes occurring in temporal proximity to the Calderon case, this time they placed particular emphasis on unrelated incidents. Doing so further strengthened the perceived undocumented immigrant–crime nexus and made it look like the homicide was part of a crime wave:

> A man whose vehicle police stopped at Hemlock and Laurel streets on Thursday night was charged with possession of crack cocaine. Police also found crack cocaine and marijuana inside the trunk of a car that they stopped on Friday night near Pine and Maple Streets. While looking into the murder, police also gained evidence that led to the arrest of two boys, one 14 and the other 17, for each firing guns at the Pine Street Playground on Friday. The younger boy tried to hide four bags of cocaine in his mouth when arrested, and might be in the country illegally and faces deportation, police said. The playground incident was not related to the murder, but police said both boys are involved in gang activity.[16]

Officials went on to put the case in the context of the national-level immigration debate. The resulting message seemed to be that familiar "border problems" are expanding to the point of afflicting this small, interior city. The lead article pointed out that "the Romeros and Cabrera were charged one day after President Bush announced a five-point plan for securing America's southern border and dealing with people in the country illegally."[17] The title of a second front-page article quoted the police chief, "Ferdinand: Time to Seal off the Border."[18] That report also recounted the alleged assailants' criminal history, mentioned that they spoke Spanish, and emphasized that the men were "born in Santo Domingo and [had] lived in New York City *before coming to Hazleton*."[19] Perhaps best communicating the underlying message that "dangerous outsiders" might be "invading" this small town was Mayor Barletta, who made an analogy to a deadly disease: "Once they cross the border, they don't stay long. They come into cities such as Hazleton. It's like a cancer."[20]

Given this perceived invasion, officials called for a get-tough approach. They showcased their agenda in a third front-page article, titled "Police Plan to Continue Intensive Patrols." Ferdinand asserted, "You are only going to see more,"[21] referring to the arrests of Romero and Cabrera. Barletta told reporters, "People won't even be able to spit on the sidewalk without worrying that a police officer will stop them."[22] As opposed to being vague, these efforts were innovative and targeted (e.g., "The mayor said he wants to use video cameras to watch high crime areas")[23] and seemingly deployed with the intent to protect "us" from "them." Barletta promised that officials were willing to "use every resource to take back *our* streets."[24]

"Who's Next?" The Official Response

A press conference induced the second stage of reporting on the Calderon case. The message remained the same: This was an isolated incident, and things were under control. When the report mentioned other crimes that had occurred in the same week as the murder, the police assured residents that "all shootings in these cases were directed at specific persons and were not random shootings. It's important to realize that."[25] Calls for additional law enforcement persisted, but officials accompanied these calls with an acknowledgment of the hard truth that they could not eliminate crime: "We hope the quick arrests made in these cases and the increased patrol activity shows citizens that although criminal activity can never be completely deterred anywhere, they are still being protected as well as possible by the Hazleton police. I would like to assure them that I don't believe Hazleton is any less safe than it was. It's unfortunate that we have these types of incidents that occur, but due to the nature of them, I don't believe there's any way to completely deter it."[26]

Whereas coverage of the Calderon homicide conveyed a sense that all was well, the second set of reports to mention the Kichline murder focused on a highly dramatized drug raid and depicted a battle that had only just begun. "Who's Next?" the headline read. The first line of the article maintained that uncompromising tone: "Hazleton's special weapons and tactics team, federal agents and state police troopers burst into homes and businesses in Hazleton and West Hazleton on Thursday looking for drugs and criminals."[27] Subsequent statements communicated further that a powerful law enforcement apparatus had been unleashed: "Police milled around the front of the store. They carried a variety of guns. Some wore ski masks, helmets and bullet-resistant vests, others wore jackets, shirts or vests saying 'DEA,' 'State Police' or simply 'Police.'"[28]

Although the raids did not appear to target any individual thought to be involved in the homicide, it is clear that they were a continuation of the racialized reaction to the Kichline murder. The report explicitly states that the raids "showed that police activity remains intense after last week's murder in the city."[29] It seems to be further implied that the "dangerous outsiders" who used and sold drugs were at the root of Hazleton's so-called unruliness and would be met with aggressive law enforcement tactics meant to restore order. Mayor Barletta—pictured in the article standing with his arms crossed, surrounded by four law enforcement officers in full gear—made this clear when the *Standard-Speaker* quoted him as saying, "For anyone who thought we were kidding this is proof: This morning we took some drug-infested criminals off the street." He went on, "I suggest if anybody in Hazleton is involved in drug sales, they need to leave or they will be visited. Who's next?"[30] Clues regarding the ethnicity of those targeted by the raids accompanied such remarks. The news report provided a list of suspects taken into custody, which featured names of obvious Latin American origin, followed by aliases.[31] These names appeared in isolation without any information about the individuals or the charges they faced. Whether it was intended or not, it is hard to deny the existence of a subtext suggesting the raids targeted Latinos.

"Alleged Killer Slipped through System": The Community Reflection

After downtown business owners expressed worry that the Calderon homicide would deter customers from frequenting their stores, Mayor Barletta held a public meeting to reassure his concerned constituents. This meeting was the subject of the third stage of reporting on the Calderon case. At the meeting, officials told residents, "You can walk anywhere in Hazleton and feel safe."[32] Rather than playing on fears, the mayor dismissed the public's worries as mere perception and invalidated linkages between Hazleton's Latina/o community and violent crime. "Out of the thousands of people who've come to Hazleton in recent years," he said, "only a couple hundred are bad people."[33] His estimate may have been arbitrary, but the mayor seems to be fostering calm rather than inciting panic.

This news report uniquely included non-officials as sources, quoting local university professors. The result was a reflective discussion about overcoming ethnic conflict and dealing with social change. Using their knowledge of local history, the professors explained misperceptions about early Italian and Polish coal mining immigrants in Hazleton and cautioned residents about reliving this tumultuous past. Barletta, too, drew parallels between worries about Latino crime and unjustified fears associated with immigrants in prior eras. "Some people fear the Hispanic population," he said, "[but] the perceptions aren't much different than the established community's ideas from years ago."[34] Those attending and reporting on this meeting discussed race/ethnicity openly and thoughtfully. They admitted that clouds of resentment might be drifting over the city; they were forthright about the irrationality of this attitude; and they worked together to come up with ways to move the city forward.

Reflections on the Kichline homicide did nothing of the sort. Coverage there came in the form of a lengthy investigative report, titled "Alleged Killer Slipped through System." The report detailed the criminal history of one of the alleged perpetrators and questioned a judge's decision not to impose high bail when police arrested him in the months leading up to the murder. The take-home message was that punitive crime and immigration policies could prevent tragedies like this. As Mayor Barletta said in the quote that concluded the article, "Maybe we'd have had one less homicide had this guy been kept in prison."[35]

From Incident to Ordinance

To sum up, when Antonio Sanchez murdered Julio Calderon, a person of color, officials deemed a law-and-order response unnecessary, dismissing the crime as little more than an unfortunate incident. But when two undocumented Latino immigrants were charged with killing a White Hazletonian, their message appeared to be that Hazleton was under siege and therefore needed to get tough on crime and undocumented immigration. Hence, whereas officials took little further action on the Calderon homicide, they continued to toil in the weeks following Kichline's murder, hoping to find, in Mayor Barletta's words, "something that we could do to *protect ourselves* in the form of an ordinance."[36]

What they found was a piece of legislation drafted by Joseph Turner of Save Our State, an organization based in California and founded in 2005, which the Southern Poverty Law Center's Intelligence Project has determined to be a "nativist extremist" organization.[37] Turner unsuccessfully pushed the ordinance in San Bernardino, hoping to, as he put it, "save California from turning into a "Third World cesspool" of illegal immigrants."[38] Making only minimal adjustments and expressing no concern with its origins, the Hazleton City Council introduced the Illegal Immigration Relief Act just thirty-six days after Kichline was murdered.

Latina/o Degradation: "If You Are Illegal, You Are a Criminal"

Debates over the ordinance took place on June 15 and July 13, 2006. Residents filled the City Council chambers on each occasion, with crowds spilling out onto the streets. From the beginning of the debates, it was clear that those with decision-making authority formed a consensus.[39] Only one of Hazleton's five bipartisan council members ultimately voted against the ordinance, and he did so out of concern that the law "would not pass legal muster."[40] And whereas "normally, council waits at least 10 days between the first and final readings of an act," in this case it "approved all readings within three days."[41]

At these meetings and beyond, the justifications officials provided for the IIRA exemplify Latina/o degradation. In fact, the meetings themselves bear striking resemblance to what the late sociologist Harold Garfinkel famously called a *status degradation ceremony*.[42] My analysis suggests that officials expanded the implications of this single criminal incident, making undocumented immigrants—and to a considerable extent, as we will see, Latinas/os more generally—"stand out as 'out of the ordinary,'"[43] a "community of anti-civility that contravenes the . . . norms of proper conduct."[44] They accused undocumented immigrants of bringing not only crime but also a host of other social and economic ills with them into Hazleton. They also seemed to imply that undesirable behavior is not so much an occurrence as it is an *essential characteristic of the entire group*—that is, what "they" *do*, given their nature. Officials therefore expressed their preference for the ordinance as "beyond any motive or doubt."[45] "Protecting" their city from this "nuisance" became the understood prerogative, without regard for empirical evidence or broader social factors.[46]

Rather than focusing on Romero and Cabrera, much of the official rhetoric at the City Council meetings linked *all* people without documentation to criminality. The logic underlying the ordinance, which contained *no stipulations specifically targeting crime*, was that by keeping undocumented immigrants out of the city, the IIRA would "eventually deter crime" in Hazleton.[47] Councilman Joseph Yanuzzi was especially up front about this. "If you are illegal, you are a criminal; that is the gist here," he said.[48] Mayor Barletta similarly spoke as though undocumented criminality was so entrenched that it was not a matter of *whether* but, rather, *where* this group would offend. "Deprived of a place to live and without family or friends who live and work in Hazleton legally," he asserted, "other illegal immigrants may . . . look elsewhere when choosing a place to commit a crime."[49] In defending the portion of the ordinance designed to punish landlords who rent to undocumented immigrants, he added, "Anybody can walk into the city right now, give the landlord $400, put their bags in a room and go shoot somebody in the head tomorrow."[50] As another example, even after prosecutors dropped the charges against Cabrera and Romero, Barletta remained insistent about their guilt and continued to link documentation status to the commission of murder. "Today, a young man is still dead, and illegal aliens got away with murder," he said. "The Illegal Immigration Relief Act can't bring back Derek Kichline, but it could help save someone else's life."[51]

By characterizing undocumented immigrants in this way, officials made it seem "inconceivable" that the Kichline homicide had unique features.[52] Their assumptions of lawlessness likewise left no room for complicating questions that might arise from a careful analysis of crime data or conversations about other issues. For example, when attorneys asked Mayor Barletta whether he had access to crime statistics prior to proposing the IIRA, he replied, "No, I did not. . . . I don't need to know how many home runs Barry Bonds has to know that [if] I throw him a bad pitch, he can knock it out of the park. I knew we had a problem here. I didn't need numbers. . . . My people in my City did not need any numbers. We knew there is a problem here in the City."[53] According to legal briefs, Councilman Yanuzzi similarly "admitted that the City Council did not receive or review any police reports, shift incident reports, crime data or statistics showing the numbers of crimes claimed to have been committed by illegal aliens, . . . [that] he was unaware of the criminal conviction of any illegal alien in Hazleton, . . . [and that the] City Council heard only from Barletta, who asserted that illegal immigration increased crime. The only crime mentioned was the Kichline homicide."[54]

As it turns out, an examination of empirical data would have revealed that the Kichline murder was not part of a broader trend. From the time immigration into Hazleton increased in 2001 until 2006, when the city passed the IIRA, crime did not surge. In fact, crime statistics from Hazleton in those years resemble patterns observed by criminologists across the United States who are forming a "scholarly consensus" that immigration does not increase crime and may actually help reduce it.[55] As was reported in legal filings submitted by the plaintiffs who later challenged the IIRA (see Chapter 3), aggregately 1,358 crimes were reported in Hazleton in 2001, compared with 1,397 in 2006—a 2.8 percent increase in the *incidence rate* for reported crimes.[56] When we take into consideration that Hazleton's population is believed to have increased substantially during this time, these figures suggest there may actually have been a decrease in Hazleton's *crime rate* over this period.[57] Moreover, these filings suggest that only 10 of the 235 drug offenders arrested in Hazleton between 2001 and 2006 were people without documentation (4.3 percent).[58] They also suggest that only "three of the 428 violent crimes [e.g., murder, rape, robbery, and aggravated assault] . . . committed in . . . Hazleton [during those years] were allegedly committed by undocumented aliens" (0.7 percent).[59] Although the mayor elsewhere claimed that 30 percent "of the gang members that were arrested in Hazleton were illegal aliens,"[60] city officials could produce only 5 *total* examples of gang member arrests between 1997 and 2006.[61] Perhaps most glaringly, of the 8,571 total arrests made in Hazleton between 2001 and 2006, people without documentation accounted for just 21 of all arrestees.[62] That's 0.25 percent.

"Illegal Immigration . . . Diminishes Our Overall Quality of Life"

In addition to the crime itself, officials used the fact that police worked overtime investigating the Kichline homicide as evidence that undocumented immigrants sap city resources.[63] Once again expanding the implications of this single case in ways that mimic the broader Latino Threat Narrative, my analysis suggests that they presented undocumented immigrants one-dimensionally and derogatorily as burdensome "takers." The text of the first proposed draft of the ordinance declares, "Illegal immigration leads to higher crime rates" *and* "contributes to overcrowded classrooms and failing schools, subjects our hospitals to fiscal hardship and legal residents to substandard quality of care, contributes to other burdens on public services, increasing their costs and diminishing their availability to lawful residents, and destroys our neighborhoods and diminishes our overall quality of life."[64]

Councilman Yanuzzi at one point complained that people without documentation use the emergency room "as their practitionery office. They go in for splinters, colds, coughs, and it overloads, and then [the hospital] has the problem of not being paid."[65] Another example of this comes from an open letter Mayor Barletta posted on the city of Hazleton's website. "Some people have taken advantage of America's openness and tolerance," he wrote. "Some come to this country and *refuse to learn English*, creating a language barrier for city employees."[66]

Neither of these statements is supported by evidence.[67] Trends on language acquisition actually suggest the opposite of what Mayor Barletta asserts.[68] Nor do they consider broader circumstances: Even if Councilman Yanuzzi's comment were accurate,[69] what does it say about access to affordable health care in our society?[70] Disengagement from such realities and complexities, however, makes space for the presentation of a narrative depicting the city as besieged (e.g., its institutions overwhelmed) by a "manipulative" (e.g., using the emergency room for petty health issues) and "stubborn" (e.g., refusing to learn English) population.[71]

As an offshoot, consider also the following exchange from an interview Mayor Barletta conducted with Kiran Chetry of CNN while the IIRA was getting national attention:

> CHETRY: You say the illegal immigrants have brought with them drugs, they brought with them crime, gangs, and that your city is overwhelmed, the police force as well as the schools and hospitals. Can you elaborate on the impact, the negative impact, that you say illegal immigrants have had on your community?
>
> BARLETTA: Yeah, absolutely. For example, English as a Second Language [ESL] in the year 2000, the budget was $500. Today, it is $1,145,000. Our small budget here in the city cannot absorb the cost of illegal immigration.[72]

Although Chetry asked about problems posed by people without documentation, Mayor Barletta's response conflates language and citizenship status.[73] Examples like this that associate non-English-speakers with illegality thus reveal one of the many ways in which this narrative extends beyond legal status. This answer also again relies on the Latino Threat Narrative's taken-for-granted assumptions while leaving out other important considerations. If increasing ESL budgets are the actual concern, for example, we might expect a conversation about demographic change, a call for assistance so that these services can be offered, or a discussion about the comparable sums of money the school board has sacrificed for the Keystone Opportunity Zone (KOZ) initiative. Instead, the focus is narrowly on how "they" have financially burdened "our" schools.

Another important piece of this response is the second sentence: "Our small budget . . . *cannot absorb the cost of illegal immigration.*" This, too, was a common refrain. When he later testified in front of the U.S. Senate at a hearing about immigration reform, Mayor Barletta said, "We are spending the little amount [of money] that [we] do have chasing illegal immigrants around the city of Hazleton."[74] It is here that we see quite clearly how the Latino Threat Narrative also propagates a racialized understanding of socioeconomic relations. Hazleton's economy is indeed struggling and has become reliant on Latina/o immigrant laborers, many of whom continue to confront low wages and difficult conditions, despite choosing the best option neoliberal capitalism has offered them (see the Introduction and Chapter 1). That structural context and the real people who confront it are absent from this rhetoric, however, replaced by virtual representations of the "economically burdensome immigrant."[75]

White Affirmation: Enter the "Small Town Defender"

Consistent with Garfinkel's notion of a status degradation ceremony, City Council debates also featured imagery of the supposedly threatening outsider "clarified by the reference it bears to its opposite, the sacred."[76] Complementing the characterization of undocumented immigrants as "murderous thug[s]"[77] who take what they do not deserve, in other words, were suggestions that they have corrupted something innocent and pure.[78] Hazleton is "under attack" *and as a result* Hazleton "deserves" protection.[79] Language that is presumably code for White in this sense stands in direct opposition to the racialized language used to vilify recent immigrants (e.g., "legal residents," "hardworking people").[80] As john powell writes, "The dominant group . . . becomes the invisible standard by which all others are (unfavorably) measured. This process defines the racial other, but it also defines the racially privileged: they are not the other."[81] I found that officials constructed a conception of Hazleton's community identity around such definitions, in this way providing Whites with *affirmation* by presenting mirror image *positive traits* as the *essential characteristics* of so-called "legal" Hazletonians.

We see this in the way officials expanded Kichline's individual victimhood. Elaborating on previous comments made to the press about undocumented immigrants being "like a cancer," the City Council debates focused not only on the "disease" but also on the metaphorical "infected" body. Mayor Barletta explained how the defilement of a once tranquil place motivated him to pass the IIRA, saying, "I am the Mayor of Hazleton. I swore an oath to protect residents of this city—the legal residents of this city. When people are gunned down outside their homes, I cannot sit by and wait for a solution. When residents are afraid to walk down the street, I cannot ignore their complaints. When children—*children*—are afraid to go to a playground, I must act."[82]

As another example, recall the specific language of the proposed ordinance. Note this time how it subtly implies "White injury":[83] "Illegal immigration . . . contributes to . . . burdens on public services . . . *diminishing* their availability to *lawful residents*"; it "*destroys our* neighborhoods," "subjects *our* hospitals to *fiscal hardship*" "*subjects . . . legal residents* to substandard quality of care," and "*diminishes our* overall quality of life."[84]

Most official statements justifying the ordinance followed this pattern. Complaints about "our" victimization always seemed to accompany references to "their" alleged depravity. When officials bemoaned those who "come to this country and *refuse to learn English*," they also harped on how this *creates "a language barrier for city employees*."[85] This is especially apparent in Mayor Barletta's speech to the City Council on July 13:

The other day, police officers responded to a simple noise complaint and found three illegal aliens. The officers who went to that scene were *taken away from* other patrols. Those three young men were not supposed to be in the United States to begin with, but the Hazleton Police Department had to *shift resources away* from other law enforcement duties to respond to that complaint. Earlier this month, city police officers *had to* physically subdue a man who later claimed he was an illegal immigrant. This man allegedly fought with *our police* and tried to *take* the gun out of the hands of one of *our detectives.*[86]

Along these same lines, officials were adamant in City Council debates and beyond that "their" criminal behavior should not be happening *here.* Mayor Barletta in particular took on the persona of a "Small Town Defender," which, not coincidentally, is the name of the organization later used to collect funds for the legal defense of the IIRA.[87] "Hazleton is Small Town, USA," he told the City Council. "We are an All-American City. We are a place where people should be able to raise their families free of fear."[88] Statements like this appear to reinforce the idea that "we" are virtuous and "they" are menacing. He went on to explain how the two men initially charged in the Kichline murder "eventually migrated into Hazleton, where they helped *create a sense of fear* in the *good, hardworking residents who are here legally.*"[89] In his testimony to the U.S. Senate, Barletta likewise asserted that "[Cabrera and Romero] should never have been in this country in the first place, *let alone in Hazleton, Pennsylvania.*"[90] This last statement obviously has no legal basis. It is not any more "illegal" to be present without authorization in Hazleton than it is in other parts of the country. Yet the message seems clear: these two men—and presumably others like them—do not belong in the United States and they most certainly are not welcome within the confines of "Small Town, USA."[91]

"Licensed to Hate": Degradation and Affirmation on the Ground

It would be one thing if this were all empty rhetoric, but degradation translates into subordination. Real people have to confront the virtual personas assigned to them, living their lives with others assuming that they are dangerous, lazy, and manipulative. To be sure, this is by no means new.[92] However, it seems to become more salient when officials freely use this rhetoric as they justify the passage of an exclusionary local law.

Indeed, a mounting body of research has found that in the wake of exclusionary local and state-level immigration legislation, Latinas/os, *regardless of their immigration or legal status*, experience intensified harassment, discrimination, and psychological distress.[93] In Hazleton, many in the Latina/o community reported experiencing increased resentment after the IIRA was passed. During the course of my research, I heard accounts about discrimination in public places and in interpersonal interactions. People told me that Latina/o residents were scolded in restaurants for speaking Spanish, called "illegal" by strangers, and discriminated against in the housing market.[94] One Latina woman I spoke with said it felt as if the IIRA gave native-born White residents a "license to hate."

Others who conducted research on Hazleton in the aftermath of the ordinance had similar findings.[95] René Flores interviewed Hazleton residents in 2007 and 2011 and found that Latina/o respondents noticed substantial differences in how they were treated following the IIRA.[96] "There's always been animosity here, but before, it was more hidden," one Colombian immigrant who has lived in Hazleton for many years told him. "After . . . the ordinance, a lot of people feel they have the right to say things . . . to yell from cars. . . . Random people that I don't even know have asked me if I'm legal!"[97] A research team working with Zogby International hosted focus groups with some Latina/o residents in June 2006 as part of a study the Greater Hazleton Area Civic Partnership commissioned the organization to conduct. In but one of several examples from that research, a Latina woman mentioned that her daughter, who had previously "felt like a native" and "even talked with a Hazleton accent" had experienced "new and emerging issues" since the IIRA passed. "Now everyone's treating [my kids] differently because of what's going on recently," she said. "My daughter is discriminated against for no reason."[98]

Signs also exist suggesting that, on the ground, many working-class White residents have embraced what Ali Behdad describes as a "*differential mode of . . . identification . . . articulated through and dependent upon the alien other.*"[99] When I conducted focus groups and interviews with ordinary, White, mostly lifelong Hazleton residents in 2009, I began by asking how the city had changed. Nearly everyone expressed, in one way or another, the feeling that the city, in the exact words of one resident, "went to hell." The most common way they articulated this was through nostalgic stories that began with phrases such as "I remember when we used to" and that ended with "But it's not like that anymore." On close inspection, I found that these stories resemble what Eduardo Bonilla-Silva calls *racial story lines* or *racial testimonies*.[100] The tales I heard were characterized by a rhetorical pattern that draws contrasts between "us," represented by the fabled past, and "them," represented by the undesirable present. Most attributed the demise of the "good old days" to "their" pathological behavior.[101] Themes from participants' remembrances evoked a city that was close-knit, quiet, obedient, honest, harmless, and hardworking. In direct contrast, tales of a corrupted contemporary Hazleton commonly featured "city people," "illegals," "a different element," and sometimes, stated frankly, Hispanics / Latinos who are characterized as strangers, loud, disobedient, manipulative, lawless, and lazy.[102] When they raised economic issues, the residents I spoke with occasionally mentioned CAN DO or the lack of high-quality jobs available in the city.[103] However, much more prominent were economic stories told using the script from the Latino Threat Narrative. A running theme among White residents was how it is unfair that Latinas/os benefit from state programs and their alleged ability to manipulate the system while "we" suffer. One man's account of shopping at the local Wal-Mart store is an illustrative example: "There was a lady at Wal-Mart who had a really monstrous cart full of stuff. She was Latino. She paid with some kind of card. At the bottom of this pile was a bag of dog food. The clerk said, 'That card won't cover the dog food.' She said OK and took the dog food back. She came back with a package of steaks. She said, 'The dog will eat steak.' I haven't bought steak in a long time."

Again, what I am describing is by no means an entirely new phenomenon. Although fears are perhaps amplified in the current historical moment, the national discourse has consistently evoked the themes of the Latino Threat Narrative for decades, and similar racial narratives have even deeper historical roots.[104] Thus, what we do not learn from these data is the particular extent to which the politics surrounding the introduction of the IIRA created, enflamed, or simply spoke to already existing attitudes. What they do seem to represent, however, is one of several examples where a community identity was articulated using conceptions of "us" and "them." Another particularly emblematic example of this is a sign that hung outside a pub at a busy intersection for several months after the city approved the ordinance. The sign contained the words "ALL LEGALS SERVED."[105] Although the pub owner may have claimed a different intent,[106] the sign's symbolism is powerful in the context of what I just described. One might even say it frighteningly bears similarities to the "White" and "Colored" placards that infamously decorated the Jim Crow South. As the sign hung all that time, seemingly declaring both who "we" are and who "we" are not, it is easy to imagine a scenario in which some passersby were reminded of their subordinate position and others of their relative privilege.

Conclusion

After spearheading the IIRA, "Mayor Lou," as many Hazletonians fondly refer to Barletta, became a local hero. His political career took off as he rode a widely felt perception that he had "the courage to address the real problem in our community."[107] In his first post-IIRA mayoral reelection bid, he won the primaries of *both* parties and went on to win the election by a landslide—the largest in Hazleton's history.[108] National prominence followed.[109] He eventually unseated the longtime incumbent Representative Paul Kanjorski in 2010 to become a member of the U.S. House of Representatives.

We can interpret Barletta's success as an example of the political rewards associated with amplifying perceptions of Latino Threat. Acknowledging looming fears, attributing them to a familiar (though false) enemy, and reassuring some concerned constituents that the bottom rung of the social ladder is not theirs to occupy all contribute to the potency of this narrative.[110]

This becomes even more apparent in the next chapter as we explore how the community reacted to pro-immigrant activists who pushed back against Latina/o degradation. As the dismissal of evidence and unwillingness to consider the broader context suggests, the politics employed up to this point have set up a debate rooted not in logic but in *identity*. When seen from this perspective, we realize that pro-immigrant, anti-degradation politics pose a threat to how those who embrace this narrative see themselves and their community.[111] Claims that the city has violated immigrants' rights or that residents have acted in discriminatory ways complicate idyllic depictions of Whiteness and compromise its psychological wage. Efforts to humanize Latina/o immigrants and problematize imagery of the "threatening outsider" similarly obstruct the view of the virtual figure on which many have come to rely to articulate who they are through differentiation. In this way, pro-immigrant activists who resist confront a rekindled alliance between political elites and a cadre of poor and working-class Whites that dishes out a one-two punch of political ambition and passion as it vigilantly opposes their activism, disavowing it as yet another attack on an "innocent small town."

3

Lozano v. Hazleton and the Defense
of White Innocence

he most visible initial opposition to the Illegal Immigration Relief
Act (IIRA) came from a trio of local Latina/o community leaders: Dr.
Agapito Lopez, Anna Arias, and Amilcar Arroyo. Lopez is a retired
ophthalmologist from Puerto Rico.[1] When I first met him, he had statistics handy to debunk claims that Hazleton's recent Latina/o immigrants
commit more crime and are a fiscal drain. "All of these are myths," he
said. "Really, we are contributing to the economy of the state."[2] Familiar
with the racial implications of the ordinance, he went on to situate his
opposition to the IIRA within a larger historical struggle "against injustice, against disparity, and against lack of representation by minorities."
He shared with me the slides from a presentation he had given at a local
college. Titled "Intolerance," the presentation linked Hazleton's passage of
the IIRA to oppressive acts from throughout U.S. history, such as slavery,
the Trail of Tears, and discrimination against immigrants in earlier eras.

Arias was born in the Dominican Republic, and she has lived in
the Hazleton area since 1992. A passionate activist, she also saw the
ordinance as "very discriminatory . . . very bigoted and racist" and "an
affront not only to the undocumented immigrants, but to the whole
Latino population [in Hazleton]."[3] Criminalization and the post-IIRA

harassment that many endured were chief among her concerns. She was also protective of people without documentation, whom in her view were being dehumanized:

> Undocumented people come into this country to work because they have a family to support, they have children to feed, and we are forgetting about that part, the human part of the whole thing. I wish that people would stop and think that if your child is hungry, you are going to do whatever it takes to feed that child and to clothe that child, to put shoes on their feet. A lot of us are not thinking about that. We are thinking, "Oh, they are breaking the law." If your child is hungry and you know that if you cross a border and find work you will be able to clothe and feed that child, you are going to do it. . . . So I would like people to remember this: An undocumented person living in the United States is human. He bleeds. He feels. He cries.

Arroyo is a native Peruvian who founded Hazleton's first Spanish-language newspaper, *El Mensajero*. He came to the United States in 1989. Although he has since become a U.S. citizen, he was undocumented for a short time after overstaying a tourist visa. In his first few years in the United States, he worked as a tomato packer; he also did a stint as a laborer in one of the local factories. The sentiments lurking below the surface of the debate over the IIRA were apparent to him, as well—including, especially, the tendency of residents to use the terms "illegals" and "Hispanics" interchangeably. He takes pride as a businessperson in the economic benefits Latinas/os have brought to Hazleton and intentionally patronizes Latina/o-owned establishments. In our conversations, he, like Arias, often put a human face on the issue. He told me stories about his own immigrant experience and used the poverty he witnessed in Peru as an example of the forces that drive migration.

This group, in short, directly challenged the prevailing narrative with a discourse that was decidedly *race-cognizant*.[4] In contrast to color-blindness, they emphasized how race and racism create different social experiences across groups. They do so empathetically out of a concern that the IIRA has adversely affected the Latina/o community and fearlessly in the face of the majority's insistence that race is not relevant to the debate. In contrast to the narrowness of the degrading "illegals" tag, Lopez, Arias, and Arroyo also placed local issues in a broader historical and social-structural context, painting a picture of complex human beings experiencing equally complex social circumstances.

Together, these leaders formed a small, local organization called the Hazleton Area Latino Association (HALA). Each of them also had an affiliation with a group known as the Hazleton Area Latino Taskforce (HALT), and all served in various capacities on local, county, and state-level boards and commissions. In the community, they led vigils, spoke out at City Council debates, and spearheaded efforts to challenge the IIRA's constitutionality in court. Picking up the story at the passage of the ordinance, this chapter chronicles the community's reactions to this group's activism. Although, as Ian Haney López observes, "We would like to believe that if the polity understood that race-baiting continues to be widely practiced, people would repudiate it,"[5] this is often not at all the case. I will contend that when this group of activists challenged the dominant narrative and questioned its myths, many opted to "reject this information and compound their support for discrimination."[6] What transpires is an often intense vilification of these Latina/o leaders and those who engage in similar work that begins during City Council arguments and persists as the debate moves into the courtroom and eventually out onto the streets.

My analysis of the response to this wave of pro-immigrant activism thus peels back another layer of the local Latino Threat Narrative. Using a pair of concepts—*White innocence* and *Latina/o abstraction*[7]—I identify a rhetorical pattern encompassed within this larger narrative to illustrate how community "insiders" tend to fend off resistance. We will see how insistence on the innocence of Whites and a refusal to acknowledge the real, lived experiences of Latinas/os reinforces the prevailing narrative. It also perpetuates existing social arrangements in several ways. Specifically, I argue that this rhetoric tries to prevent race-cognizance from entering the debate by chiding those who evoke it and that it almost unconditionally casts immigrants' rights claims and legal mobilizations as unacceptable.[8] When efforts to bring about racial justice are delegitimized as such, I show not only how potential pro-immigrant mobilizations are quelled but also how previous constructions of Hazleton's collective identity are reaffirmed as the majority adds pro-immigrant activists to the list of "enemies" who have allegedly corrupted this small town.

"I Could Accuse You of Racism": White Innocence and Latina/o Abstraction

In challenging the ordinance before the City Council, Arias began her testimony by contrasting the words recited in the Pledge of Allegiance with what she saw as a contrary reality underlying the IIRA: "liberty and justice for some."[9] She went on to highlight the contradiction of Hazleton's passing an exclusionary ordinance in a "nation of immigrants." Questioning myths about immigrants' draining city resources and disproportionately committing crime was also her ambition.[10] Her testimony was as direct as could be. At one point, she warned the council members that if they passed the law, Hazleton "would go down in history as the first Nazi city in the country."[11] After a council member chimed in with the question, "Do you believe that this ordinance is divisive?" she responded, "It is very divisive. Yes, sir. It is divisive, and it is creating hatred and racism in the community. We had a family already whose trash was not picked up just for the mere fact that they were Latinos. . . . Don't you think that is divisive enough?"[12]

Arias's claims did not sit well, to put it mildly. Later in the meeting, a former Hazleton resident provided the following testimony in response:

A lot of our speakers are underscoring [Derek Kichline] being fatally shot on Chestnut Street over somebody's garbage being late. I'm very appalled at that. There is a group called the Hazleton Area Latino Task Force,[13] and I don't know why the word "Latino" is in there. It is an immigration relief act; it is not a Latino immigration [relief act]. . . . That being said, I really, really feel after reading the newspapers that HALT is the cause of a lot of these problems. They are telling the Latino community that we are against all of them, not just the illegals. It is almost like blackmail. They are blackmailing our community with litigation threats. I'm hearing them all night. We're threatened about our economy going down, litigation. It has to come to an end. We survived for many years before this mass immigration came into Hazleton. We're going to survive again. As to HALT, I just want you to know blackmail is a crime, just like being illegal is a crime. . . . You're threatening Hazleton, threatening everybody else and I think it is wrong.[14]

Agapito Lopez's testimony covered an array of issues. He evoked the history of U.S. immigration, spoke about the economic circumstances that drive migration, called the IIRA unenforceable, and pointed to immigrant-led economic revitalization. Most controversial were statements he made about assimilation. "I think you have the wrong word," he told a councilmember who asked whether he thought recent immigrants would assimilate. "It is not 'assimilate,' because assimilation means that we convert ourselves automatically into Anglos. We will never convert ourselves into Anglos. We will *culturalize*. We will learn the language, we will learn the laws, we will follow the laws, but we will never assimilate."[15]

Councilwoman Evelyn Graham seemed perturbed by this statement and the anti-IIRA resistance more generally, as is reflected in the following comments she made during the conclusion of the July 13 council meeting:

> Dr. Lopez, I have tried twice to explain to you the serious problems we face, and you have dismissed these problems by insisting they are just the result of a different culture. You seem to believe that we must accept them. When I and the mayor tried to give you and Amilcar Arroyo examples of troubles in the community which we believe are caused by illegal aliens, your response was to discount "illegal" as just a word that changes with time. You belittle any implications of criminality. You show no desire to help solve the problems and will not even discuss them. I must confess, I am dismayed by this attitude. I was hoping that you would help build the bridge we need. Based on your statements in front of City Council . . . I could accuse you and Anna Arias of racism. You, not the mayor or council, are the ones who are inciting segregation instead of encouraging integration. I believe it is you who are practicing divisiveness. Look into your hearts and you may find that you are advocating separatism. . . . I believe that most of Hazleton's immigrants came here to become a part of the community and build a better life, a new life. I believe they seek unity rather than diversity. And I believe that you, the mayor, City Council, and community leaders owe it to them and future legal immigrants to get behind them and encourage their adaptation to a new life and a loyalty to America, their new home. We welcome them. And you do them a disservice when you deliberately misrepresent our actions for your own purposes.[16]

The applause these words prompted rivaled the standing ovation Mayor Barletta received when he walked in the door that evening. Graham likely struck a chord because what she said embodied the rhetorical pattern that would characterize how the majority countered claims for immigrants' rights throughout the debate. Namely, I have found that resistance to pro-immigrant activism in Hazleton closely resembled what the legal scholar Thomas Ross has called "White innocence" ("the insistence on the innocence or absence of responsibility of contemporary whites") and "Latina/o abstraction" ("the rhetorical depiction of [Latina/os] in an abstract context, outside of any real or rich social context").[17] Deeply rooted in U.S. legal and racial history and patterned a lot like the broader Latino Threat Narrative, this rhetoric

- denies that Latina/os experience harm (and usually claims that they benefit);
- emphasizes the absence of a racial motive; and
- raises concerns about Whites' injury and the loss of their way of life.[18]

Notice, for instance, how the former Hazleton resident who was appalled by Arias's comments used the unrelated murder of Derek Kichline to make her claim appear petty, effectively invalidating discrimination against Latinas/os as a serious concern. Graham's comment similarly elevated fears about criminality among undocumented immigrants without actually addressing the claims Lopez and Arias made about the IIRA's effect on the Latina/o community. Each also denied that race was a factor and scorned attempts to bring it into the conversation. Graham dwelled on the "illegal" versus "legal" distinction and decried efforts to complicate it; the former Hazleton resident advocated erasure of the word "Latino" from the pro-immigrant organization's name. Once this rhetoric takes race and the negative effects of the ordinance off the table, those who support the IIRA seem innocent, and any antagonisms from the opposition begin to look like unfair attacks. As a result, the ideology of White injury prevails again. Indeed, it was Lopez and Arias whom they presented as "the cause of a lot of these problems." We also see musings about litigation threats and suggestions that the *White* (inferring from the comment, "We survived for many years before this mass immigration") Hazleton community is a victim of "blackmail." Graham likewise presented the city as victimized by HALA's so-called divisive, segregationist, and borderline racist demands.

The power of this rhetoric, therefore, is that it makes the decision to pass the IIRA appear all the more justified. Joining "crime-prone" and "burdensome" undocumented immigrants on the list of those who pose a threat to Hazleton are now "self-interested" activists who allegedly disrupt community harmony by considering litigation and bringing race into a "race-less" debate. A comment Mayor Barletta made to open the July 13 City Council meeting provides another example of this pattern. Note in this statement how the mayor seems to strongly deny racial intent. He also leverages the Latino Threat Narrative in a way that turns accusations of racism and intolerance levied against him upside down. The backlash against "special rights" activists and the crackdown on "undocumented criminals" are in this way folded into a single narrative in which the mayor and members of his community occupy the role of the injured party:

> Over the past month or so, we have been accused of being racist, intolerant, and unfair. But let me repeat what I have been saying all along . . . Illegal is illegal! We do not care where they come from, we do not care what language they speak, but an illegal alien is not welcome in Hazleton! . . . On a personal note, I have been accused of not only being a racist, but also doing this for other reasons, for political gain, or to help other elected officials. I am personally offended by those accusations, not because they insult me, I am offended because they insult the family of Derek Kichline, who was allegedly gunned down—murdered—by four [*sic*] illegal aliens. They insult the children who are no longer allowed on the Pine Street Playground because an illegal alien fired a gun there. They insult the fathers and mothers, brothers and sisters, sons and daughters, of those in our community who are addicted to the drugs sold by illegal immigrants.[19]

Lozano v. Hazleton

Once it was clear that they were making little headway locally, members of HALA began contacting "other people that have dealt with this," as Lopez recalled when we spoke, including groups at the local, state, and national levels. After recruiting allies, they convened a "strategic meeting" at a local

Mexican restaurant. It was there, Lopez further explained, that they made the decision to file a lawsuit against the city:

> This strategic meeting was done with all the Latino representatives from northeastern Pennsylvania, and that included lawyers like the lawyers from the Community Justice Project in Harrisburg and, of course, representatives from the ACLU [American Civil Liberties Union]. . . . So these organizations and these lawyers and people in the community that were worried about this ordinance, we got together. There were about sixty or seventy persons coming from New York, coming from Harrisburg, coming from Philadelphia, and we made a strategic meeting in which we divided into groups and we searched for opinions on different topics and we wrote them on a big notebook on the wall. We wrote the suggestions of everybody. . . . The lawyers in the group, they said we have to do something legal. We have to stop this ordinance in a legal way. . . . They said they had to challenge this ordinance.

At the very least, such a lawsuit held promise in its potential to defeat the IIRA. The ordinance may already have done some damage, but fears loomed that once enforcement began, the situation would get worse. Turning to the law could also generate collective action. As sociolegal scholars who study legal mobilization often point out, regardless of whether groups are victorious in court, merely filing a lawsuit often benefits less powerful groups because it allows them to see their plight through a new, legalistic lens.[20] In other words, a high-profile lawsuit could provide local Latina/o residents with a stronger, more culturally resonant vision of the IIRA as *impinging on immigrants' rights.*[21]

A team of attorneys from the ACLU, the Puerto Rican Legal Defense and Education Fund (PRLDEF), and other firms did ultimately file a lawsuit against Hazleton. Their argument was that the IIRA violated equal protection and due process rights and usurped the federal power to regulate immigration.[22] Litigators chose Pedro Lozano, a local landlord, as the lead plaintiff in the case. Joining him were other individuals and organizations who felt harmed by the IIRA.[23] After they submitted the suit, courts issued a restraining order that kept Hazleton from enforcing the ordinance until Judge James Munley of the Middle District Court in Scranton, Pennsylvania, assessed its constitutionality in *Lozano v. Hazleton* in the spring of 2007.

Even though the debate was taken into a formal legal setting, the arguments at trial reflected those heard outside of the courtroom. The plaintiffs called a number of witnesses who spoke about the harm they felt the IIRA's symbolic passage inflicted. Lopez took the stand first. He testified about widespread fear within the immigrant community. "I had contact with these people," he said. "I could see their anguish. I could see their fear. I could hear their worries."[24] Others echoed his points. Jose and Rosa Lechuga testified that the restaurant they owned suffered from a loss of revenue because potential customers were fearful of frequenting closely monitored Latina/o-owned establishments. Lozano explained that his tenants had moved out after learning about the IIRA. Jose Molina of the Pennsylvania Statewide Latino Coalition gave an account of a meeting held soon after the IIRA was passed at which a number of concerned community members aired grievances. His testimony depicted a climate of fierce hostility. At that meeting, Molina said, some Latinas/os reported racial profiling by police; one person said that someone had thrown a brick through the window of a Latino-owned business; and many people expressed more general fears of taking part in day-to-day activities because of the possibility of being targeted by law enforcement or hate groups.

Kris Kobach headed Hazleton's legal team. A prominent national figure in the movement calling for increased immigration restrictions, he has had a hand in some of the most controversial initiatives implemented across the United States in recent years.[25] In defending the IIRA, my analysis suggests that he and other attorneys representing Hazleton followed the innocence / abstraction script. In his opening statement, Kobach painted Hazleton as the victim, asserting that undocumented immigrants have "played a very destructive role in Hazleton's history."[26] He added, "With a wave of illegal immigration in recent years, Hazleton has seen new criminals and new sorts of crime."[27] The city's budget, he told the judge, was "busting at the seams" because of undocumented immigrants, who, among other things, caused police to spend "innumerable hours . . . identifying perpetrators."[28] In passing the IIRA, he said, Lou Barletta was simply trying to protect his cherished way of life, doing something that "needed to be done to preserve the city that he grew up in, the city that he loved, and the city that he took an oath to protect."[29]

In studying the transcript of the *Lozano* trial, I also observed Hazleton's attorneys denying racial motivations. They did this by frequently pointing out the lack of explicit references to race / ethnicity in the ordinance and in the mayor's discourse. "Can you agree that nowhere in the ordinances is the word 'Latino' or 'Hispanic' ever referenced?"[30] Hazleton's lawyers asked Molina during the cross-examination. The attorney Harry Mahoney similarly pressed Lopez:

MAHONEY: Let me read to you, sir, what the Mayor said in part, "But I can read hundreds of stories from residents, former residents and people across America who have seen illegal aliens destroy their towns and their quality of life. As the Mayor, I see how illegal aliens are sapping our City resources. Enough is enough." Did I read that correctly, Doctor?

LOPEZ: Yes, sir.

MAHONEY: And on the next page . . . the Mayor said, "Over the past month or so, I have been accused of being racist, intolerant and unfair, but let me repeat what I have been saying all along[:] [I]llegal is illegal. We do not care where they came from[,] [w]e do not care what language they speak, but an illegal alien is not welcome in Hazleton[!] Those who are here illegally continue to drain City resources." Did I read that correctly, Doctor?

LOPEZ: Yes, sir.

MAHONEY: Would I be correct, Doctor, in characterizing the Mayor's comments throughout his remarks on July 13, 2006, at the City Council meeting as being directed not against immigrants, but against illegal aliens and illegal immigrants?[31]

Even when presented with examples of overt racism that occurred in the community, the defendant's attorneys seemed to brush race aside. The plaintiffs presented as evidence three pieces of hate mail that Lopez had received in the months he was protesting.[32] Hazleton attorneys countered that these letters were separate from the IIRA, implying they were simply the work of a few "bad apples," not an indication of a hostile climate. "There is going to be people with prejudices against ethnic groups whether there is ordinances or not, isn't that right?"[33] Lopez was asked.[34]

I found that, exemplifying abstraction, the defendants rarely took testimony from Latinas/os about harm they have endured seriously and often dismissed it outright. Throughout the trial, they sought to portray the ordinance as harmless by, for example, questioning the financial practices of the Lechugas and Lozano. One may argue that this is understandable to an extent, considering that Hazleton's legal team would need to disassociate the IIRA from such harms to win the case.[35] However, less excusable are instances of outright dehumanization. When the plaintiffs' attorney Thomas Wilkinson questioned Councilman Yanuzzi, he asked him why he did not commission a study to explore the issue of crime committed by people without documentation and about the potential for unintended consequences. Yanuzzi compared the IIRA to a "pooper scooper law," then refused to backtrack after Wilkinson problematized his remarks. The exchange went this way:

> YANUZZI: Every ordinance I pass or every law I make, somebody is going to be hurt. There is no 100 percent, and to have studies done—I mean, I passed the pooper scooper law, and what am I going to do, study that? We just can't have consultants come in every two minutes.
>
> WILKINSON: Well, when you're doing a pooper scooper law, you're not evicting people.
>
> YANUZZI: It's an ordinance. It's a law. It's the same thing as this.
>
> WILKINSON: So removing these people from town who were working, living, employed is just the same thing as removing something off the sidewalk?
>
> YANUZZI: Well, you're talking about a person that is, first off, illegal.[36]

Return of the "Small Town Defender"

Ultimately, Judge Munley agreed with the plaintiffs, signaling what was at least a temporary victory for Hazleton's Latina/o community. In an opinion that ran for more than two hundred pages, he declared, "The genius of our Constitution is that it provides rights even to those who evoke the least sympathy from the general public. In that way, all in this nation can be confident of equal justice under its laws. . . . Hazleton, in its zeal to control the presence of a group deemed undesirable, violated the rights of such people, as well as others in the community. Since the United States Constitution protects even the disfavored, the ordinances cannot be enforced."[37]

"The whole town should be celebrating," Lopez exclaimed, echoing the jubilance many in the Latina/o community felt after the decision.[38] Caution tempered the excitement, however. Perhaps knowing that mobilizing in favor of immigrants' rights remained an uphill battle, many expressed somberness, as well. "It is a beautiful day. Justice has spoken," Arias told the press, before holding back and reflectively questioning, "But did we really win? Did we really win?"[39] What would transpire warranted her guardedness: The only mobilization that ultimately gained steam was one that *opposed* Judge Munley's ruling.

As some celebrated, other Hazleton residents took news of the decision as a most unwelcome development. A declaration in an oversize font decorated the front page of the June 27, 2007, edition of the *Standard-Speaker*: "STRUCK DOWN." Officials and attorneys quoted in that morning's news suggested that Judge Munley's ruling was an illegitimate, unfair attack on a small community that was trying to do what was right. Mayor Barletta again positioned himself as a *small town defender*. This time, it was attorneys and litigating organizations from whom he vowed to protect his city. In his version of events, Hazleton was the underdog confronting multiple threats.[40] As he did when he postured as a local-level general in the war on crime, in reacting to the *Lozano* decision Mayor Barletta seems to portray himself as ready to lead his constituents through the sizable challenge their "small city . . . faces when it chooses to take on the powerful, special interest groups and lobbyists."[41] He told reporters, "This fight is far from over. Hazleton will not back down."[42] In a subsequent speech, he spoke to the swirling perception that this decision had victimized the people of Hazleton, again reminding his constituents that, as their leader, he would fight back: "The ACLU and their 25 lawyers thought that this little city would roll over and back down, but we're not going to back down."[43] Kobach also portrayed Hazleton as the less powerful entity as he vowed to continue the crusade. "We expected to be down at halftime," he said, "but we expect to win in the end."[44] Hazleton's legal adversaries had a "special advantage" in the case, he elaborated, calling Munley's ruling "the paradigm of judicial activism" and complaining, "It is clear we were not only battling [the plaintiffs in the case], but a hostile court as well."[45]

Mobilizing in Opposition to *Lozano:* Voice of the People, USA

In response to the legal defeat of the IIRA, many residents from Hazleton and surrounding areas sprang into action. Frustrations with pro-immigrant activists and the *Lozano* decision most notably led to the formation of the grassroots organization Voice of the People, USA (VOP).[46] The following account provides a glimpse of how the momentum immigrants' rights activists generated prompted a counter-mobilization:

> I saw [Mayor Barletta] on TV speaking the same language I am. . . . Then I see where the ACLU is taking him to court. Then this is playing out in the courts. Then I hear during his trial [that] the ACLU and . . . La Raza and a couple other militant organizations are going to be staging a protest outside of the courthouse in Scranton on Public Square. . . . So I pull over and I go out and here is all the pro–illegal immigration activists—not immigration activists, [but] *illegal* immigration activists. . . . I said, "Something has to be done here. There has to be a counter-demonstration, a counter show of support for *legal* immigration and against *illegal*." So I went ahead and made a couple of phone calls. . . . I called talk radio and said, "Look, tomorrow I am going to have a rally in support of Mayor Lou Barletta and the IIRA."[47]

Another activist similarly recounted, "I'm trying to drive through Hazleton and I see the street closed down because illegals [were] protesting. . . . I didn't appreciate that. But all you heard was this hatred being shot at Barletta. [In a subsequent encounter with Mayor Barletta], I came up to him and I told him, I made him a promise. I said, 'I don't know how and I don't know when and I don't know where, but I'm going to do something to support you.'"[48]

It was therefore the *challenge to* rather than the *passage of* the IIRA that activated those who participated in this mobilization. The first activist went on to admit:

> If there was no rally there that day and I didn't hear the misrepresentation and the lies, I probably would not have been activated, mobilized. But that is what really got me. . . . [When the ordinance passed], I was like, "OK, here is a guy that is standing up, Lou Barletta. Here is a guy that is doing something good." . . . I never called him. I never said, "Hey, Mayor, what's going on? I wish you luck." I just saw him in some newscast and I thought, "Here is a guy that is doing something that needs . . . well, not initially, needed support." I thought he had his own [City Council] supporting him;

he had the people of Hazleton supporting him. It really came to a head when I was driving just happenstance through Scranton, saw the Fox News trucks, went over and saw the people there and I listened to what they had to say and I was, like, "Wait a minute! This viewpoint is skewed!"

As another activist comparably recalled, "At the time, when [the IIRA] was first passed . . . , I supported it, but I was like everybody else. I supported it, but I was, like, 'I support [Mayor Barletta],' but OK, I just kind of watched it play out. . . . Then as everything else was going on—[the city of Hazleton] getting sued and everything else and all of the problems [Mayor Barletta] was encountering with that—that is when we decided to give him support."

After announcing its intentions to take to the streets and hold rallies, VOP began attracting likeminded citizens very quickly. The group's sentiments, it turns out, were widely shared. "I got, like, a hundred e-mails from people who agreed with my letter [announcing plans to hold a rally] . . . saying that they wanted to do something," one organizer recalled. "Next day, three hundred e-mails. . . . By the end of that week, we had over 1,500, and it kind of just spun. By the time we had our first rally we had 400,000 e-mails. So it's just, like, this big, big thing."

My interviews with those who got involved suggest that many, indeed, had been thinking along these lines but did not choose to act collectively until VOP and others mobilized in response to *Lozano*. One woman had previously made phone calls to elected officials about undocumented immigration, but it was not until she read the "article [saying] that anybody that wanted to do something about illegal immigration should meet" that she joined an organization. Another eventual activist was not politically involved at all before attending VOP rallies. He told me that he had been watching Fox News and Lou Dobbs's program on CNN before he learned what VOP was doing and decided to take part. A third activist had been thinking just a bit about immigration issues but was motivated by VOP's letter in the newspaper to start "researching statistics and information regarding illegal immigration and how it is affecting society and the economy." Another person admitted to having political views that aligned with VOP's but did not become an activist until the mobilization began: "I remember my mother reading the paper and saying, 'Oh, there's an anti-illegal immigration rally in Scranton.' And I said, 'Really? . . . Why don't we all go?' So I called up my friend . . . and we got together and . . . spent an afternoon making signs. We got markers and everything. We went to the rally, and I was thinking, 'You know, this is a lot of fun.'"

With emphatic support pouring in, VOP went on to host a number of well-attended rallies in the subsequent months. More than two thousand people reportedly attended one of the group's first demonstrations, an event staged in front of Hazleton City Hall. The organizers claim that it was the biggest crowd ever assembled to oppose undocumented immigration. The rally featured "some of the die-hard supporters from Hazleton," as well as "a lot of people [who] were traveling from other parts of the state."[49] The success of this initial event, as one activist explained, allowed VOP to "get this thing rolling, rolling, rolling." Just a week later, the activists assembled in Scranton; in August, they rallied in nearby Freeland, Pennsylvania; in September, they were making speeches on the steps of the Pennsylvania Capitol Building in Harrisburg. The rallies generated even more publicity and support. News outlets sought interviews with VOP's founding members; similar groups in other states asked for help so they could hold rallies of their own; and many local residents embraced VOP. The group became, as at least one organizer likes to describe it, "the mayor's unofficial street team."

Whose Law? The Legal Consciousness of Pro-IIRA Activists

Two particularly noteworthy characteristics emerge from my analysis of these activists' discourse. The first is the way those who mobilized in opposition to *Lozano* think and talk about law—that is, their *legal consciousness*.[50] Throughout the campaign, activists employed legalistic rhetoric, often framing their efforts as a defense of the rule of law. "We are trying to make a point here: U.S. law," one participant told me. "That is what we are arguing. We are arguing in favor of the law." Mirroring the innocence/abstraction rhetoric described above, as well as findings from research in a variety of other contexts,[51] however, my interpretation is that it was not always that straightforward. I found these activists were prone to dismiss the rights claims and legal filings of pro-immigrant groups, depicting them as demands for "special," as opposed to equal, rights. In contrast, they presented themselves as victimized by this alleged "special treatment" while viewing the majority's evocations of rights and mobilizations of law as acceptable, and even as necessary to ensuring the persistence of community harmony (e.g., the IIRA was thought to have restored order, while *Lozano* was seen as an overreach).

To illustrate, some activists followed Mayor Barletta and Kobach in declaring Judge Munley's decision illegitimate. One accused him of falling asleep during testimony at the trial; another called his decision a case study in why term limits are important; a third deemed the decision "legally stupid" and called the restraining order prohibiting the city from enforcing the IIRA "illegal." Another activist began by declaring full support for the Fourteenth Amendment when it conforms to a generic, color-blind worldview but pulled an about-face when its application no longer fit that vision: "So if Chinese came across the border illegally, you'd be like, 'Yeah, OK, as long as they are not Mexican.' No. Principle dictates it doesn't matter who you are. . . . Law applies equally to everybody. That's the Fourteenth Amendment, and that's what Judge Munley ruled on, [the] Fourteenth Amendment. Which is wrong. . . . Munley is totally, totally. . . . His decision is just ludicrous. I don't agree with it at all."

My analysis reveals that race shaped this discourse, as well. "If we would just enforce our laws, then, of course, stuff like this wouldn't be happening," one activist told me in reference to Hazleton's supposed problems with undocumented immigration. Yet later in the interview, this respondent shunned efforts to enforce antidiscrimination laws:

> There is a gentleman in Mountaintop; he is a lawyer. . . . He had a big large sign up [that is visible when] going into Hazleton. [It said] something to the effect that "if you don't speak English and you have a problem, it could be . . . discrimination. Call me." And then it had it all in Spanish. . . . He was telling them if they committed a crime, he could get them out of it. That is basically what he was saying on the billboard. Now, nobody tells me if I commit a crime, they will get me out of it.

Notice how this activist denies the possibility that Spanish-speakers living in Hazleton might actually face discrimination and seems to assume that people in this population are criminals. This activist also reports feeling slighted as a White person for not benefiting from antidiscrimination law, which in this case is presented as a "special" legal protection that is akin to a free pass for lawlessness.

A second activist I spoke with brought up the killing in 2008 of Luis Ramirez, an undocumented Mexican immigrant whom a group of White teenage high school football players beat to death in nearby Shenandoah, hurling racial slurs as they carried out the attack. They called Ramirez a "fucking Spic" and told him, "This is Shenandoah. This is America. Go back to Mexico."[52] Initially, an all-White jury acquitted the teens of the most serious charges.[53] But after urging from immigrants' rights groups such as the Mexican American Legal Defense and Education Fund (MALDEF),[54] as well as reports of a police cover-up,[55] the U.S. Justice Department intervened and ultimately convicted two of Ramirez's killers of a hate crime.[56]

The activist strongly disputed MALDEF's efforts to seek justice for Ramirez in the case, saying: "It was just unbelievable. They wanted to lynch these kids—MALDEF and all of them. First of all, MALDEF has no right in our legal system. This is our country, not the Spanish country. You know what I mean? What right does MALDEF have to put their nose in our legal system?" This comment speaks for itself: The selective acceptance of law is explicit (i.e., *"our"* legal system"), and the rhetorical inversion epitomizes White innocence and Latina/o abstraction, making a mockery of past racial oppression by calling a group of racially motivated Whites who beat a person of color to death the *victims of a lynching.*[57]

Amplified Resentment

The second noteworthy characteristic of this wave of activism is its tendency to amplify resentment and ratchet up the stakes of the debate.[58] Concerns about undocumented immigrants and "special rights" claimants stretched beyond the streets of Hazleton: Activists now warned of a threat to the nation. We see this in the pronounced displays of patriotism at VOP rallies. These events had titles such as "Save America, Save Hazleton," "Pro-America and Immigration Enforcement Rally," and "Loyalty Day Rally." Each began with a reciting of the Pledge of Allegiance and ended with a collective singing of "God Bless America." American flags—draped over participants, waving on small wooden sticks, printed on T-shirts and ties, appearing on speakers' lapel pins—were commonplace, as were other patriotic insignia, including VOP's red, white, and blue logo featuring an eagle.

People without documentation remained the prime target, but speakers at the rallies added even more "enemies" to the growing list of threats, including politicians with whom they disagreed, "big government," welfare recipients, and the "liberal media." "This all goes together," one activist told me. The goal of this movement, as another put it, was "combating everything and anything anti–United States of America."

Even as concerns expanded, the rhetorical pattern remained the same. Many who participated in this mobilization claimed that undocumented immigration rampantly victimized "American citizens." A member of the Americans for Legal Immigration Political Action Committee (ALIPAC), based in North Carolina,[59] spoke at the rally outside Hazleton City Hall. He warned the crowd about the dangers associated with bringing "a million people from these gang-ruled areas where there is no law." He also callously portrayed immigrants as agents of contagion, claiming that there are "four to ten [tuberculosis] cases rushing across our border every night."[60] Signs held by participants at another rally also amplified the perception of Latino Threat. One greatly exaggerated the extent to which "they" fiscally burden "us," reading, "$90 Billion dollars a year is spent on illegal aliens for welfare and social services paid by American taxpayers."[61] Another vastly overhyped the threat of violent crime, claiming that "48,000 American citizens [have been] murdered by illegal aliens since 9/11."[62]

Such elevated risks, the activists suggested, call for an elevated response. Those who participated in VOP rallies tended to advocate very strict immigration control. A banner that read "WHERE'S THE FENCE? CLOSE THE BORDERS IN 90 DAYS!" served as the backdrop for most events. Many speakers favored deportation as a policy response. One rally attendee held up a sign that read, "Gallon of Gas: $3.69, Purchase of a Gun: $419.00, Deportation: PRICELESS!" Another wore a "Border Patrol" T-shirt. A table at one event advertised the website "exporttheimport.com." And in an especially visceral display of these sentiments, videos of the protests show another attendee wearing a T-shirt that says, "Not in My Neighborhood, Motherfucker."[63]

This wave of activism also featured denials of racial motivations, bolstered by particularly strong assertions that *Latinas/os* were acting in "racist" ways. "Racist groups . . . such as La Raza and MALDEF . . . try to be very intimidating," one activist told me, before contending, to the contrary, that "real Americans know it has nothing to do with the color of their skin or the accent that comes out of the voice. But the Hispanics are the ones who are racist. They are the ones who are racist. They see everything in color, and if you are not brown, then you don't count."

Indeed, accusations of racism seemed to fuel the fire of those who participated in this mobilization. "Who are the ones making this about race?" one speaker shouted at a rally. "They are!" the crowd shot back. "Do we as Americans have to stand for this anymore?" the speaker yelled, prompting from the crowd an enthusiastic "No!" One participant told me that the rallies were envisioned as an opportunity to empower people who "are afraid to speak out" in the face of resistance from immigrants' rights activists: "Nobody wants to be called a racist and that is what I think it all comes down to."

In several other examples, one can similarly see this group of activists relishing the notion that they are standing up for themselves.[64] A speaker opened one of the rallies by congratulating attendees for showing up, saying, "You overcame fear. You overcame condemnation. You are standing up for your town, [for] your state, for your country, and for yourself." Another hollered the rhetorical question "Ladies and gentlemen, are you afraid?" to which the crowd responded with a forceful, collective "Hell, no!" "We will never, ever live in fear again," a third activist passionately promised. A fourth participant ended his speech by shouting with vigor, "We are in the right on this issue, and don't let anybody tell you otherwise!"

In my analysis, I found that the obfuscation of Latina/o harm was also a common occurrence in this mobilization.[65] Unlike those who simply ignored or denied it, however, rally attendees occasionally asserted that those who experienced such harm *deserved it*. When Arroyo showed up at the rally outside of City Hall hoping to cover it for *El Mensajero*, at least one protestor verbally assaulted him, calling him a "traitor" and shouting, "Go home! . . . We don't want you here!" The *Pittsburgh Post-Gazette* later asked the woman who reportedly led the verbal assault about the incident, and she replied, "Somebody had to confront him for that. He has the right to free speech, but he has to be prepared to pay the consequences."[66] VOP's decision to host an anti–undocumented immigrant rally in Shenandoah only a little more than six weeks after the group of White teenagers killed Luis Ramirez represents what I would consider an even more poignant example of this. Although that rally began with a moment of silence for the deceased young man, it quickly became clear that at least a few in the crowd were not at all sympathetic. At one point after a speaker brought the incident up, shouts emerged from the audience: "He got what he deserved! He was an illegal!"[67]

Conclusion

Although fervent, this mobilization maintained momentum for only a short time. Not long after hosting several rallies in the summer of 2007, VOP's influence and visibility began to wane. Its rallies attracted smaller crowds; the group took its website down, and when VOP announced it would be protesting in Shenandoah, Mayor Barletta reportedly had a staff member ask its members to stop displaying his political insignia at their events.[68] Despite this, it is hard to deny that activists participating in this mobilization—and, for that matter, their predecessors who fended off resistance in the courtroom and in the council chambers—left their mark.

At the most basic level, efforts to counter immigrants' rights demoted race cognizance in favor of color-blindness, effectively keeping the unique lived realities of Latina/o residents out of the conversation. When activists turned to the law as a last resort, they experienced a similar fate. Supporters of the IIRA used "special rights" politics to delegitimize their claims, limiting the possibility of a wider pro-immigrant mobilization in the process. *Lozano,* as a result, leaves an important formal legal legacy, defeating a potentially harmful local ordinance and setting precedent that may block similar initiatives elsewhere.[69] Yet on the ground, as I have demonstrated, it prompted a counter-mobilization in defense of White innocence.

On another level, these mobilizations both reinforced and expanded the prevailing Latino Threat Narrative. When pro-immigrant activists, attorneys, and others challenged the rhetoric that surrounded the IIRA, their opponents used the rhetorical device of innocence / abstraction to turn those challenges around. Like "racial jujitsu,"[70] I have argued that they twisted demands for immigrants' rights into "evidence" that pro-immigrant activists and others pose a threat and therefore belong on the margins of the community. To quote the sociolegal scholars Jonathan Goldberg-Hiller and Neal Milner, who have identified a similar pattern in other contexts, I argue that supporters of the IIRA characterized those who challenged the ordinance as "morally dangerous, irrational, profligate people whose very rights claims become indicators of [their] general unseemliness."[71] More White affirmation, meanwhile, emerges from these politics, as "insiders" are depicted—again, in direct contrast to demoted "outsiders"—as "community-oriented," "color-blind," and "egalitarian."

In the next chapter, I reveal one other important implication of this mobilization. We will see how it had what law and society scholars call *constitutive effects*—that is, it shaped the course of action subsequent activists were willing and able to take.[72] As dust from the IIRA settled, Latinas/os in Hazleton continued to endure institutional barriers and the like. But what will become apparent is that to avoid backlash, activists now face pressure to adhere to the terms that IIRA supporters and the politicians they rallied around have set. Such terms overlook economic circumstances, portray supporters of the IIRA innocently, depict "criminals," "system milkers," and immigrants' rights activists as Hazleton's primary burden, and harshly stigmatize any efforts to bring about social justice that are deliberately pro-Latina/o.

4

"All We Can Do Is Show Them We Are a Respectable Bunch"

Sergio, Juan, and I peered up at the large white banner we had just finished taping to the coarse cement wall in the basement of a local church.[1] "It looks straight," I remarked. Juan agreed. "No, no, no. I think that side is still a little lower," Sergio declared. He pointed to the wall, prompting us to climb back onto the metal folding chairs to make adjustments. I think Juan and I both knew that the banner was indeed slightly crooked, but to us it was close enough. After all, we still had a lot of preparation work we needed to do that morning, and we had already climbed off and onto those chairs a half-dozen times. We nevertheless scaled the event furniture once more. This time, to Sergio's delight, Juan and I leveled the banner with precision. The name of the organization proudly revealed itself in English and Spanish: "Concerned Parents of the Hazleton Area; Padres Preocupados del Area de Hazleton." "Perfect!" Sergio yelled from below.

Under normal circumstances, I might have found Sergio's persistence irritating, but the day before I had learned just how important this first anniversary celebration was to members of the Concerned Parents of the Hazleton Area (CPH). As I sat and listened in the back of their humble office under glowing florescent lights, group members reviewed for the final time plans they had been carefully making for months. One of a handful of White, native-born Hazleton residents involved in this coalition of concerned Latina/o and White citizens sat at the head table and reviewed a list of people CPH planned to thank and acknowledge at the start of the formal ceremony. "We want to make sure we don't miss any of the 'special' people," the volunteer remarked with an equal blend of seriousness and humor. I smiled from my seat in one of the white plastic lawn chairs they were using to accommodate the larger-than-normal group of about twenty people. The chair was one of many such unconventional office supplies that filled an atmosphere that was at once makeshift and professional. All members were volunteers, and all items—including the chairs—were donations. The group was functioning on a budget of practically zero.

To my right were two posters propped upright on a table featuring some of the appearances CPH had made in the local press since its founding in 2008. Normally displayed at the office's entrance, the posters were ready for transport to the celebration for the public to see and "learn about the achievements and progress [CPH] has made."[2] A photo of the group doing volunteer work accompanied one of the articles; another depicted members discussing ways to curb violence in the city; a third was a hot-off-the-press article announcing the next day's event that featured a photo of the group's president busy at work.

In addition to a formal ceremony meant to thank volunteers and some local officials, the anniversary event was to include a number of information tables at which attendees could learn about and meet with representatives from colleges, libraries, museums, and the like. The entire community was invited, and CPH hoped guests would represent Hazleton's population. Indeed, it was clear to me that the group envisioned a cosmopolitan event, at which new Latina/o families mingled with longtime White residents as all enjoyed the prepared program. There were empanadas at one end of the refreshment table and Senape's Pitza, which has been a local food staple in Hazleton for decades, at the other. An FBI agent was to give the keynote address, discussing topics of crime prevention and rights violations. All presentations were in English and Spanish. Every detail of the celebration, in short, conformed to the mission under which CPH had operated for the past year: to "build a bridge" between established local institutions and residents and Hazleton's new immigrants.

The idea to form CPH emerged from a discussion between a small group of Latina/o parents and a school board member. Both had been searching for ways to solve persistent problems facing Hazleton's immigrant community, and both agreed that a liaison of sorts was necessary. "We seen that there was a need—that there was nobody, no organization, to advocate for people who are looking for a place, at least to find direction," one group member told me.[3] Originally, CPH focused on the schools, prioritizing language barriers that kept parents uninformed about their children's educational progress. It quickly became apparent, however, that the community faced challenges greater than the group initially realized. Recognizing "there was more needs than the ones that was presented at the beginning that needed to be taken care of first," CPH members found themselves handling a wide variety of social service tasks in the community. As they like to describe it, their office became a "headquarters" where people could report any type of problem. "Our magic word," CPH members like to say, is "How can we help?"

With a small group of committed volunteers and the occasional high school student fulfilling community service requirements, CPH worked tirelessly at its bridge building mission in its first few years. Its volunteers visited schools to mentor students, serve as translators, and reduce truancy.[4] Many volunteers also monitored students as they walked home, making sure there were no after-school fights. Sometimes they served as student advocates, successfully lobbying to get a traffic light installed at a busy intersection, and persuading city officials to provide students with discounts on public buses. Adults have reaped the benefits of CPH's work, as well. Several community members have taken the computer literacy courses held at the group's office, and their translating service has been the most in demand. Volunteers routinely accompany non-English-speakers to the hospital, doctors' offices, and attorneys' offices as needed.[5]

CPH thus provides a clear example of doing immigrant advocacy against all odds. Even though the group lacked resources and confronted a dearth of infrastructure to accommodate Hazleton's growing immigrant population, it has successfully managed to offer many previously nonexistent services and, as we will see, has taken steps toward changing the dialogue around immigration issues in Hazleton.[6] Yet as I recount the group's experience of navigating the post-IIRA political climate in this chapter, what emerges in the shadow of these impressive accomplishments is a set of limitations that earlier mobilizations and dominant ideologies have imposed. Relying on participant observation and interviews with group members,[7] I document how a dilemma long confronted by racial justice activists takes on particular significance in the context of emergent local immigration politics.[8] I show how CPH, on one hand, has achieved success by avoiding contentious issues and dodging backlash. This has continued to be the case as the group has greatly expanded its efforts in recent years. On the other hand, I consider how dominant ideologies and prior mobilizations have limited what these activists can say and do in a way that also limits their ability to pose serious challenges to the prevailing narrative and, ultimately, to the unequal social arrangements it protects. My exploration of CPH's activism therefore is intended to illuminate the extent to which the Latino Threat Narrative is hegemonic, accommodating resistance and exerting its power even when not forcefully evoked.

"We Don't Want Special Privileges"

The day of the first anniversary celebration, I parted from Sergio and Juan soon after we hung the banner. I was to join another volunteer to help retrieve donated food items before having lunch on my own. The three of us planned to reconvene after that to tie up a few loose ends before the event kicked off at two o'clock.

I was the first of our small group to return that afternoon, so I mingled for a bit with the church pastor and a group of teenage volunteers who lined a metal table in the kitchen of the church basement preparing the event's food. I wondered silently what was keeping Sergio and the others. In due time they arrived, and the answer became apparent: The men had traveled home to clean up, replacing the polo shirts and khaki pants they had worn in the morning with dapper black suits and ties. In my judgment, their original outfits seemed perfectly suitable for the day's festivities. The modest church basement, with its low ceilings and dusty tile floors, seemed unworthy of formal apparel; although when more group members arrived in similar attire, I felt the effect and realized the extent to which image control is a vital part of CPH's approach.

Most every action they took in preparation for the event was an effort, as was pointed out in the meeting the day before, "to show that we are becoming a prominent, respected organization." Members dressed well and invited guests with high local profiles because they "care about . . . influencing people in town so that they can be more welcoming of people no matter what." CPH thus embraces "the idea of [making] sure that people have a good image of us." The "us" here is not just members of the organization; they are working to improve the image of the "immigrant community in general. Because if [members of the broader community] don't have a good image [of immigrants], then it is easier for them to think [they] are bad." One volunteer told me that he often coaches the city's new immigrants along these lines: "I tell them, 'All we can do is keep working hard, showing them that we are a respectable bunch.'" On that point others agreed, noting in response to a question about the IIRA that "when the mayor sees we are making progress, he will probably change his mind and take out the [Illegal] Immigration [Relief] Act. Let's show him we are better."

CPH seems to have adopted a similar strategy when it comes to some of the key issues from this debate. Rather than challenging the racialized criminalization of immigrants, it has taken a less controversial anticrime approach. In its early years, CPH helped bring a chapter of the citizen crime-fighting group the Guardian Angels to Hazleton.[9] Offering English courses has also become a top priority, as opposed to engaging in hot debates about language acquisition and assimilation.

What stood out most to me is the great care CPH has taken to avoid sounding overtly pro-Latina/o. One member I interviewed made his intentions clear from the beginning: He is involved because he cares about what is good "not just for the Latino community, but for the whole community." To that end, he asked, "If we [do] not open the door for the whole community, why would we expect the whole community to open the door for us?" Other group members echoed this sentiment. "CPH is a mixed group, not just Latino," one interviewee said. Therefore, when people are discussing problems facing the city with CPH, "[they] want to listen as a group, not as ... Latino[s]." This is why the group's policy is "*anyone* can come, bring their concern, and we can work together." Some went as far as to agree that race-cognizance amounts to "reverse discrimination." When we discussed the origins of the group, one member explained the rationale behind calling the group the Concerned Parents of the Hazleton Area rather than the name they initially chose, the Latin Parents Association: "Oh my goodness, we don't want to separate." Others agreed, noting, "If it was only for Latinos, it wouldn't be fair; then [CPH] discriminates [against] White people." Another member put it this way: "The Hispanic community has to learn that we are here, and this is not our house. We have to learn to accept this country, accept its language, accept its customs. If we help these

Hispanic people learn about what is the rule—not in the Hispanic community, what is the rule in the Hazleton community—all the community is going to benefit."

While they admit that "we all disagree, all of us," when it comes to the IIRA, one can see from these examples how CPH's public persona is non-antagonistic. The group avoids mixing politics with volunteer work and tries to let its actions do the talking as much as possible. This is obviously a significant departure from their pro-immigrant predecessors. CPH is up front about this. Although they have collaborated and maintained relationships with members of the Hazleton Area Latino Association, some who work with CPH consider its members "more militant than we are"; another told me, "We want to be the people who bridge the gap, where, like Anna Arias and Dr. Lopez, I think they look more at the Hispanics." My time around CPH members led me to see this divergence as a difference in strategy more so than opinion.[10] My impression was that members of the group were not only aware of the continued salience of race but also deeply committed to alleviating racial inequality in Hazleton. The way they talk about and act on such issues, however, suggests they remain cognizant of impending "colorblind attacks that tar the first person to directly mention race with the charge of racism," and perhaps for this reason join in on the "insistence that race should not be discussed."[11]

It is hard to deny that treading lightly across contentious terrain and thus avoiding backlash has been a key to CPH's success. But the paradox is that when activists are pushed into a position of operating within the confines of what the majority deems discursively permissible, their capacity to contest dominant narratives is limited. It becomes hard to challenge Latina/o degradation and to problematize the distortions inherent in the ideology of White injury. In contrast to some who contend that compromise of this sort is equivalent to "finding a middle a ground,"[12] my analysis suggests that despite pro-immigrant groups making some meaningful progress, the local debate over immigration remains squarely on the majority's ideological turf.

It is true, in other words, that CPH has been able to pursue and make gains pertaining to immigrant rights and racial justice by relying on what resembles a "post-racial" rhetoric.[13] However, they do so while the ideological assumptions inherent in the Latino Threat Narrative remain taken for granted as truth.[14] A general anticrime approach, for example, while perhaps having its benefits, is limited to the extent that the Latino Threat Narrative's characteristic racialized criminalization evades critique.[15] A noncontroversial focus on teaching English similarly enables CPH to avoid criticism while also providing an important, in-demand service. However, assimilationists remain undeterred from using English as a marker of belonging, and those non-English-speakers who do not take such courses remain susceptible to accusations that their "refusal" to learn is what burdens the city. As another example, we can attribute part of CPH's success to their placing of some distance between themselves and "more militant," race-cognizant activists. Yet doing so also means not interrogating the majority's defense of White innocence and its vilification of those who tried to call attention to discrimination (see Chapter 3).

The constitutive effects of prior mobilizations and the Latino Threat Narrative more generally thus have CPH in a difficult spot. The reality is that making these sorts of concessions is one of the few options available for immigrants and their advocates. What confounds matters even further is that when they do concede to the majority's demands, they have no guarantee that the majority will concede to theirs. Indeed, CPH confronts no small task: It is seeking to demonstrate through its actions that issues such as criminality, a widespread "refusal" to learn English, and wanting "special privileges" are untrue in a context where perception has already won out over reality on these issues. As the social commentator Mychal Denzel Smith painfully admits, "You can do everything 'right,' obey all of the rules, be exemplary in every way, and racism still does its work."[16] Even as CPH and the community members with whom they are involved align with the anticrime perspective of the majority, for example, dominant, deeply rooted associations between recent Latino immigrants and crime have persisted on the ground.[17] In some cases, people have already experienced how learning English is not enough to dislodge misperceptions, either.[18] And despite CPH's "post-racial" approach, many continue to see them as a group that is narrowly pro-Latina/o and therefore unwilling to be a part of the community. One White CPH member mentioned that people sometimes privately stigmatize those who engage in this work: "I mean, it's hard to come out [to White peers] because you say [that you are a member of CPH] to some people and they look at you like you're the most [awful] person in the world. [They say], 'Why do you do this? Look at what you're bringing into this community.'" This is something I heard a lot of from pro-IIRA activists. Although they did not necessarily publicly oppose the work CPH is doing, many barely adjusted their rhetoric when this group came up in conversation. To some, they too were merely supporting "illegals."[19]

The Hazleton Integration Project

After establishing itself, CPH received a massive boost when a celebrity emerged with local ties and an interest in getting involved. Joe Maddon, who was then the manager of Major League Baseball's Tampa Bay Rays,[20] returned to his native Hazleton in December 2010 "disappointed" after noticing that "things had changed a lot."[21] Maddon is particularly fond of his upbringing in Hazleton, noting that he cannot recall "one bad day growing up [t]here."[22] What disturbed him most was that "neighbors from different backgrounds were not interacting and had begun to fear each other's differences."[23]

During that visit, members of CPH invited Maddon to a holiday potluck gathering hosted by a Latina woman who provides day care from her home. At the gathering, the story goes, "merengue music blared," "Spanish conversation flowed around him . . . , [and] children ran about, weaving among adults who talked, laughed, and shared cuisine from the Dominican Republic, Guatemala, and Peru."[24] The experience reminded Maddon of "his days growing up on 11th Street in an apartment building that housed four families." The "moment I saw that," he recalled, "I said to myself, 'That's it. This is what we're missing here.'"[25] In a different interview, he said, "That was my seminal moment. [W]e're the same, we just speak a different language."[26]

Maddon acted quickly, helping to establish what would become CPH's parent organization, the Hazleton Integration Project (HIP).[27] In December 2011, he hosted the first ethnic dinner fundraiser and sports memorabilia auction. Maddon made the event appealing by inviting some of his players and other baseball stars, including the Hall of Famer Yogi Berra and the Latino players Tino Martinez and Carlos Peña. With increasing fanfare, he has hosted similar events every year since.[28] Money from meal tickets and items sold at auction has helped fund HIP initiatives, along with grants and donations from various agencies accrued thanks in large part to Maddon's social capital.[29]

The crowning achievement of HIP at the time of this writing is the creation of the Hazleton One Community Center. In contrast to CPH's small, rudimentary office space, HIP has renovated a spacious former school building capable of providing an array of services. I visited the center soon after it opened in 2013 and was struck by how lively it was, even as a work in progress. The doors constantly swung open, it seemed, as individuals and families came and went. Even though some of the gym's overhead lights still needed repair, basketballs bounced all around. Kids and adults filled the bleachers waiting to get in on a pick-up game. Down the hall, children were reading in a former classroom that is now a library of donated books. All of this activity made it easy to see the potential that filled several still vacant rooms. Those who showed me around explained detailed plans for each one, rattling off a long list of forthcoming offerings in areas that ranged from culture to recreation.[30]

The mission of the center is to provide a place "where economically disadvantaged children can participate in a wide variety of free or afford-able educational, cultural and athletic activities."[31] Many who frequent the center are poor: One staff member told me the center keeps a collection of basketball shoes in the office so those who cannot afford a pair can still play. On a deeper level, HIP leaders see the community center as a place to foster integration. As the organization's president has explained, "This is not a place that is only for immigrants. And it is not just an open gym either. The very explicit goal of this place and of this effort is clear: It is to bring two currently much separated communities together. . . . The larger mission of integration will guide us in everything that we do. Services are one thing; integration is another. It's a longer range goal."[32]

In slight contrast to CPH's "post-racial" approach, public declarations from HIP tend to evoke what we might call *multiculturalism*.[33] The over-arching idea is that the community needs to embrace ethnic differences to save Hazleton from the divisiveness that is tearing it apart. Maddon told the *Standard-Speaker*, "If we can't bring this community together, it's going to die."[34] When the ESPN program *Outside the Lines* profiled Mad-don's efforts, he similarly specified, "We are not using the word 'immigra-tion'; this is about *integration*. This is about bringing people together."[35] Reflecting on his return to a now divided community, as another example, Maddon said, "There was the Anglo side and the Hispanic side and the disconnect. You could feel it."[36] To ease such tensions, "we need to absorb our Hispanic brothers and sisters to bring this town back to what it used to be. . . . Too many times it's about skin color that's different or food that's different or music that's different. But that's what makes it so exciting—the diversity, the vibrancy. I like these people a lot."[37] Hence, Maddon sees the strategy as simple: "Communication comes first. Then, you sit down and break bread together. From there, trust begins to build. That's how you get to the World Series and that's how you bring a community together."[38]

One of the clearest examples of this multicultural approach is HIP's emphasis on the potential of children to overcome social conflict.[39] The logic is that adults' capacity to bring about racial/ethnic harmony is limited because they are set in their ways. Children, in contrast, will "engage in activities together, the barriers of unfamiliarity will crumble and friendships will form." Maddon added, "When the kids come [to the community center], the parents will [also] come and hopefully all that superficial nonsense will go away. It starts with the kids."[40]

Many people in Hazleton find Maddon's narrative of unity refreshing.[41] He and his organization have brought a new perspective to the debate, which gained traction thanks at least in part to his local popularity.[42] The people of Hazleton are proud to have one of their own in such a high-profile position, especially someone who remembers his roots and is apt to mention his hometown on the national stage.[43] It therefore should not come as a surprise to learn that HIP has enjoyed minimal opposition and a great deal of support, even from those seemingly uninterested in issues of immigrant integration.[44]

The result of all this has been impressive progress. Accommodative infrastructure is beginning to emerge along with symbolism that suggests inclusivity.[45] But, again, I want to point out that even under the leadership of a local celebrity, HIP still needs to traverse some difficult political terrain. While Maddon's capital provides a lift, his popularity remains dependent on his actions, both in Hazleton and on the national level. The expectation is that he, as a sports star, will give back to his community without being "overly political."[46] As much as locals adore him, sentiments can easily shift if it appears that he is posing a threat to the status quo. Thus, while what HIP brings to the table may be fresh, I think it is also important to understand that the organization still confronts a political reality in which acceptance is granted "*on the condition*" that activists and members of marginalized groups frame their practices in terms that the majority deems acceptable.[47]

It is likely that HIP is cognizant of the balance it needs to strike; its multicultural stance evokes race/ethnicity, but only to a certain extent.[48]

The public comments we just saw from Maddon and other HIP representatives discuss how there are problematic divisions across racial/ethnic lines but shy away from *politicizing* such differences and from discussing their hierarchical nature. HIP has also contributed to a shift in the local debate by speaking in terms of *community harm*. Their organizational rhetoric may not point directly to anti-Latina/o discrimination, but by implying that *Hazleton as a whole* is suffering from racial/ethnic conflict, they depart in an important way from prior narrow emphases on White victimization.

In this way, HIP has managed to *get to the metaphorical edge* of the discursive boundary the majority has imposed. But what are the implications of not being able to cross that threshold? One is that color-blindness continues to be understood as the preferred way of talking about race. Even in this more inclusive rhetoric, problems are attributed to "superficial nonsense" and differences in "aesthetic domains" such as language and food preferences.[49] Privilege and power, degradation and affirmation remain absent from the conversation on racial/ethnic conflict. The discourse of community harm likewise *encompasses* the ideology of White injury. Statements such as "There was the Anglo side and the Hispanic side and the disconnect" indicate that "they" have harmed "us" as much as "we" have harmed "them." Judith Goode refers to this as the "false ideology of equality," wherein "Whites . . . are included as just another category representing different but equivalent, unranked cultural/behavioral traits."[50] The gain, in other words, comes in the form of a first-of-its-kind widespread local acceptance of the notion that Hazleton's recent Latina/o immigrants *have* faced resentment. But because activists are compelled to frame the politics surrounding the IIRA as an even-handed disagreement, those who advocated exclusion are able to maintain their innocence, stand by their claims of White victimization, and keep their power concealed. Rather than a story of officials propagating racialized imagery of criminality and burdensomeness, for example, what emerges is a version of events where existing racial/ethnic rifts look like "natural occurrences."[51] As Eduardo Bonilla-Silva writes, although the majority in a case like this may be willing to admit they said some harsh words, we often see such concessions made only when there is a corresponding acknowledgment that "*they* (racial minorities) do it too."[52]

A similar idea applies to the ideological constraints subtly imposed on HIP's plan to foster integration among children. Again, it admirably brings an inclusive attitude to the forefront. Yet what it is unable to do is draw attention to the *deep-seated nature of racial inequality*. When race *is* part of the discussion, the dominant racial ideology in the United States demands that people talk about it in interpersonal, as opposed to systemic or institutional, terms. This is a preference that the historian Charles Payne notes has its roots in the Confederacy, where "good" race relations were used as evidence to blur power differentials. We continue to see this today, Payne adds, "when contemporary college students reduce race to who eats lunch with whom instead of, say, who gets access to higher education."[53]

To put that another way, whereas cross-racial/ethnic bonds may indeed develop among local kids, symbolic prohibitions on race-cognizant discourse make it especially difficult to draw attention to the harsh reality that children are not immune from the systemic racism that has endured with each successive generation in America.[54] Among many other disparities,[55] Latina/o youth still confront criminalization at an early age,[56] endure lingering local hostilities (see Chapter 2), and, compared with their White peers, are less likely to have access to high-quality education.[57] Institutional barriers also remain all too real among adults in post-IIRA Hazleton. As of January 2015—almost a decade and a half since significant Latina/o migration to the city began—there are still *no* Latinas/os in public office.[58] In the local school district, where the ratio of White to Latina/o students is fast approaching 1:1, almost *all* teachers—a full 99.6 percent—identify as White.[59] This figure would have represented a disparity *before* large numbers of Latina/o immigrants began arriving. It is also especially troubling when we consider that teaching remains one of the few opportunities for professional employment in Hazleton.

Neoliberal Accommodation and the Persistence of Divide and Conquer Politics

As several people began to flock into the anniversary celebration, the big question on the minds of CPH members was whether Mayor Lou Barletta would accept their invitation to attend the event. His was one of the names read off the list of "special people" the day before. It was interesting to me at the time that while none of the members of the group was quite sure about whether Barletta would come, they had made plans to accommodate him, just in case.

Sure enough, the mayor arrived in the church basement shortly after 2:00 P.M. Compared with the spruce CPH members, he showed up underdressed, wearing a polo shirt, khaki shorts, and a pair of loafers rather than his usual political attire. Someone whispered to me at the event that "he must be going to the golf course after this."[60]

Once attendees ate and took in the information booths, the formal ceremony commenced. In what resembled an act of reconciliation, a CPH member offered Mayor Barletta the microphone for a speech. It was at this moment that I really began to question just how high this group's work was on the mayor's political agenda. It seemed as though he arrived without a prepared speech, and when it came time for the formal presentation, he was sitting near the back of what was a fairly large crowd, blending in. My observation from an adjacent seat was that the offer seemed to startle him; but, in no position to turn it down, he approached the podium to say a few words. His speech lasted about one minute, and his comments were limited to a few generic statements about the great work CPH has done. Others agreed with my assessment that the mayor was brief and perhaps unenthusiastic. When I attended the next CPH meeting, the buzz about the event seemed to be concerned with the mayor's actions, and there was much talk consistent with the observations I had made. "He looked uncomfortable,"[61] one member said as we mingled before the meeting.

It is hard to know for sure, but with regard to how city officials received CPH, particularly in those early years, this may have been par for the course. One group member confided to me that officials rarely dismissed the group outright, especially in public—after all, supporting an all-volunteer organization that wants to make the city a better place for children is a political no-brainer—but their sense was also that few were willing to throw their weight behind the group in pursuit of visible, meaningful change.

Since Maddon came on board, the situation has been a bit different. With so many residents pulled by the baseball celebrities in their midst, politicians seem more willing to support HIP. As congressman, Barletta traveled home from Washington, DC, to attend the community center's ribbon-cutting ceremony. He also consistently makes the trip for the annual fundraising dinner and memorabilia auction. HIP has praised his efforts as "wonderfully supportive."[62] Joe Yanuzzi, who became Hazleton's mayor after Barletta vacated the seat, was also present when the community center opened. And he, too, is a regular at the annual fundraising event, having even played the role of "guest server," dishing out symbolic meals that feature Italian, Polish, and Hispanic cuisine.[63]

Simultaneously, however, I would argue that one can still hear echoes of the Latino Threat Narrative in the recent rhetoric of these officials. As a member of the U.S. House of Representatives, Barletta has blamed the failure to pass immigration reform on the "[Barack Obama] administration's reckless release of thousands of criminal illegal immigrants."[64] In an article the *New York Times* published in 2013, he was quoted comparing undocumented immigrants to "water [on a] sinking ship."[65] In 2014, he told a radio host at the Hold Their Feet to the Fire rally, sponsored by the Federation for American Immigration Reform (FAIR), "There may not be anything more dangerous than [giving] amnesty to millions of people."[66] He has also openly discussed the prospect of impeaching President Obama in the context of his supposed failure to enforce immigration laws[67] and has proposed cutting off federal funding to "sanctuary cities," claiming that they are making the United States into a "Third World country."[68] Yanuzzi, too, remained steadfast as mayor in his refusal to withdraw the IIRA, even as legal costs continued to mount.[69] Moreover, when interviewed in 2012 for the ESPN segment that profiled HIP, Mayor Yanuzzi openly suggested a link between Hispanic residents in Hazleton and violent crime, stating, "There was a lot of violent crime, things that we never experienced. I mean . . . the Hispanic community, and this is not an insult, but . . . [*claps hands*] as soon as something happens, somebody gets stabbed, somebody gets cut."[70]

One interpretation of these recent developments is that the community is making progress despite there being a few bumps in the road. Continuing the argument I have been making, I want to complicate that idea by considering how what we are seeing may actually be indicative of the malleability of divide and conquer politics.[71] Especially relevant to such an argument is Derrick Bell's concept of *interest convergence*. Analyzing the case of school desegregation, he famously asserted that, on occasion, there will be support for "racial remediation" on the condition that such actions "will secure, advance, or at least not harm societal interests deemed important by . . . whites."[72] Given what we know about the lure of the Latino Threat Narrative, there is little reason to believe that the emerging popularity of multiculturalism diminishes its utility as a political tool that attracts many poor and working-class Whites.[73] That said, Bell's thesis also sheds light on why multiculturalism may simultaneously gain traction under the right conditions: In addition to being unthreatening, it provides an opportunity for members of the majority to position themselves and their community as egalitarian and nonracist. From this angle, then, we might say that those who trumpet Latino Threat might find they also benefit from dabbling in multiculturalism because it bolsters their claims about innocence and color-blindness.[74]

At a structural level, it is also important to keep in mind that the politics of divide and conquer are not about *race hatred* but, rather, about *using race to create divisions*. Maintaining the existing system therefore does not require keeping *all* Latinas/os, or Latina/os *in particular*, down. Instead, the prerogative is to construct a group of what Lester Spence refers to as "exceptions" who are degraded and made to appear as fundamentally distinct from those who are affirmed and granted inclusion.[75] Thus, although it champions inclusivity, there is still space within a multiculturalist narrative to construct binaries *within* immigrant groups—legal versus illegal, multilingual versus monolingual, hard worker versus burdensome, activist versus community member.

Indeed, there is a long history in the United States of a few individuals from otherwise excluded groups being granted social and material benefits and given the privilege of having their voices heard as long as they do not question existing power structures.[76] Fredrick C. Harris has likewise emphasized how the elite embrace of multiculturalism in more recent years has served to reward nonantagonistic behavior.[77] When those in power embrace members of marginalized groups for their willingness to cooperate, in other words, the subtext is often that a corresponding *unwillingness to cooperate* (e.g., engagement in race-cognizant activism) is the reason others remain on margins.

There is an economic undercurrent here, as well. I have already discussed how the Latino Threat Narrative ignores the structural sources of economic inequality but, at the same time, *acknowledges* economic conditions with individualistic and racialized assertions that those who allegedly seek "shortcuts" (e.g., "unfairly" receiving government services, etc.) are economically harming "hard workers" who "follow the rules" (see the Introduction). Despite its appearance as a vastly different approach, similar politics are possible under the form of multiculturalism that emerged at the tail end of this debate. It, too, avoids discussions of "the need for political struggle" to combat the structural sources of economic inequality.[78] Add to that the still taken-for-granted notion that, to succeed, members of excluded groups should simply avoid "shortcutting" behavior by working hard and getting along. The result, quoting Harris, is a neoliberal steering of "'unrespectables' away from making demands on the state to intervene on their behalf and toward self-correction and the false belief that the market economy alone will lift them out of their plight."[79]

This last point takes on particular salience when we also consider that corporations have lined up to support HIP.[80] Perhaps the most telling example of this came in 2014 when Cargill "donated $10,000 to the Hazleton Integration Project to assist in [its] efforts to provide low-cost educational, cultural, and athletic activities to the area's residents and children."[81]

It is again worth acknowledging the small victory here. HIP can make this amount of money go a long way. But this act of generosity does not exist in a vacuum. As discussed in Chapter 1, neoliberalism's "rollback" approach has been responsible for the decline of state-sponsored social services, and its "rollout" agenda has produced laws such as the Keystone Opportunity Zone (KOZ) initiative. As a number of scholars have noted, groups such as HIP are filling social service gaps created by neoliberal policy all over the world.[82] In this respect, one can argue that this gesture reinforces neoliberal ideology by encouraging the continued existence of an organization that does not threaten the prevailing economic order and that has filled the socially devastating void that is the result of neoliberal cuts to state-funded social services.

On receiving the gift, a HIP representative said that "corporate sponsors like Cargill are our life-blood."[83] Yet Cargill could also be relying on HIP to forge a relationship that masks its business and employment practices and enhances its local image. Indeed, KOZ provides Cargill with financial rewards in the form of tax cuts that likely dwarf the value of the donation.[84] At the same time, it is easy to see how the meager pay and difficult conditions offered by many of the companies that employ recent immigrants in Hazleton may be contributors to the poverty that HIP is working to alleviate.[85] Similar to patterns evident across the United States,[86] some residents who frequent the community center are unemployed, but many have jobs in Hazleton's new industries and still struggle to get by.[87] When corporations donate money to groups like HIP, they appear separate from these economic realities, creating the appearance that they are working on the side of, rather than in opposition to, people in poverty. As Paul Kivel writes, institutionalizing social service providers is favorable to many corporations because it helps "convince people that tremendous inequalities of wealth are *natural* and *inevitable*."[88] Corporate "generosity," in other words, propagates a vague conception of the poor, diverting our collective gaze from poverty *as it relates to wealth* and leading the public "to expect that inevitably there will be people without enough to eat."[89] In discussing the donation, a company representative said, "Cargill loves to take an active role in investing both time and money back into our community. . . . [It's] part of our culture."[90] Seen this way, Cargill looks like a local company that "cares" rather than a profit-maximizing multinational conglomerate that wields immense power with an increasingly firm grip on the global food system.[91]

Conclusion

At this point, we have come full circle. Corporate cost cutting and a market-centric ideology have helped transform Hazleton's economy as low-wage industries replaced decent-paying manufacturing jobs. I argue that providing cover to the corporations and economic elites that have benefited from such arrangements is a narrative that scapegoats Latinas/os and urges poor and working-class Whites to enjoy their relative racial privilege rather than contest their economic misfortunes. At first, efforts to push back against this met harsh resistance. Later, those efforts confronted the malleability of this ideology as it intermixed depoliticized corporatism and hardline racial appeals with corporate benevolence and support for multiculturalism. Indeed, this chapter in particular shows that neoliberal ideology and the Latino Threat Narrative that works in its favor represent expansive, hegemonic modes of governance. Prior mobilizations evoking these ideologies not only accomplished the objectives of the moment; they also placed limitations on subsequent efforts. Thus, after years of social conflict and several mobilizations around a high-profile law, economic arrangements remain relatively unchanged in Hazleton and, despite some important progress in the realm of providing social services and encouraging integration, racial inequality remains robust.

One reading of this and the previous chapter is that activists face a perpetual Catch-22: demand racial justice and provoke backlash, on one hand, or acquiesce and risk reifying existing arrangements, on the other. Similarly, some may read a critical analysis of various approaches as a pessimistic assessment that fails to provide an alternative. My response would be that the activists' dilemma is in fact very real, and nuanced approaches rather than a silver-bullet policy response are required to overcome this impasse. To that end, what I offer in the Conclusion is not a top-down legislative strategy but, rather, a lens for interpreting the story I have told in a way that translates into social action from below. With a sharper collective understanding of how dominant ideologies work, coupled with the will to put such an understanding to use as we actively strive to free ourselves from these arrangements, I think we can indeed widen the scope of possibilities as we work toward ultimately subverting the politics of divide and conquer. As an attempt to foster that, I turn to an example from Hazleton's history that I see as but one strategy for inspiring ordinary people to develop more innovative and authentic approaches to attaining racial and economic justice in our communities.

Conclusion

Recovering Authenticity

The oppressed . . . discover that without freedom they cannot exist authentically. Yet, although they desire authentic existence, they fear it. The conflict lies in the choice between being wholly themselves or being divided; . . . between human solidarity or alienation; between following prescriptions or having choices; between being spectators or actors; between acting or having the illusion of acting through the action of the oppressors; between speaking out or being silent, castrated in their power to create and re-create, in their power to transform the world.
—PAULO FREIRE, *Pedagogy of the Oppressed*

If history is to be creative, to anticipate a possible future, without denying the past, it should, I believe, emphasize new possibilities by disclosing those hidden episodes of the past, when, even if in brief flashes, people showed their ability to resist, to join together, occasionally to win.
—HOWARD ZINN, *A People's History of the United States*

In his book *A Forgetful Nation*, Ali Behdad argues that the United States suffers from "historical amnesia" on issues of immigration. It is "akin to the Freudian notion of negation in which disavowal is accompanied by a supplementary act of acknowledgement." While we may be aware of historical brutalities against immigrants, as a nation we are continually "encouraged to believe that contemporary events were utterly different from those of the past." As a result, we move through the present "culturally desensitized," ever willing to identify our collective selves in contrast to the "threatening [immigrant] other."[1]

As immigration law and politics localize, important questions arise regarding how Behdad's insight pertains to local collective memories and the formation of community identities. Hazleton has a long history of struggle between labor and capital, "insiders" and "outsiders"—a struggle with which, I think it is safe to say, most longtime residents are familiar.[2] Nevertheless, recent events showed few signs of class-consciousness, and the virtual figure of the "threatening immigrant" became the means through which localized conceptions of "us" and "them" were forged. I say this not to blame ordinary people or to dwell on the irony of the past repeating itself but, rather, following Zinn, to draw attention to the "new possibilities" that the past affords us. Deep engagement with history, in other words—particularly those "brief flashes" in which "people showed their ability to resist"—has the potential to liberate by offering an alternative to "cultural desensitization."[3] Seeing the present in new ways can inspire new forms of action and, ultimately, new ways to see our situations and ourselves. With *sensitized* identities, we can approach without fear that "authentic existence" to which Freire refers.

In this concluding chapter, I recount a well-known event from Hazleton's history: the "Lattimer Massacre." Rather than drawing academic comparisons between what happened then and what is happening now,[4] I discuss how reconnecting with such events can help us contest prescriptive assertions of local identity.[5] Specifically, I make the case that historical re-engagement is one method that can prompt us to become actors rather than spectators, to connect to and confront reality rather than dabble in imaginary worlds that shield us from it, and to work toward collective liberation rather than serving a system that keeps so many of us down.

The Lattimer Massacre

John Bodan, a youthful coal miner, was one of thirty-five strikers who formed a picket line in front of the Honey Brook colliery, located just outside Hazleton, on August 14, 1897.[6] The picket was a response to a new policy that Gomer Jones, a forty-two-year-old superintendent for the Lehigh and Wilkes-Barre Coal Company, recently announced. Jones was a mining veteran with thirty-five years of experience in the industry, first employed at age seven. The historians Donald Miller and Richard Sharpless describe Jones as having a reputation for being "a hard-nosed boss";[7] one mining official called him the "worst slave-driver who ever set foot in the coal region."[8] This brought him no shame. He took great pride in getting the most out of his workers, particularly the Slavs, "for whom he expressed open contempt."[9] His focus was on restoring "discipline in the mines and [operating] them in such a manner that the company could continue in business."[10] As Michael Novak, author of *The Guns of Lattimer*, frankly put it, "Gomer Jones was hired to make the mine owners money. Ten hours a day the men were supposed to work; ten hours of production he wanted from them."[11]

Jones's policy created a central location for mining mules: Rather than feeding and caring for the animals individually across expansive coalfields, he tried to cut costs for his company by consolidating their upkeep. To the mule drivers, who were typically immigrants and children, this proposition was troubling. The company paid them only for the time they were in the mines with the mules. Under the new policy, they would have to leave home an hour early to retrieve their mules and arrive home an hour late after returning the animals to the stable. Jones just added two hours to their workday without any compensation.[12]

The workers decided to picket after Jones ignored their initial protest. Having little tolerance for defiance—"When I give orders I expect them to be obeyed and do not permit miners to do exactly as they please,"[13] he said—Jones was enraged. He had a "righteous and violent temper" and "his voice often exuded contempt."[14] When he learned they were picketing, he armed himself with a crowbar and approached the line. He singled out Bodan among the thirty-five strikers and attacked him with the bar, "beating him upon his shoulders."[15] A scuffle broke out, and eventually young Bodan and those who came to his aid were able to take control of Jones's weapon. They beat Jones in retaliation until another supervisor intervened. At once irate with Jones's brutality and empowered after prevailing in the scuffle, the strikers immediately blew the whistle that signaled work stoppage. "As news of the incident spread, 800 workers marched off their jobs."[16]

When Catholic miners celebrated the Assumption that Sunday, news of the event spread through various ethnic communities. Workers saw Jones's actions as especially troubling because they represented a continuation of an ongoing pattern of mistreatment. Coal markets had been struggling, and coal operators, as they so often did, passed the burdens of this to the workers. Many miners were no longer getting the full-time wages they needed to survive. Coal companies also rescinded their promise to pay workers twice per month, giving them their wages at the end of the month instead. This was significant because it caused many workers to go into debt with the mining companies. When their wage envelopes finally came, miners would pay off as much of the debt as they could, cover the rent on their company-owned homes, and settle bills at the company store, leaving them with virtually nothing. Beyond laying bare their destitution, payday also reminded immigrant workers—whom mine bosses continued to regard as "docile and stupid"[17]—of their subordinate position. The state legislature had recently passed the Campbell Act, an anti-immigrant measure that "taxed anthracite mine operators three cents a day for each adult immigrant employee on their payrolls."[18] True to form, mine operators also refused to let this tax be a burden, deducting the three cents per day from the wages of their immigrant employees.

After the weekend's festivities further stirred things up, there were more protests on Monday. "More than 350 angry mine workers marched to each of the Lehigh and Wilkes-Barre collieries and systematically shut them down," Miller and Sharpless recount.[19] Their numbers soon swelled to more than three thousand. When a large group crowded into a meeting hall later that day to plan their next move, the multiethnic nature of the protests became apparent. Strikers gave speeches in multiple languages, and the group chose a Slovak and an Italian—members of the two most recent immigrant groups—to head a committee they formed. Here they also articulated their first set of demands: increased wages and the removal of Gomer Jones. The picket line Bodan sat in had now transformed into a force with which folks much higher in the coal hierarchy would need to reckon. As the *Hazleton Evening Standard* reported, "The Strike now in progress on the South Side has furnished an object lesson that it will be well for the operators in this section to make note of. The day of the slave driver is past and the once ignorant foreigner will no longer tolerate it."[20]

Surely, mine operators already had their eye on the situation. In the Hazleton area, independent coal mine owners such as Ario Pardee and George Markle oversaw expansive empires that extended into other realms, including banking, railroading, and iron. They typically worked in tandem as "lords of a small fiefdom" to protect their wealth and power.[21] These two coal barons in particular were self-made men and among the richest in the country at the time. Some might call them intensely focused; others would say they were uncompromising. Pardee, the *Hazleton Plain Speaker* once reported, had "an iron will that brooked no contradictions. . . . [H]e swerved not a hair's breadth from the direct line of his business interests."[22] As Miller and Sharpless similarly observe, both were "secure in the world they had made and were convinced of the superiority of their ways. This caused them to develop a certain attitude, in practice more autocratic than paternalistic, toward people under their influence or control. As [George's son] John Markle put it, they believed that their power and wealth made them 'trustees' for their fellow men, with responsibility '*for the proper use of them.*'"[23]

Unsurprisingly, Pardee and Markle both "forcefully resisted all attempts by the mine workers to organize."[24] When strife periodically surfaced in the decades before this particular uprising, "the strategy of the corporations was devastatingly simple: starve the workers into submission."[25] Asserting absolute refusal to concede, they would simply wait until workers could no longer survive without the mines. Community members did their best to challenge these tactics. Acts of goodwill kept miners fed. Non-striking miners, relief agencies, and even small businesses—fueled by "resentment that had developed over the years because of the domination of the economy by the independent operators"[26]—contributed what they could to the strikers. Relief efforts could go on for only so long, however, as the reality of operators' owning so much and everyone else so little eventually, like a magnet, pulled strikers back to the job. In response to such strong-arm tactics, some miners retreated to seek work elsewhere in the region. The barons eventually adapted to this, as well, collaborating with other mine bosses to fire and blacklist those who tried to subvert their power.

In addition to exploiting economic necessity, coal barons took advantage of, and helped create, ethnic divisions. It was common for them to bring "immigrants into the anthracite fields to divide and weaken the labor force."[27] When an allied group of twenty thousand miners struck after failed negotiations in 1887, for example, the powerful independent mine operators kept their mines open, hoping to lure Slavic and Italian immigrants back to work. When, to their surprise, the immigrants expressed solidarity with the strikers, the owners brought in workers from outside the region, and rumors spread that they were making efforts to import other immigrant groups. When strikes resurged in 1902, as another example, coal barons distributed propaganda such as this in an attempt to break the strike by pitting other ethnic groups against the Irish:

> Who is going to take care of you? Who gives your friends and relatives good chambers? Are they your countrymen? No, all Irish. Do [union leaders] John Mitchell, [John] Fahy, [Thomas] Duffy, and [Thomas] Nicholls work for you? No, for themselves and their own class, the Irish. They use you and your countrymen to win their battle. . . . The men who own the mines and pay you are better friends to you than those who lied to you and are still lying.[28]

Workers themselves often did the barons a favor by intensifying the divisions among them. Many recent Slavic and Italian immigrants were reluctant to join labor organizations; for this reason, they were viewed with scorn by many established ethnic groups, such as the English, Germans, Welsh, and Irish, who saw the new immigrants as "wage-cheapening laborers easily controlled by management."[29] In fact, John Fahy, a leader of the United Mine Workers, was a firm supporter of the Campbell Act. He thought it would keep the coal companies from using immigrants to undercut the wages of those ethnic groups that made up his union.[30]

The 1897 strike would be one of the exceptions, however. Although English-speakers were not on board when the mostly Slavic and Italian workers gathered at the hall to strategize, they did join their ranks in time. Given his support for the Campbell Act, Fahy, accounts suggest, was particularly hesitant to come back to the coal region when he heard about the protests. What he happily found when he returned, however, was that there was little animosity toward him. Strikers instead directed their resentment toward the companies that passed costs down to immigrant workers.[31] With the help of additional antagonism from mine bosses, including a failure to take action against Gomer Jones, the movement continued to gain steam, and the group of workers, who now had union backing but remained led by immigrants, added to their list of demands.[32]

The formation of a coalition between immigrants and "English-speakers" changed the game. As Miller and Sharpless write, in addition to fearing the "possible sabotage and destruction of valuable mining properties," the owners were "concerned about the growing willingness of the English-speaking miners to align with the immigrants. [Having] used the Slavs and Italians against the English-speaking miners in the past[,] the growing solidarity of the various ethnic groups was an ominous development in terms of the operators' future relations with labor."[33] Still unwilling to make any concessions, especially amid an economic depression, the mine owners hastily organized a secret meeting of their own on August 31. Perhaps an indication of what they discussed at that gathering, the local press noticed on that same day "500 Winchesters had arrived in the Coxe Company offices and that 300 more were on their way to A. Pardee and Company."[34]

The mine operators also summoned Luzerne County's Sheriff James L. Martin. Like others occupying middle-class status in the anthracite coal region during this era, Martin "owed [his] livelihood to the coal barons" and "knew whom he had to please if he wanted to remain sheriff" and avoid returning to the mines.[35] Miller and Sharpless write, "The message Martin received was clear: the owners wanted a strike broken and they didn't care how it was done."[36] He promised to enlist the help of other powerful men who were in a similar position. After navigating a few legal loopholes,[37] he formed a posse of eighty-seven volunteers. Most were professional men of English, Irish, and German ancestry "whose careers were intimately bound up with the fortunes of the coal operators."[38] Upon enlistment, Martin handed each deputy a new rifle and "three-inch, metal piercing bullets as well as buckshot loads."[39]

The strikers, meanwhile, continued to advance their cause. On September 3, they organized an eleven-mile march from nearby McAdoo to Hazleton. An Italian immigrant, the story goes, spontaneously prompted the movement of "over a thousand men, brandishing pokers, fence pickets, and clubs" after he shouted, "Vendetta!"[40] In what would become their characteristic marching formation, the strikers fashioned a column behind a leader who carried an American flag, under which the strikers felt both "patriotic" and "protected."[41]

To the great frustration of Martin and his deputies, momentum continued to pick up later that week, with the number of strikers increasing to as many as ten thousand. On the evening of Thursday, September 9, miners from Lattimer, a coal community bordering Hazleton's northeastern corner, contacted the strikers, wanting to join them. Lattimer was the last of Pardee's mines that was still operating, which made this communication especially important. The strikers figured that if they were to shut it down, the coal barons just might concede.[42]

The next morning, a group of three hundred Polish, Slovak, and Lithuanian immigrants gathered to march from Harwood, southwest of Hazleton, through the city and into Lattimer. Determined to be nonviolent, the leaders insisted that strikers discard all items, including walking sticks, before they departed. Soon after they set off, the group encountered Martin and his armed posse in Hazleton. A fight broke out, and one of the deputies took the American flag from the protestors and tore it. Hazleton police intervened and determined that the protestors, much to Martin's chagrin, could lawfully continue to march as long as they took a less disruptive route around the city. Martin and his frustrated posse boarded a trolley with plans to meet the protestors in Lattimer. The defiance of the miners by this point had enflamed the deputies. Conversations on that trolley ride suggested that violence was imminent. "I bet I drop six of them when I get over there," someone overheard one man boasting.[43]

Figure 1.1. Miners marching toward Lattimer, September 10, 1897. (MG-273 Charles H. Burg Collection, "Strikers on the March." Courtesy of Pennsylvania Historical Museum and Commission, Pennsylvania State Archives.)

With a torn flag leading the way, the protestors approached Lattimer, where Martin and his posse awaited (Figure 1.1). When they finally met, Martin made the first move. With one hand holding a drawn pistol and the other signaling "stop," he shouted, "You must stop marching and disperse. This is contrary to the law and you are creating a disturbance. You must go back. I won't let you go to the colliery."[44] This was enough to freeze those in the front of the line, Miller and Sharpless recount, but many who lagged behind did not see or hear Martin's demand. Someone from the crowd then shouted, "Go ahead!" and the group moved forward again.[45]

Martin physically pulled one of the marchers out of the line, but when others came to his aid, it was clear that this, too, was futile. Now especially distressed, and with the group continuing past him, Martin apparently attempted to shoot one of the strikers, but his pistol failed to fire. After that, Novak describes how "someone—two of the marchers claimed it was Martin—shouted 'Fire!' and 'Give two or three shots!'"[46] These words prompted an all-out barrage from the deputies, who relentlessly cast a fury of bullets into the unarmed crowd. "Steven Jurich, the Slovak flag bearer, was the first man hit, a bullet shattering his skull."[47] "O Joj! Joj! Joj! He cried in the ancient Slovak cry to God," Novak writes.[48] The deputies proceeded to gun down many of Jurich's comrades before they could react.[49] Others fled, but they, too, became targets. According to Miller and Sharpless's account, some were shot even as they retreated "as far away as 300 yards."[50] Witnesses heard deputies shouting, "Shoot the sons of bitches!"[51] When the firing ended, many marchers had entry wounds in their backs. "A number of the sixteen-cartridge Winchester magazines were completely emptied. A witness claimed that at least 150 shots were fired." What remained was a "horrible scene of carnage"[52] overwhelmed by "blood, smoke, road dust, and cries of anguish."[53]

Estimates vary, but at least nineteen people were killed and thirty-two more were wounded by the onslaught allegedly perpetrated by Martin's posse, which would come to be known as the "Lattimer Massacre." The coal barons' hired guns had done their job of breaking the strike at all costs, and, as is especially apparent from the deputies' actions when they left the scene, they reasserted their superiority over their immigrant victims. Some deputies kicked the defeated marchers as they lay on the ground, helplessly bleeding. Another rejected a victim's plea for water, offering instead an ethnic slur: "We'll give you hell, not water, Hunkies!"[54] As they climbed back aboard the trolley, the deputies laughed and joked about how many strikers they had hit.[55]

A week after the massacre, the *Hazleton Daily Standard* published the poem "The Ballad of the Deputies," which included this verse:

> If the courts of justice shield you
>   And your freedom you should gain,
> Remember that your brows are marked
>   With the burning brand of Cain.
> Oh, noble, noble, deputies
>   We always will remember
> Your bloody work at Lattimer
>   On the 10th day of September.[56]

In reading this poem while reflecting on recent events, it is hard not to fixate on the line "We always will remember." The temptation is to read it as a glaring inaccuracy. If one thing is clear from the preceding chapters, it is that the important lessons from Lattimer have not been on our collective minds. Yet when read not as a literal promise but simply as a call to keep alive the fighting spirit of the miners, the line emits a strong sense of hope with implications for the present: *What if we did remember?* Just how expansive is the realm of possibilities?

This history serves, on one hand, as a cautionary tale: It lays bare the tendency of economic elites to protect their interests at all costs, exposes how nonelites often aid in such efforts to avoid their own impoverishment, and reminds us that interpersonal and legal hostility toward immigrants is age-old. It also provides inspiration: From this history, we learn about poor and working people's agency and their capacity for resistance. The ending was tragic, to be sure, but the panic felt by the coal barons when previously divided ethnic groups rallied is one of the best examples one can find to illustrate the power that comes from working-class solidarity.[57]

When we bring these lessons to bear on the present, we can start to see existing circumstances through a new lens. The contemporary captains of industry suddenly look much like their forebears as they pass the economic burdens of globalization down to ordinary workers. Our accumulating debts and the working conditions many endure today begin to resemble those of the miners over whose lives the coal companies exerted almost total control. This history also begins to put migrant illegality into perspective, both as a legal tool used to control labor and as pejorative phrase.[58] Indeed, after reading this story it becomes easier to comprehend how Latina/o degradation and White affirmation represent a modern-day form of divide-and-conquer propaganda.

These new visions, in turn, open up new possibilities for action. With John Bodan's legacy restored, we may decide to protest corporate decisions that cut costs to the detriment of working people. Now familiar with the comradery that existed between small businesses and miners, we may start to envision new coalitions and devise new strategies to protect our local economy from corporate domination.[59] Newly aware of how community members once provided relief to destitute miners to spite those responsible for their destitution, we may take steps to immunize our own relief efforts from co-optation. Moved by the loyalty of those immigrants who refused offers to work during a strike, we may reject the race to the bottom and its practice of awarding jobs to the lowest bidder.[60] Repulsed by the deputies' post-shooting actions, we may give up on our insistence that subtler forms of contemporary degradation be called something other than what they are. Deeply appreciative of all it took for the strikers to get to Lattimer and of all that stood in their way, we may begin reaching across lines of difference in the pursuit of a similar journey. With imagery of the miners marching toward Lattimer with that torn flag etched in our minds, we may express enthusiasm about the prospect of immigrants, the poor, people of color, women, and members of other historically marginalized groups leading today's struggle,[61] and we may begin to understand why it is important that they do.[62]

The prescriptive forms of thought and action I have described throughout this book have embedded in them an element of deception that reinforces race-based and class-based oppression. By leaving out the details, narrow promises of jobs provide cover for a political-economic ideology designed to keep wealth concentrated in the hands of a few.[63] Color-blind ideology incorrectly suggests that race no longer matters while the Latino Threat Narrative reduces human beings to "virtual characters"[64] and sly rhetoric, which "transforms things into their opposites," causes "real human suffering to [vanish]."[65] Renderings of Hazleton as Small Town, USA, draw heavily on nostalgia, "a collective dream that facilitates a primitive exchange of sentiments, while inhibiting a realistic appraisal of contemporary social relations."[66] Out of this comes a collective White identity that is "nothing but oppressive and false"[67]—constructed vis-à-vis false enemies and used to blur economic realities.

In sharp contrast, *authenticity* characterizes this new realm of possibilities. With awareness that this is an ongoing struggle, we become empowered to *re-politicize* neoliberalism, asking difficult questions and demanding truthful answers about economic policy, participating in educative political action, and hosting economic forums that share real stories from the bottom rather than sanitized rhetoric from the top.[68] Mindful of racial hierarchies and familiar with continuities in the immigrant experience, we rise up to confront race rather than hiding behind a color-blind façade: seeing and naming degradation, interrogating Whiteness, demanding a non-hostile space where people of color can "recount their experiences with racism,"[69] and working to forge class-based unity without putting race on the back burner.[70] We also remain vigilant about co-optation, closely guarding the "free spaces" we create from those who threaten to water down their richness.[71] This new realm of possibilities, in short, encompasses Freire's notion of "'*the practice of freedom*,' the means by which men and women deal critically and creatively with reality and discover how to participate in the transformation of their world."[72]

As he considers healthier forms of historical engagement, Behdad acknowledges that forgetting is not inherently a bad thing. Sometimes we need to forget in order to "transcend historical traumas and avoid being psychologically paralyzed."[73] For all of the inspiration it provides, the line "We always will remember" from "The Ballad of the Deputies" may thus actually be an overstatement. The horrors of Lattimer need not forever plague our minds. Behdad's key point, however, which he makes by quoting the philosopher Slavoj Žižek, is that "in order really to forget an event, we must first summon up the strength to remember it properly."[74] What I am describing is admittedly difficult work. Nostalgia is easier than confronting the gritty reality of a postindustrial city stripped of its worth by generations of barons. The inclination in a culture in which racism is so deeply rooted is to fall back on innocence and abstraction rather than confront privilege and oppression. When it comes to understanding the historical antecedents of complex economic policy, "spectating" often seems preferable to "acting." But our pressing problems are not going anywhere without authentic confrontation and truly democratic participation. Our past will continue to haunt us until we remember it well enough to apply its lessons to the present day. In time, we can forget. The problem is the ideologies that protect oppressive social structures urge us to do so before we are ready.

Appendix A

Data and Methods

The research I conducted for this book uses a combination of ethnographic and archival methods. I was in and out of the field from 2007 until 2013. Following Michael Buroway's conception of "the extended case method,"[1] I continually refined my research questions as I collected new data and interpreted it in a broader social and theoretical context. What follows is a chapter-by-chapter breakdown summarizing the data I collected, explaining my analysis strategy, and delineating how my thinking came together over the course of this project.

CHAPTER 1

In 2007 when I decided to study this case, I had been learning a lot about the political economy of immigration. I therefore saw it as important to begin by exploring Hazleton's recent economic history in more depth. From reading Thomas Dublin and Walter Licht's *The Face of Decline*,[2] which I consider the seminal book on this topic, I learned about an archive CAN DO maintains at its headquarters in downtown Hazleton. This source proved instrumental in helping me construct the short history of CAN DO that appears in Chapter 1. The organization granted me access to the archive for several days in December 2007 and again in July 2008. At the time I studied it, the collection consisted of twenty-two temporary-ordered "books," covering the period from CAN DO's founding in the mid-1950s to the present day. The archive resembles a scrapbook; it contains mostly newspaper clippings, but a variety of other materials are scattered throughout. Consistent with what others have said about archival research, I found the longitudinal nature of this resource invaluable for shedding light on historical progression and change[3]—particularly, in my case, identifying the political economic shifts of the 1980s as a turning point for CAN DO—and ultimately for contextualizing Hazleton's passage of the Illegal Immigration Relief Act (IIRA).

I cross-checked and further pursued some of my findings from the archive in a number of ways. In particular, I traveled to Harrisburg to view Hazleton's application for Keystone Opportunity Zone (KOZ) status,[4] and I spoke informally with a public official who is familiar with the initiative. Pertaining to CAN DO specifically, I accessed and analyzed some of the materials the group shares with the public that are not in the archive (e.g., self-published books, annual reports, a fiftieth anniversary DVD), reviewed documents describing the local board meetings at which CAN DO pitched the KOZ initiative, and interviewed the organization's current president. To gain perspective from outside of the organization, I also interviewed seven "economic activists"—local residents who at one time or another have spoken publicly about local economic development issues.[5]

CHAPTER 2

Familiar with what had been transpiring in Hazleton before my research officially began, I was already aware that the murder of Derek Kichline had been the catalyst for the IIRA. This led me to review local newspaper articles about the crime, which, I found, contained glaring similarities to what Stanley Cohen famously termed a "moral panic."[6] To ensure that this was not simply how the press in this small city typically responds to homicides, I sought out a comparable case and found that the murder of Julio Calderon in 2005 had several factual similarities with the important exception of the race/ethnicity of the victim. Thus, the content analysis in the first part of Chapter 2 is of the *Standard-Speaker*'s coverage of these two cases. The *Standard-Speaker* is Hazleton's primary newspaper and, to my knowledge, was the only outlet to cover the two cases in depth. Because my focus was on how race shaped the reaction, I chose only articles that appeared after police identified the suspects. Realizing the richness of the reports that immediately followed each crime compared with those published later, which only mention the crimes in passing,[7] I decided to include only articles printed less than one month after police identified a suspect in each case. Importantly, all the reporting I analyzed took place before any determination of guilt or innocence.

I also obtained, transcribed, and analyzed audiotapes from the Hazleton City Council meetings that took place on June 15 and July 13, 2006. Although several themes emerged from this analysis,[8] what I focus on in this chapter is how officials forged symbolic, racialized linkages between particular groups and particular behaviors and traits. The rather seamless transition from how the media covered the Kichline murder to how officials discussed the issue of undocumented immigration at the meetings is what led me to flag this theme as important. Once my argument began to take shape, I turned to other sources for additional illustrative examples. Transcripts from the *Lozano v. Hazleton* trial and comments public officials made in other venues (i.e., in the national media, in front of the U.S. Senate) following the IIRA's passage were particularly useful in this regard.[9]

I used a combination of methodologies to make the observations that appear at the end of Chapter 2 regarding how the IIRA has affected life on the ground—namely, my ethnographic field notes;[10] interviews with activists (see below); focus groups and interviews I conducted with ordinary, longtime White Hazleton residents;[11] and reports from other scholars.[12] Within each of these data sources, I looked for instances in which people's accounts of discrimination or their stories about a changing city bore resemblance to the degradation and affirmation narratives that I found were coming from above.

CHAPTER 3

Data I use in Chapters 3 and 4 come from in-depth, semi-structured interviews with activists on both sides of the debate over the IIRA. In all, I interviewed twenty-four activists, mostly in 2009, twelve of whom I would call "pro-IIRA" and twelve of whom were generally opposed to the ordinance.[13] I began by recruiting participants with high visibility (e.g., who were mentioned in newspaper reports, who testified at City Council meetings) and continued to recruit using snowball sampling.[14] These interviews helped me learn more about the events that transpired; indeed, they provide a lot of the substance of the stories I tell in these chapters. However, my primary focus remained on these activists' *narratives*.[15] I wanted to understand local actors' position vis-à-vis prevailing ideologies. To quote Anne Swidler, "I was less interested in *what* people thought than in what resources they had available to *think with*, and how they mobilized those resources."[16] How did they put to use, contest, or work within the narratives that tend to dominate discussions about race, social class, law, and immigration in the United States? And how did this shape the subsequent course of action they were willing and able to take?

In both chapters, I supplemented interviews with other data. In Chapter 3, I analyzed the transcripts of the *Lozano* trial. I found this source especially useful for unpacking the rhetorical patterns that I saw emerging from the local response to immigrants' rights activism. I also thought it was quite telling that the formal rhetoric used in the courtroom mirrored the discourse used in other settings. In the chapter, I also relied on video footage from five of the public rallies Voice of the People, USA, hosted from June to September 2007. The video was available on the Internet and it represents most, but not all, such events.[17] I downloaded and watched each video; transcribed the text of all of the speeches; and took notes on relevant audio and visual cues, such as the content of attendees' signs and the audiences' responses.[18] In all, I downloaded more than six hours of footage and analyzed the transcripts of thirty-eight speeches.

CHAPTER 4

In addition to interviews with activists, Chapter 4 relies on participant observation with the Concerned Parents of the Hazleton Area. I attended several of the group's meetings and events between April and June 2009. My discussion of more recent activity (i.e., the Hazleton Integration Project) draws mostly from news reports. However, I did seek out updates on that group's progress and visited the community center on two occasions in 2013.

Appendix B

Full Text of the Illegal Immigration Relief Act

ORDINANCE 2006-18
ILLEGAL IMMIGRATION RELIEF ACT ORDINANCE

BE IT ORDAINED BY THE COUNCIL OF THE CITY
OF HAZLETON AS FOLLOWS:

SECTION 1. TITLE
This chapter shall be known and may be cited as the "City of Hazleton Illegal Immigration Relief Act Ordinance."

SECTION 2. FINDINGS AND DECLARATION OF PURPOSE
The People of the City of Hazleton find and declare:

    A. That state and federal law require that certain conditions be met before a person may be authorized to work or reside in this country.

    B. That unlawful workers and illegal aliens, as defined by this ordinance and state and federal law, do not normally meet such conditions as a matter of law when present in the City of Hazleton.

    C. That unlawful employment, the harboring of illegal aliens in dwelling units in the City of Hazleton, and crime committed by illegal aliens harm the health, safety and welfare of authorized U.S. workers and legal residents in the City of Hazleton. Illegal immigration leads to higher crime rates, subjects our hospitals to fiscal hardship and legal residents to substandard quality of care, contributes to other burdens on public services, increasing their cost and diminishing their availability to legal residents, and diminishes our overall quality of life.

D. That the City of Hazleton is authorized to abate public nuisances and empowered and mandated by the people of Hazleton to abate the nuisance of illegal immigration by diligently prohibiting the acts and policies that facilitate illegal immigration in a manner consistent with federal law and the objectives of Congress.

E. That United States Code Title 8, subsection 1324(a)(1)(A) prohibits the harboring of illegal aliens. The provision of housing to illegal aliens is a fundamental component of harboring.

F. This ordinance seeks to secure to those lawfully present in the United States and this City, whether or not they are citizens of the United States, the right to live in peace free from the threat [of] crime, to enjoy the public services provided by this city without being burdened by the cost of providing goods, support and services to aliens unlawfully present in the United States, and to be free from the debilitating effects on their economic and social well being imposed by the influx of illegal aliens to the fullest extent that these goals can be achieved consistent with the Constitution and Laws of the United States and the Commonwealth of Pennsylvania.

G. The City shall not construe this ordinance to prohibit the rendering of emergency medical care, emergency assistance, or legal assistance to any person.

SECTION 3. DEFINITIONS

When used in this chapter, the following words, terms and phrases shall have the meanings ascribed to them herein, and shall be construed so as to be consistent with state and federal law, including federal immigration law:

A. "Business entity" means any person or group of persons performing or engaging in any activity, enterprise, profession, or occupation for gain, benefit, advantage, or livelihood, whether for profit or not for profit.

  (1) The term "business entity" shall include but not be limited to self-employed individuals, partnerships, corporations, contractors, and subcontractors.

  (2) The term "business entity" shall include any business entity that possesses a business permit, any business entity that is exempt by law from obtaining such a business permit, and any business entity that is operating unlawfully without such a business permit.

B. "City" means the City of Hazleton.

C. "Contractor" means a person, employer, subcontractor, or business entity that enters into an agreement to perform any service or work or to provide a certain product in exchange for valuable consideration. This definition shall include but not be limited to a subcontractor, contract employee, or a recruiting or staffing entity.

D. "Illegal Alien" means an alien who is not lawfully present in the United States, according to the terms of United States Code Title 8, section 1101 et seq. The City shall not conclude that a person is an illegal alien unless and until an authorized representative of the City has verified with the federal government, pursuant to United States Code Title 8, subsection 1373(c), that the person is an alien who is not lawfully present in the United States.

E. "Unlawful worker" means a person who does not have the legal right or authorization to work due to an impediment in any provision of federal, state or local law, including but not limited to a minor disqualified by nonage, or an unauthorized alien as defined by United States Code Title 8, subsection 1324a(h)(3).

F. "Work" means any job, task, employment, labor, personal services, or any other activity for which compensation is provided, expected, or due, including but not limited to all activities conducted by business entities.

G. "Basic Pilot Program" means the electronic verification of work authorization program of the Illegal Immigration Reform and Immigration Responsibility Act of 1996, P.L. 104-208, Division C, Section 403(a); United States Code Title 8, subsection 1324a, and operated by the United States Department of Homeland Security (or a successor program established by the federal government).

SECTION 4. BUSINESS PERMITS, CONTRACTS, OR GRANTS

A. It is unlawful for any business entity to recruit, hire for employment, or continue to employ, or to permit, dispatch, or instruct any person who is an unlawful worker to perform work in whole or part within the City. Every business entity that applies for a business permit to engage in any type of work in the City shall sign an affidavit, prepared by the City Solicitor, affirming that they do not knowingly utilize the services or hire any person who is an unlawful worker.

B. Enforcement: The Hazleton Code Enforcement Office shall enforce the requirements of this section.

(1) An enforcement action shall be initiated by means of a written signed complaint to the Hazleton Code Enforcement Office submitted by any City official, business entity, or City resident. A valid complaint shall include an allegation which describes the alleged violator(s) as well as the actions constituting the violation, and the date and location where such actions occurred.

(2) A complaint which alleges a violation solely or primarily on the basis of national origin, ethnicity, or race shall be deemed invalid and shall not be enforced.

(3) Upon receipt of a valid complaint, the Hazleton Code Enforcement Office shall, within three business days, request identity information from the business entity regarding any persons alleged to be unlawful workers. The Hazleton Code Enforcement Office shall suspend the business permit of any business entity which fails, within three business days after receipt of the request, to provide such information. In instances where an unlawful worker is alleged to be an unauthorized alien, as defined in United States Code Title 8, subsection 1324a(h)(3), the Hazleton Code Enforcement Office shall submit identity data required by the federal government to verify, pursuant to United States Code Title 8, section 1373, the immigration status of such person(s), and shall provide the business entity with written confirmation of that verification.

(4) The Hazleton Code Enforcement Office shall suspend the business permit of any business entity which fails to correct a violation of this

section within three business days after notification of the violation by the Hazleton Code Enforcement Office.

(5) The Hazleton Code Enforcement Office shall not suspend the business permit of a business entity if, prior to the date of the violation, the business entity had verified the work authorization of the alleged unlawful worker(s) using the Basic Pilot Program.

(6) The suspension shall terminate one business day after a legal representative of the business entity submits, at a City office designated by the City Solicitor, a sworn affidavit stating that the violation has ended.

   (a) The affidavit shall include a description of the specific measures and actions taken by the business entity to end the violation, and shall include the name, address and other adequate identifying information of the unlawful workers related to the complaint.

   (b) Where two or more of the unlawful workers were verified by the federal government to be unauthorized aliens, the legal representative of the business entity shall submit to the Hazleton Code Enforcement Office, in addition to the prescribed affidavit, documentation acceptable to the City Solicitor which confirms that the business entity has enrolled in and will participate in the Basic Pilot Program for the duration of the validity of the business permit granted to the business entity.

(7) For a second or subsequent violation, the Hazleton Code Enforcement Office shall suspend the business permit of a business entity for a period of twenty days. After the end of the suspension period, and upon receipt of the prescribed affidavit, the Hazleton Code Enforcement Office shall reinstate the business permit. The Hazleton Code Enforcement Office shall forward the affidavit, complaint, and associated documents to the appropriate federal enforcement agency, pursuant to United States Code Title 8, section 1373. In the case of an unlawful worker disqualified by state law not related to immigration, the Hazleton Code Enforcement Office shall forward the affidavit, complaint, and associated documents to the appropriate state enforcement agency.

C. All agencies of the City shall enroll and participate in the Basic Pilot Program.

D. As a condition for the award of any City contract or grant to a business entity for which the value of employment, labor or, personal services shall exceed $10,000, the business entity shall provide documentation confirming its enrollment and participation in the Basic Pilot Program.

E. Private Cause of Action for Unfairly Discharged Employees.

(1) The discharge of any employee who is not an unlawful worker by a business entity in the City is an unfair business practice if, on the date of the discharge, the business entity was not participating in the Basic Pilot Program and the business entity was employing an unlawful worker.

(2) The discharged worker shall have a private cause of action in the Municipal Court of Hazleton against the business entity for the unfair business practice. The business entity found to have violated this subsection shall be liable to the aggrieved employee for:

(a) three times the actual damages sustained by the employee, including but not limited to lost wages or compensation from the date of the discharge until the date the employee has procured new employment at an equivalent rate of compensation, up to a period of one hundred and twenty days; and

(b) reasonable attorney's fees and costs.

SECTION 5. HARBORING ILLEGAL ALIENS

A. It is unlawful for any person or business entity that owns a dwelling unit in the City to harbor an illegal alien in the dwelling unit, knowing or in reckless disregard of the fact that an alien has come to, entered, or remains in the United States in violation of law, unless such harboring is otherwise expressly permitted by federal law.

(1) For the purposes of this section, to let, lease, or rent a dwelling unit to an illegal alien, knowing or in reckless disregard of the fact that an alien has come to, entered, or remains in the United States in violation of law, shall be deemed to constitute harboring. To suffer or permit the occupancy of the dwelling unit by an illegal alien, knowing or in reckless disregard of the fact that an alien has come to, entered, or remains in the United States in violation of law, shall also be deemed to constitute harboring.

(2) A separate violation shall be deemed to have been committed on each day that such harboring occurs, and for each adult illegal alien harbored in the dwelling unit, beginning one business day after receipt of a notice of violation from the Hazleton Code Enforcement Office.

(3) A separate violation of this section shall be deemed to have been committed for each business day on which the owner fails to provide the Hazleton Code Enforcement Office with identity data needed to obtain a federal verification of immigration status, beginning three days after the owner receives written notice from the Hazleton Code Enforcement Office.

B. Enforcement: The Hazleton Code Enforcement Office shall enforce the requirements of this section.

(1) An enforcement action shall be initiated by means of a written signed complaint to the Hazleton Code Enforcement Office submitted by any official, business entity, or resident of the City. A valid complaint shall include an allegation which describes the alleged violator(s) as well as the actions constituting the violation, and the date and location where such actions occurred.

(2) A complaint which alleges a violation solely or primarily on the basis of national origin, ethnicity, or race shall be deemed invalid and shall not be enforced.

(3) Upon receipt of a valid written complaint, the Hazleton Code Enforcement Office shall, pursuant to United States Code Title 8, section 1373(c), verify with the federal government the immigration status of a person seeking to use, occupy, lease, or rent a dwelling unit in the City. The Hazle-

ton Code Enforcement Office shall submit identity data required by the federal government to verify immigration status. The City shall forward identity data provided by the owner to the federal government, and shall provide the property owner with written confirmation of that verification.

(4) If after five business days following receipt of written notice from the City that a violation has occurred and that the immigration status of any alleged illegal alien has been verified, pursuant to United States Code Title 8, section 1373(c), the owner of the dwelling unit fails to correct a violation of this section, the Hazleton Code Enforcement Office shall deny or suspend the rental license of the dwelling unit.

(5) For the period of suspension, the owner of the dwelling unit shall not be permitted to collect any rent, payment, fee, or any other form of compensation from, or on behalf of, any tenant or occupant in the dwelling unit.

(6) The denial or suspension shall terminate one business day after a legal representative of the dwelling unit owner submits to the Hazleton Code Enforcement Office a sworn affidavit stating that each and every violation has ended. The affidavit shall include a description of the specific measures and actions taken by the business entity to end the violation, and shall include the name, address and other adequate identifying information for the illegal aliens who were the subject of the complaint.

(7) The Hazleton Code Enforcement Office shall forward the affidavit, complaint, and associated documents to the appropriate federal enforcement agency, pursuant to United States Code Title 8, section 1373.

(8) Any dwelling unit owner who commits a second or subsequent violation of this section shall be subject to a fine of two hundred and fifty dollars ($250) for each separate violation. The suspension provisions of this section applicable to a first violation shall also apply.

(9) Upon the request of a dwelling unit owner, the Hazleton Code Enforcement Office shall, pursuant to United States Code Title 8, section 1373(c), verify with the federal government the lawful immigration status of a person seeking to use, occupy, lease, or rent a dwelling unit in the City. The penalties in this section shall not apply in the case of dwelling unit occupants whose status as an alien lawfully present in the United States has been verified.

SECTION 6. CONSTRUCTION AND SEVERABILITY

A. The requirements and obligations of this section shall be implemented in a manner fully consistent with federal law regulating immigration and protecting the civil rights of all citizens and aliens.

B. If any part of provision of this Chapter is in conflict or inconsistent with applicable provisions of federal or state statutes, or is otherwise held to be invalid or unenforceable by any court of competent jurisdiction, such part of provision shall be suspended and superseded by such applicable laws or regulations, and the remainder of this Chapter shall not be affected thereby.

ORDINANCE 2006-19
OFFICAL ENGLISH ORDINANCE

**BE IT ORDAINED BY THE COUNCIL OF THE CITY
OF HAZLETON AS FOLLOWS:**

SECTION 1. TITLE

This chapter shall be known and may be cited as the "City of Hazleton Official English Ordinance."

SECTION 2. FINDINGS AND DECLARATION OF PURPOSE

The People of the City of Hazleton find and declare:

A. That the English language is the common language of the City of Hazleton, of the Commonwealth of Pennsylvania and of the United States.

B. That the use of a common language removes barriers of misunderstanding and helps to unify the people of [the] City of Hazleton, the Commonwealth of Pennsylvania, and the United States, and helps to enable the full economic and civic participation of all its citizens, regardless of national origin, creed, race or other characteristics, and thus a compelling government interest exists in promoting, preserving, and strengthening the use of the English language.

C. That proficiency in the English language, as well as in languages other than the English language, benefits the City of Hazleton both economically and culturally and should be encouraged.

D. That, in addition to any other ways to promote proficiency in the English language, the government of the City of Hazleton can promote proficiency in English by using the English language in its official actions and activities.

E. That in today's modern society, the City of Hazleton may also need to protect and preserve the rights of those who speak only the English language to use or obtain government programs and benefits.

F. That the government of the City of Hazleton can reduce costs and promote efficiency in its roles as employer and as a government of the people, by using the English language in its official actions and activities.

SECTION 3. OFFICIAL ENGLISH DECLARATION

A. The English language is the official language of the City of Hazleton.

B. The City Council, Mayor, and officials of the City of Hazleton shall take all steps necessary to insure that the role of English as the common language of the City of Hazleton is preserved and enhanced.

C. The government [of the] City of Hazleton shall make no policy that diminishes or ignores the role of English as the common language of the City of Hazleton.

D. Official actions of the City of Hazleton that bind or commit the City of Hazleton or that give the appearance of presenting the official views or position of the City of Hazleton shall be taken in the English language, and in no other language. Unofficial or non-binding translations or explanations of official actions may be provided separately in languages other than English, if they are appropriately labeled as such and reference is made to a method to obtain the official action; unless otherwise required by federal law or the law of the Commonwealth of Pennsylvania, no person has a right to such an unofficial or non-binding translation or explanation, and no liability or commitment of the City of Hazleton shall be based on such a translation or explanation.

E. No ordinance, decree, program, or policy of the City of Hazleton or any of its subdivisions shall require the use of any language other than English for any documents, regulations, orders, transactions, proceedings, meetings, programs, or publications, except as provided in Section 4.

F. A person who speaks only the English language shall be eligible to participate in all programs, benefits and opportunities, including employment, provided by the City of Hazleton and its subdivisions, except when required to speak another language as provided in Section 4.

G. No law, ordinance, decree, program, or policy of the City of Hazleton or any of its subdivisions shall penalize or impair the rights, obligations or opportunities available to any person solely because a person speaks only the English language.

SECTION 4. EXCEPTIONS

The City of Hazleton and its subdivisions may use a language other than English for any of the following purposes, whether or not the use would be considered part of an official action:

A. To teach or encourage the learning of languages other than English.

B. To protect the public health or safety.

C. To teach English to those who are not fluent in the language.

D. To comply with the Native American Languages Act, the Individuals with Disabilities Education Act, the Voting Rights Act, or any other federal law or law of the Commonwealth of Pennsylvania.

E. To protect the rights of criminal defendants and victims of crime.

F. To promote trade, commerce, and tourism.

G. To create or promote mottos or designations, inscribe public monuments, and perform other acts involving the customary use of a language other than English.

H. To utilize terms of art or terms or phrases from other languages which are commonly used in communications otherwise in English.

SECTION 5. PRIVATE USE PROTECTED

The declaration and use of English as the official language of the City of Hazleton should not be construed as infringing upon the rights of any person to use a language other than English in private communications or actions, including the right of government officials (including elected officials) to communicate with others while not performing official actions of the City of Hazleton.

SECTION 6. INTERPRETATION

Nothing in this ordinance shall be interpreted as conflicting with the statutes of the United States, or the laws of the Commonwealth of Pennsylvania.

SECTION 7. SEVERABILITY

If any part or provision of this Chapter, or the applicability of any provision to any person or circumstance, is held to be invalid by a court of competent jurisdiction, the remainder of this Chapter shall not be affected thereby and shall be given effect to the fullest extent practicable.

Notes

PREFACE

1. As Spencer Soper and Matt Birkbeck reported, "News vans and satellite trucks circled City Hall on Friday. [Hazleton Mayor Lou] Barletta's secretary, Cherie Homa, ordinarily fields calls from residents upset about potholes and stray garbage cans. But on Friday, the interview requests poured in from CNN, Fox News and *The O'Reilly Factor*": Spencer Soper and Matt Birkbeck, "Hazleton Gears Up to Keep Illegals Out," *Morning Call*, July 15, 2006.

2. *Lou Dobbs Tonight*, CNN, transcript available at http://transcripts.cnn.com/TRANSCRIPTS/0705/02/ldt.02.html.

3. Monica W. Varsanyi, "Immigration Policy Activism in U.S. States and Cities: Interdisciplinary Perspectives," in *Taking Local Control: Immigration Policy Activism in U.S. Cities and States*, ed. Monica W. Varsanyi (Stanford, CA: Stanford University Press, 2010), 3. Notably, this "flood" included "pro-immigrant" initiatives, as well: see, e.g., the "Welcome Dayton—Immigrant Friendly City" initiative, available at http://www.welcomedayton.org.

4. Proposition 187 sought to deny services such as health care and public education to people without documentation. For analyses, see Lisa Marie Cacho, "'The People of California Are Suffering': The Ideology of White Injury in the Discourse of Immigration," *Cultural Values* 4 (2000): 389–418; Kitty Calavita, "The New Politics of Immigration: 'Balanced-Budget Conservatism' and the Symbolism of Proposition 187," *Social Problems* 43, no. 3 (1996): 284–305.

5. See Leo R. Chavez, *The Latino Threat: Constructing Immigrants, Citizens, and the Nation* (Stanford, CA: Stanford University Press, 2008), 132–176.

6. As Leif Jensen acknowledges in a report prepared for the Carsey Institute in 2006, "For many decades urban areas have been, and they remain, the destination of choice

for the nation's immigrants. Recent evidence suggests, however, that many immigrant groups are dispersing away from traditional gateway cities. Many small towns and cities in every region of the country are contending with new challenges and opportunities brought by rapid increases in their immigrant populations": Leif Jensen, "New Immigrant Settlements in Rural America: Problems, Prospects, and Policies," Carsey Institute, 2006, available at http://scholars.unh.edu/cgi/viewcontent.cgi?article=1016&conte xt=carsey, accessed December 22, 2014. See also Katharine M. Donato et al., "Changing Faces, Changing Places: The Emergence of New Nonmetropolitan Immigrant Gateways," in *New Faces in New Places: The Changing Geography of American Immigration*, ed. Douglas Massey (New York: Russell Sage Foundation, 2008), 75–98.

7. Massey, *New Faces in New Places*.

8. Muzaffar Chishti and Claire Bergeron report, "By September 2006, six other towns had adopted Hazleton-type ordinances, including Valley Park, Missouri, and Riverside, New Jersey. Farmers Branch, Texas, followed suit in November 2006. Though there is no comprehensive database of all local-level immigration enforcement laws considered post-Hazleton, estimates suggest that between July 2006 and July 2007, U.S. towns and counties actively considered 118 immigration enforcement proposals. And between 2000 and 2010, 107 U.S. towns, cities, and counties had approved local immigration enforcement ordinances." They then summarize subsequent state-level activity:

> States meanwhile also began stepping into the immigration enforcement arena. Arizona was first, enacting a 2007 law requiring all businesses to use the federal E-Verify system to ascertain that new employees were authorized to work. . . . Three years later, Arizona enacted SB 1070, a sweeping immigration enforcement measure designed to drive unauthorized immigrants out of the state. The law required state and local police officers to inquire about immigration status if they had reasonable suspicion that the person they stopped was an unauthorized immigrant. SB 1070 made it a state crime for immigrants not to carry proof of immigration status or for [unauthorized immigrants] to work, and it allowed state officers to arrest without a warrant anyone believed to be deportable based on past criminal offenses. Following SB 1070's enactment, five states—Utah, South Carolina, Indiana, Georgia, and Alabama—enacted legislation patterned on SB 1070. (Muzaffar Chishti and Claire Bergeron, "Hazleton Immigration Ordinance that Began with a Bang Goes Out with a Whimper," Migration Policy Institute, Washington, DC, March 28, 2014, available at http://www .migrationpolicy.org/article/hazleton-immigration-ordinance-began-bang-goes out-whimper, accessed March 18, 2015)

9. Clifford Geertz, *The Interpretation of Cultures* (New York: Basic Books, 1973), 3.

10. Gary Alan Fine, "The Sociology of the Local: Action and Its Publics," *Sociological Theory* 28, no. 4 (2010): 355.

11. See, e.g., Ali Behdad, *A Forgetful Nation: On Immigration and Cultural Identity in the United States* (Durham, NC: Duke University Press, 2005).

12. This is a direct quote from a resident and each of these themes came up in my research when longtime White residents spoke about their immigrant ancestors.

13. On this issue, I agree with Lani Guinier and Gerald Torres, who focus on an "aspirational and motivational project" that

emphasizes bottom-up movements rather than top-down technocratic policy solutions. We are not opposed to law reform, nor do we dismiss all public policy agendas or bureaucratic reform movements as optimistic or naïve, although we do worry about their often unintended consequences. Our concern is that law reform and technical fixes have claimed too much of our attention. Our goal is to restore some balance to the dynamic relationship between insider strategies that depend on elites manipulating zero-sum (I-win/you-lose) power and outsider strategies that emphasize the role for grassroots organizations to experiment with alternative forms of resistance leading to greater access and accountability. (Lani Guinier and Gerald Torres (*The Miner's Canary: Enlisting Race, Resisting Power* [Cambridge, MA: Harvard University Press, 2002], 17)

14. Joe R. Feagin and Hernán Vera, *Liberation Sociology*, 2d ed. (Boulder, CO: Paradigm, 2008), 1.

15. Ibid.

16. Ibid., 2.

17. Ibid., 2–3. They write, "Some social science research emphasizes its policy relevance for those at the helm of the nation state or large corporations. The research of liberation sociology, in contrast, is generally defined by its usefulness to those who are oppressed and struggling for their liberation. Commitments to alleviating human suffering—or to peace, human rights, social justice, and real democracy—politicize the practice of sociology no more than the commitments that assert indifference, value-free methods, or neutral knowledge."

18. For a compelling empirical demonstration of this phenomenon, see Michael I. Norton and Dan Ariely, "Building a Better America—One Wealth Quintile at a Time," *Perspectives on Psychological Science* 6 (2011).

19. Palmer's full quote follows:

What we are seeing in our time is the rise of what I've come to call the "empty self." By that, I mean a self . . . that is no longer able to find authority from within and so must import authority from without. This is the kind of self that lives very fearfully in the world because emptiness is a fearful place to be and is therefore constantly looking for ways to prop up his or her own life and easily settles for leadership that both manipulates fear and promises to give that person a sense of identity that doesn't come from within but comes from without. Something is going on in our democracy that has led people to vote against their own economic interests and even their own personal interests in order to fill an emptiness with the appearance of power and security. "*We live in a world of terrorism, but I am the guy who can make you safe.*" Well, that one needs to be thought about with some care. And it can only be thought about by people who have enough sense of identity that comes from within themselves, enough sense of personal authority and ground on which to stand that they can do what patriots need to do, which is to be critical of their country at points where it needs critique—stand on their own ground as citizens and pull our country back to safety. If patriotism becomes our way of filling our own emptiness, then you can't do what a true patriot needs to do, which is to have a *lover's quarrel* with your own country, with your own political system. I think democracy has always depended on people who are standing independently and are able to have that lover's quarrel with something they love too much to let it sink to its lowest life form. So the empty self is a threat, I think, to fundamental democratic values and processes. (Parker Palmer, "Inner Authority and Democracy," interview, available at https://www.youtube.com/watch?v=xVmt7FouwGo, accessed March 21, 2015)

20. Parker Palmer, interview by Bill Moyers, February 20, 2009, available at http://www.pbs.org/moyers/journal/02202009/transcript2.html, accessed December 22, 2014.

21. Rita Hardiman and Bailey Jackson, "Conceptual Foundations for Social Justice Education," in *Teaching for Diversity and Social Justice*, 2d ed., ed. Maurianne Adams, Lee Anne Bell, and Pat Griffin (New York: Routledge, 2007), 41. Feagin and Vera similarly write about liberation sociology:

> We call for the reassertion of a sociological practice designed to empower ordinary people through social science research and knowledge. By having better access to critical sociological knowledge, people will be in a better position to understand their personal and familial troubles, make better sense of the world we live in, plan their individual and collective lives, and relate in egalitarian and democratic fashions to others within and outside their own nation state. This includes being in a better position to struggle for individual and collective human rights. A broad-based democracy can be fully developed in our era only if key types of knowledge are made available to all, not just to those at the top of the socioeconomic pyramid and their professional servants. (Feagin and Vera, *Liberation Sociology*, 10)

INTRODUCTION

1. The full video is available at http://www.cbsnews.com/news/welcome-to-hazleton, accessed July 30, 2015.

2. Compare this with Leo Chavez's observation that "since the Mexican-American War, immigration from Mexico and other Latin countries has waxed and waned, building in the early twentieth century, diminishing in the 1930s, and building again [in] the post-1965 years. These migrations paralleled those of other immigrant groups. But Mexicans in particular have been represented as the quintessential 'illegal aliens,' which distinguishes them from other immigrant groups. Their social identity has been plagued by the mark of illegality, which in much public discourse means that they are criminals and thus illegitimate members of society undeserving of social benefits, including citizenship": Leo R. Chavez, *The Latino Threat: Constructing Immigrants, Citizens, and the Nation* (Stanford, CA: Stanford University Press, 2008), 3.

3. A similar image is presented later in this broadcast. With the narrator describing the IIRA as "an ordinance that punishes businesses or landlords who give work or shelter to illegal aliens," we see the rear view of a person in a dark green jacket with the hood up walking down a sidewalk on a dark, rainy day. Chavez insightfully describes the significance of such depictions:

> Media spectacles transform immigrants' lives into virtual lives, which are typically devoid of the nuances and subtleties of real lived lives. . . . It is in this sense

that the media spectacle transforms a "worldview"—that is, a taken-for-granted understanding of the world—into an objective force, one that is taken as "truth." In their coverage of immigration events, the media gave voice to commentators, pundits, informed sources, and man-on-the-street observers who often invoke one or more of the myriad truths in the Latino Threat Narrative to support arguments and justify actions. In this way, media spectacles objectify Latinos. Through objectification (the process of turning a person into a thing) people are dehumanized, and once that is accomplished, it is easier to lack empathy for those objects and to pass policies and laws to govern their behavior, limit their social integration, and obstruct their economic mobility. (ibid., 5–6)

4. To be sure, the telecast goes on to feature dissenting voices. Indeed, the story attracted attention because the national media considered it *controversial*; that element adds to the newsworthiness of the case. My point, however, is not simply that they presented only one side of the debate. Rather, following Chavez, I am pointing out that assumptions about race and place are so taken-for-granted that even when journalists and others strive for objectivity, they employ problematic imagery. For example, on an episode of *Lou Dobbs Tonight* hosted live from Hazleton, Dobbs embraced the notion of a "two-sided" debate while indiscriminately accepting the idea that "illegal immigration" is a *crisis*, saying, "Tonight, we're going to examine this community's efforts to deal with the harsh realities of illegal immigration. We will tell you about the facts of our national illegal immigration crisis. And we will have a vigorous and open debate, with all viewpoints represented, and some potential solutions to the crisis, with our audience here, with advocates on both sides of this issue": see "Broken Borders," *Lou Dobbs Tonight*, CNN, available at http://transcripts.cnn.com/TRANSCRIPTS/0705/02/ldt.02. html, accessed December 22, 2014.

5. Chavez, *The Latino Threat*, 2

6. Ibid.

7. Recognizing the dehumanizing nature of referring to human beings as "illegal," I avoid using the phrase "illegal immigrant" (and variations thereof, such as "illegal alien") and refer instead to "people without documentation" or "undocumented" or "unauthorized" immigrants, except when one of the phrases is part of a quotation or part of the rhetoric I am critically analyzing. Avia Chomsky, for example, notes that the phrase "illegal immigrant" has been condemned by the United Nations High Commission on Human Rights because "it contradicts the spirit and violates directly the words of the Universal Declaration of Human Rights which clearly states in Article 6 that '[e]veryone has the right to recognition everywhere as a person before the law'": Avia Chomsky, *"They Take Our Jobs!" and Twenty Other Myths about Immigration* (Boston: Beacon, 2007), 58. Notably, the Associated Press has also changed its stylebook to avoid use of this term: see Lawrence Downes, "No More 'Illegal Immigrants,'" *New York Times*, April 4, 2013.

8. The introduction to the text version of the *60 Minutes* telecast that I am analyzing here points out, "Not that long ago [illegal immigration] was a problem in a half dozen border states; today it impacts virtually the entire country": see http://www.cbsnews .com/news/welcome-to-hazleton. Lou Dobbs presented a similar angle in his "Broken Borders" episode, saying, "Hazleton is a small community nearly 2,000 miles from our southern border with Mexico. But, while it's far from our border, it's at the center of our illegal immigration and border security crisis."

Along these lines, my use of the word "seeps" and the phrase "stem the tide" here is an intentional attempt to describe the prevailing narrative. Otto Santa Ana powerfully describes how frequently used metaphors of immigrants as "dangerous waters" contribute to the dehumanization of immigrants, writing, "The major metaphor for the process of the movement of [a] substantial number of human beings to the United States is characterized as IMMIGRATION AS DANGEROUS WATERS. . . . The DANGEROUS WATERS metaphors do not refer to any aspect of the humanity of the immigrants. . . . In contrast to such nonhuman metaphors for immigrants, U.S. society is often referred to in human terms": Otto Santa Ana, *Brown Tide Rising: Metaphors of Latinos in Contemporary American Public Discourse* (Austin: University of Texas Press, 2002), 72–73.

9. These concepts have their roots in Chavez's notion of the Latino Threat Narrative, as well as in the work of other critical race, LatCrit, and immigration scholars. In addition to Chavez's *The Latino Threat*, I am especially influenced by the concepts of "white innocence" and "black abstraction" in Thomas Ross, "The Rhetorical Tapestry of Race: White Innocence and Black Abstraction," *William and Mary Law Review* 32, no. 1 (1990): 1–36 (see Chapter 3). Lisa Marie Cacho's concept of the "ideology of White injury" has also helped me develop this framework: see Lisa Marie Cacho, "'The People of California Are Suffering': The Ideology of White Injury in Discourses of Immigration," *Cultural Values* 4 (2000): 389–418. Ian Haney López's concepts of "dog whistle politics" and "strategic racism" also were instrumental in shaping my thinking: see Ian Haney López, *Dog Whistle Politics: How Coded Racial Appeals Have Reinvented Racism and Wrecked the Middle Class* (New York: Oxford University Press, 2014). Departing slightly from the concepts these scholars use, I employ the terms "degradation" and "affirmation" to draw attention to how the uplifting of one group and the demoting of another form the basis of divide and conquer politics.

A few other notes on terminology: My focus in this book is on *racialization*—the (mostly top-down) process of attaching meanings to particular racial categories and the consequences thereof. Accordingly, as I use the term "Latina/o" throughout the text, I remain cognizant that it encompasses people from various ethnic and historical backgrounds, as well as some who may also self-identify as White. For instance, Hazleton's recent immigrants arrived mostly from the Dominican Republic, Mexico, and Peru, but they also came from, among other Latin American countries, Ecuador, Colombia, Argentina, Honduras, Guatemala, and Nicaragua: see "Ethnic Changes in Northeastern Pennsylvania: With Special Emphasis on Recent History within the City of Hazleton," Joint Urban Studies Center, July 2006, available at http://www.institutepa.org/pdf/research/diversity0906.pdf, accessed July 29, 2015. However, in this context, the encompassing term is appropriate because it is used to explain a *shared experience of racialization*.

This is also the reason I focus primarily on Latinas/os and Whites and not members of other ethnic/racial or immigrant groups who are also residents of Hazleton, albeit in much smaller numbers. This is not to deny that other residents inhabit, experience, and shape the city; it has to do with how the debate I studied racialized these two groups in particular.

The same applies to my use of the term "race" as opposed to "ethnicity." As Laura Gómez explains, race, as a socially constructed phenomenon, has "the quality of *assignment*. . . . [R]acial group membership is assigned by others, and particularly by members of the dominant group." Ethnicity, in contrast, has "the quality of *assertion*. . . . [E]thnic group membership is chosen by members of the ethnic group. . . . Used in this way, race involves harder, less voluntary group membership" (although, to be sure, undesirable racializations can be—and often are—contested): Laura Gómez, *Manifest Destinies: The Making of the Mexican American Race* (New York: New York University Press, 2007), 2.

My use of the term "White" recognizes that "Whites [also] constitute a socially defined racial group, albeit with heterogeneous origins"—hence, my capitalization of the term: see Amy C. Steinbugler, Julie E. Press, and Janice Johnson Dias, "Gender, Race, and Affirmative Action: Operationalizing Intersectionality in Survey Research," *Gender and Society* 20 (2006): 822–823. Here, too, my focus is on the process whereby particular meanings are assigned to this particular racial category. The key difference, however, is that the racial hierarchy enables Whites to be much more involved in the "assignment" process and that White racialization tends to draw links between Whiteness and characteristics that are widely understood as positive and that are *articulated through* the negative characteristics the dominant group often assigns to and associates with subordinated groups. Understood this way, we realize that a phrase such as "reverse racism" is actually a contradiction in terms. The tendency is often to equate "racism" with "prejudice," but when we take the history of race relations and the profound power differentials that linger today into account, we realize that these terms are distinct in that prejudice amounts to individual malice, whereas racism can be carried out only with the backing of institutional and cultural power structures.

Note also that I write with the understanding that meaning is usually assigned to particular racial categories *implicitly*. For example, when I argue that the community "embraces a White identity," I am aware that very few people will explicitly state this. Indeed, many may not even be aware that this is what is happening. I make such interpretations despite this, however, because what I have observed is a widespread *embrace of the set of meanings* attached to Whiteness (made possible by a parallel embrace of the set of meanings attached to, in this case, Latinas/os) that are constructed in the context of a racially charged debate. In this regard, I follow a chorus of leading scholars who point out that, although overt racial degradation and affirmation may have become socially unacceptable after the Civil Rights Movement in the United States, this does not mean that public debates are now void of racialized communication. Especially when used in particular contexts and in particular ways, code words such as "illegal immigrant," "hardworking Americans," and "Small Town, USA," are often laden with race and conjure either negative connotations about people of color or idyllic depictions of Whites. Again, even though the utterer of such phrases never mentions race per se and may deny that race had anything to do with the statement, I acknowledge in this book that we still communicate race by speaking in code and that doing so is highly consequential. For more on this, see Michelle Alexander, *The New Jim Crow: Mass Incarceration in an Age of Colorblindness* (New York: New Press, 2012); Derrick Bell, *And We Are Not Saved: The Elusive Quest for Racial Justice* (New York: Basic, 1989); Eduardo Bonilla-Silva, *Racism without Racists: Color-Blind Racism and the Persistence of Racial Inequality in America* (Lanham, MD: Rowman and Littlefield, 2006); Joe R. Feagin, *Systemic Racism: A Theory of Oppression* (New York: Routledge 2006); Ian Haney López, "Post-racial Racism: Racial Stratification and Mass Incarceration in the Age of Obama," *California Law Review* 98 (2010): 1023–1074; Michael Omi and Howard Winant, *Racial Formation in the United States: From the 1960s to the 1980s* (New York: Routledge, 1986).

Another caveat: One of the aims of this book is to problematize both the negative racialization of Latinas/os and the overwhelmingly positive racialization of Whites. In doing so, my intent in no way is to speak derogatively about *individuals* or to deny that those who identify as White are not "good people." Instead, I problematize these racializations because I see them as socially harmful. Again, because positive White racialization is coherent only when juxtaposed with negative assertions about the racial "other," it can have seriously detrimental implications. Similarly, when I problematize the "White injury" trope, my intent is not to say that White working-class people have not experienced *any* harm or endured *any* difficult social conditions. Quite the contrary: I want to emphasize that many are indeed going through some very difficult times. My point is that, contrary to dominant perceptions, the evidence overwhelmingly points to this being *class*-based as opposed to race-based harm. Thus, I see an embrace of White identity as harmful to poor and working-class White people, too—a group with whom I notably identify—because it keeps many of us from understanding our actual position in the social structure. All of this is to say that I recognize that my use of the term "White" may catch some readers off-guard, especially given that Whiteness is usually unacknowledged and "transparent": see Barbara Flagg, *Was Blind, but Now I See: White Race Consciousness and the Law* (New York: New York University Press, 1997). However, my sentiment is that it is important for those of us who are White to resist the inclination to recoil at critical analyses of racial ideology, because ultimately seeing and asking questions about White racialization is more socially productive for all of us.

10. Pat Rubio-Goldsmith and colleagues, for example, have found that simply "appearing Mexican" was the best predictor of being mistreated by immigration authorities: Pat Rubio-Goldsmith, Mary Romero, Raquel Rubio-Goldsmith, Manuel Escobedo, and Laura Khoury, "Ethno-Racial Profiling and State Violence in a Southwest Barrio," *Aztlán: A Journal of Chicano Studies* 34, no. 1 (2009): 93–123. See also, e.g., Mary Romero, "Racial Profiling and Immigration Law Enforcement: Rounding Up the Usual Suspects in the Latino Community," *Critical Sociology* 32, nos. 2–3 (2006): 447–473; Kevin R. Johnson, "'Aliens' and the U.S. Immigration Laws: The Social and Legal Construction of Nonpersons," *University of Miami Inter-American Law Review* 28 (1996): 269.

11. Derrick Bell, as a comparable example, describes how Blacks lack "racial standing" to "discuss . . . negative experiences with racism" unless "publicly [disparaging] or [criticizing] other blacks who are speaking or acting in ways that upset whites": Derrick Bell, *Faces at the Bottom of the Well: The Permanence of Racism* (New York: Basic, 1992), 111, 114.

12. For example, research on the relationship between immigrants and crime consistently shows that immigrants do not increase crime and may actually help reduce it: see, e.g., Matthew T. Lee and Ramiro Martinez Jr., "Immigration Reduces Crime: An Emerging Scholarly Consensus," *Sociology of Crime, Law and Deviance* 13 (2009): 3–16. Yet as Chapter 2 shows, undocumented immigrant criminality was presented as a "truth" through the course of this debate. Similarly, many claim that immigrants disproportionately use social services but do not contribute by paying taxes. This is untrue, as well. As Chomsky points out, "Immigrants, no matter what their status, pay the same taxes that citizens do—sales taxes, real estate taxes (if they rent or own a home), gasoline taxes. Some immigrants work in the informal economy and are paid under the table in cash, so they don't have federal and state income taxes, or social

security taxes, deducted from their paychecks. So do some citizens. In fact every time the kid next door babysits, or shovels the snow, he or she is working in the informal economy": Chomsky, *"They Take Our Jobs!"* 36. Even undocumented immigrants who work in the formal economy by presenting false Social Security numbers do pay Social Security taxes. In these instances, Chomsky continues, "The only ones who lose anything when workers use a false social security number are the workers themselves. Taxes are deducted from their paychecks—but if they are undocumented, they still have no access to the benefits they are paying for, like social security or unemployment benefits": ibid., 37–38.

13. Almost never, for example, does this narrative point to the various harms associated with living one's life, as Susan Bibler Coutin put it, "physically present but legally absent": Susan Bibler Coutin, *Nation of Emigrants: Shifting Boundaries of Citizenship in El Salvador and the United States* (Ithaca, NY: Cornell University Press, 2007), 9. The narrative also ignores the contributions undocumented immigrants make, including the production of those goods and services on which many in wealthy nations have come to rely. We also rarely see an acknowledgment of the complex nature of U.S. immigration law, including the challenges associated with gaining authorized presence, the various statuses that exist in between the simplistic legal-versus-illegal binary, and the historical antecedents to today's laws, which clearly show that racial exclusion and economic exploitation have long been central prerogatives (see below). Similarly, the story is usually an individualistic one in which people make poor choices in violating the law. Rarely does the narrative consider the structural factors that prompt migration.

14. As Joe Feagin notes in a historical overview of anti-immigrant nativism in the United States:

> Contemporary attacks on immigrants do not represent a new social phenomenon with no connection to past events. Anti-immigrant nativism in North America is at least two centuries old. . . . Historically, and on the present scene, nativists have stressed to varying degrees four major themes. One common complaint is that certain "races" are intellectually and culturally inferior and should not be allowed into the country, at least not in substantial numbers. Nativists have often regarded immigrant groups as racial "others" quite different from the Euro-American majority. A second and related theme views those who have immigrated from racially and culturally inferior groups as problematic in terms of their complete assimilation to the dominant Anglo culture. A third theme, articulated most often in troubled economic times, is that "inferior" immigrants are taking the jobs and disrupting the economic conditions of native-born Americans. A fourth notion, also heard most often in times of fiscal crisis, is that immigrants are creating serious government crises, such as by corrupting the voting system or overloading school and welfare systems. (Joe Feagin, "Old Poison in New Bottles: The Deep Roots of Modern Nativism," in *Immigrants Out! The New Nativism and the Anti-immigrant Impulse in the United States*, ed. Juan F. Perea [New York: New York University Press, 1997], 13–14)

15. Cacho, *Social Death*, 6.
16. Chavez, *The Latino Threat*, 43.

17. Howard Winant, "Behind Blue Eyes: Whiteness and Contemporary U.S. Racial Politics," in *Off White: Readings on Race, Power, and Society*, ed. Michelle Fine, Lois Weis, Linda C. Powell, and L. Mun Wong (New York: Routledge, 1997), 48.

18. Chavez makes this point in the context of citizenship. He writes, "The targeting of immigrants allows citizens to reaffirm their own subject status vis-à-vis the immigrant Other": Chavez, *The Latino Threat*, 17.

19. john a. powell, *Racing to Justice: Transforming Our Conception of Self and Other to Build an Inclusive Society* (Bloomington: Indiana University Press, 2012), 53.

20. It is here that the *local* nature of the Latino Threat Narrative becomes perhaps most apparent. Chavez's analysis produced a similar set of binaries—for example, citizen–noncitizen, native–foreigner, inside the nation–outside the nation—that articulated conceptions of "us" and "them" in the context of *the nation* rather than *the city*: see Chavez, *The Latino Threat*, 128.

21. Cacho, "The People of California Are Suffering."

22. Ibid., 393. As an illustration of this idea, consider the following example: When campaigning for president in 2012, Mitt Romney said, "My dad, as you probably know, was the governor of Michigan and was the head of a car company. But he was born in Mexico . . . and had he been born of Mexican parents, I'd have a better shot at winning [the presidency]. But he was unfortunately born to Americans living in Mexico. . . . I mean, I say that jokingly, but it would be helpful to be Latino." Romney presents himself here as victimized because of his (White) race. Yet the reality is that—in addition to many other institutional disparities—when it comes to political representation, Latinas/os "are still grossly underrepresented in proportion to their population numbers," holding 3.3 percent of all elected positions even though they make up 16 percent of the U.S. population: see Vanessa Cárdenas and Sophia Kerby, "The State of Latinos in the United States," Center for American Progress, Washington, DC, August 8, 2012, available at https://www.americanprogress.org/issues/race/report/2012/08/08/11984/the-state-of-latinos-in-the-united-states, accessed May 26, 2014.

23. To be sure, there are other lines of difference (e.g., gender, sexuality, and religion) along which divisions are forged. Arlene Stein, for example, provides an account of a local-level debate around religion and sexuality that emerges from a political economic context very similar to the one I describe here: Arlene Stein, *The Stranger Next Door: The Story of a Small Community's Battle over Sex, Faith, and Civil Rights* (Boston: Beacon, 2012).

24. See, e.g., Kitty Calavita, "The New Politics of Immigration: 'Balanced Budget Conservatism' and the Symbolism of Proposition 187." *Social Problems* 43, no. 3 (1996): 284–305; Kitty Calavita, "U.S. Immigration and Policy Responses: The Limits of Legislation," in *Controlling Immigration: A Global Perspective*, ed. Wayne Cornelius, Takeyuki Tsuda, Philip Martin, and James Hollifield (Stanford, CA: Stanford University Press, 2004), 55–81.

25. See, e.g., Roger Daniels, *Coming to America: A History of Immigration and Ethnicity in American Life* (New York: HarperCollins, 2002); Leobardo F. Estrada, Chris Garcia, Reynaldo Flores Macis, and Lionel Maldonado, "Chicanos in the United States: A History of Exploitation and Resistance," *Daedalus* 110, no. 2 (1981): 103–131.

26. As a 2013 report from the Pew Research Center points out:

The United States is the world's leader by far as a destination for immigrants. The country with the next largest number is Russia with 12.3 million. The U.S. total of 40.4 million, which includes legal as well as unauthorized immigrants, represents 13% of the total U.S. population in 2011. While the foreign-born population size is a record, immigrants' share of the total population is below the U.S. peak of just under 15% during a previous immigration wave from 1890 to 1920 that was dominated by arrivals from Europe. The modern wave, which began with the passage of border-opening legislation in 1965, has been dominated by arrivals from Latin America (about 50%) and Asia (27%). ("A Nation of Immigrants: A Portrait of the 40 Million, Including 11 Million Unauthorized," Pew Research Center, January 29, 2013, available at http://www.pewhispanic .org/2013/01/29/a-nation-of-immigrants, accessed December 22, 2014)

27. See Calavita, "The New Politics of Immigration"; Calavita, "U.S. Immigration and Policy Responses," 64; emphasis added. See also Kitty Calavita, *Immigrants at the Margins: Law, Race, and Exclusion in Southern Europe* (New York: Cambridge University Press, 2005).

28. Justin Akers Chacón and Mike Davis explain the situation in Mexico in the context of, among other neoliberal developments, the implementation of the North American Free Trade Agreement (NAFTA):

It is in the context of . . . roughshod capitalist development of Mexican agriculture and its integration into the world market—primarily through its orientation toward the United States—that we must understand the establishment of patterns of cross-border migration. The subordination of Mexican capitalism to U.S. imperialism and the global institutions of neoliberalism set the stage for further economic convulsions. Out-migration serves as a release valve for the socially dislocated. This by-product was welcomed by a U.S. market eager to absorb not only Mexican imports, but also its reserve armies of labor, since migrants could be paid less and leveraged against unionized workers. (Justin Akers Chacón and Mike Davis, *No One Is Illegal: Fighting Racism and State Violence on the U.S.-Mexico Border* [Chicago: Haymarket, 2006], 110)

The story is similar in other Latin American countries, including the Dominican Republic. Chomsky writes:

[The Dominican Republic] was colonized first by Spain, then by the United States. (The U.S. invaded and occupied the Dominican Republic from 1916 to 1924 and again in 1965.) The first U.S. occupation brought about massive dispossession and transfer of Dominican land into the hands of U.S.-owned sugar plantations; the second brought about the modern version of colonialism . . . in which the governments of poor countries are forced to create low-wage, low-tax, low-regulation environments for the benefit of U.S. corporations. . . . The United States has the highest standard of living in the world, and it maintains it by using its laws, and its military, to enforce the extraction of resources and labor from its modern version of colonies, with little compensation for the populations. It is no wonder that people from these countries want to follow their resources to the place where they are being enjoyed. (Chomsky, *"They Take Our Jobs!"* 56)

See also, e.g., Helen I. Safa, "Women and Globalization: Lessons from the Dominican Republic," in *The Spaces of Neoliberalism: Land, Place and Family in Latin America,* ed. Jacquelyn Chase (Bloomfield, CT: Kumarian, 2002), 141–158; Ronald L. Mize and Grace Peña Delgado, *Latino Immigrants in the United States* (Malden, MA: Polity, 2012); David Bacon, *The Right to Stay Home: How U.S. Policy Drives Mexican Migration* (Boston: Beacon, 2014).

29. Calavita is writing about Italy but makes a point with relevance to the contemporary global economy more generally when she says, "Immigrants are useful to Italian employers precisely because they are *different* from locals. . . . [T]heir lack of integration into Italian society and culture is a critical ingredient of their flexibility. . . . [T]hey work for wages and under conditions that locals increasingly shun. . . . It is by definition their *Otherness* that is useful": Calavita, *Immigrants at the Margins,* 64–65.

30. Haney López, *Dog Whistle Politics,* 47. He elaborates:

For almost everyone, it is wrenching to encounter, let alone participate in, the level of intense suffering associated with driving persons from their homes or forcing people into bondage. If, however, we can convince ourselves that our victims are not like us—do not feel pain the way we do, are not intelligent and sensitive, indeed are indolent, degenerate, violent, and dangerous—then perhaps we're not doing so much harm after all; indeed, more than protecting ourselves, maybe we are helping the benighted others. And how much better, in terms of excusing our own self-interest, if it turns out that forces beyond anyone's control (and hence beyond our moral responsibility) doom these unfortunate others to subservience; if, say, God or nature [or law] fixed their insuperable character and determined their lot in life.

31. What I am describing here is consistent with the critical race theory notion of *differential racialization*: "At one point, for example, society may have had little use for blacks but much need for Mexican or Japanese agricultural workers. At another time, the Japanese, including citizens of long standing, may have been in intense disfavor and removed to war relocation camps, while society cultivated other groups of color for jobs in war industry or as cannon fodder on the front" (Richard Delgado and Jean Stefancic, *Critical Race Theory: An Introduction* [New York: New York University Press, 2012], 9).

32. Nicholas P. De Genova, "Migrant 'Illegality' and Deportability in Everyday Life," *Annual Review of Anthropology* 31 (2002): 438.

33. Romero, "Racial Profiling and Immigration Law Enforcement," 468.

34. Calavita, *Immigrants at the Margins,* 154.

35. As Calavita notes, "The structural transformations in the economy that reproduce a continued demand for immigrants *at the same time* contribute to restrictionist sentiment": Calavita, "U.S. Immigration and Policy Responses," 64. In an informative journalistic piece, Saket Soni similarly calls immigrant workers "the canaries in the coal mine," experiencing the negative effects of contingent labor as it gradually becomes the norm in the United States:

Immigrant workers have long experienced vulnerability and instability, and have long been treated as disposable by their employers. Today, roughly one-third of American jobs are part-time, contract or otherwise "contingent." And the number of contingent workers in the United States is expected to grow by more than one-third over the next four years. That means more and more families are without the benefits of full-time work, such as health insurance, pensions or 401(k)s. And more of us are without the employment certainty that leads to economic stability at home—and to the consumer spending that drives the economy.

In addition, while we are working harder and longer, wages are stagnant. Between 2000 and 2011, the US economy grew by more than 18 percent, while the median income for working families declined by 12.4 percent. Once upon a time, workers shared the economic prosperity of their employers: until 1975, wages accounted for more than 50 percent of America's GDP. But by 2013, wages had fallen to a record low of just 43.5 percent of GDP. Overall compensation, which factors in healthcare and other benefits has also hit bottom. Immigrants know where this downward spiral leads. (Saket Soni, "Low-Wage Nation," *The Nation*, January 20, 2014, 4)

36. Hazleton's unemployment rate has also been consistently high compared with Pennsylvania's. For example, during the summer that the IIRA was passed (August 2006), Hazleton's unemployment rate was 6.6 percent, whereas Pennsylvania's was 4.6 percent. The median income in Hazleton, as of 2012, was $31,295, which is also below the state and national median. And like many cities across the United States, Hazleton has struggled with budgetary issues that have led the city to consider the sale of public utilities to private companies: see, e.g., David P. Sosar, "Water Authority for Sale: Disadvantages of Selling City Assets to Purge Budgetary Deficits," *International Journal of Humanities and Social Science* 1, no. 18 (2011): 134–142.

37. See, e.g., Jill Weigt, "Compromises to Carework: The Social Organization of Mothers' Experiences in the Low-Wage Labor Market after Welfare Reform," *Social Problems* 53, no. 3 (2006): 322–351.

38. Sociologists have long understood that communities strongly reassert their collective identities at moments of uncertainty, especially when the dominant group feels threatened by the combination of demographic change and economic decline. For a particularly relevant example of this, see David Engel, "The Oven Bird's Song: Insiders, Outsiders, and Personal Injuries in an American Community," *Law and Society Review* 18, no. 4 (1984): 551–582.

39. Haney López, *Dog Whistle Politics*, 35–37.

40. See, e.g., Katherine Beckett, *Making Crime Pay: Law and Order in Contemporary American Politics* (New York: Oxford University Press), 1997, 40–42.

41. Haney López, *Dog Whistle Politics*, 121.

42. Michael Powell and Michelle García, "Pa. City Put Illegal Immigrants on Notice," *Washington Post*, August 22, 2006.

43. Haney López provides an overview of the history of this tactic and its present usage, writing:

The new racial politics presents itself as steadfastly opposed to racism and ever ready to condemn those who publicly use racial profanity. *We fiercely oppose racism and stand prepared to repudiate anyone who dares utter the n-word.*

Meanwhile, though, the new racial discourse keeps up a steady drumbeat of subliminal racial grievances and appeals to color-coded solidarity. *But let's be honest: some groups commit more crimes and use more welfare, other groups are mainly unskilled and illiterate illegals, and some religions inspire violence and don't value human life.* The new racism rips through society, inaudible and also easily defended insofar as it fails to whoop in the tones of old racism, yet booming in its racial meaning and provoking predictable responses among those who immediately hear the racial undertones of references to the undeserving poor, illegal aliens, and sharia law. (Haney López, *Dog Whistle Politics*, 3–4).

44. As Beckett notes, "To a certain extent this effort has been guided by electoral considerations: the New Right, based primarily in the Republican party, has rearticulated racial meanings in such a way as to encourage defections from the Democratic party. . . . But the New Right's 'authoritarian-populist' project is aimed, more broadly, at discrediting state policies and programs aimed at minimizing racial, class, and gender inequality and strengthening those that promise to enhance the states' control of the troublesome": Beckett, *Making Crime Pay*, 42–43.

45. Alexander uses this term in her discussion of the parallel politics that characterized slavery, Jim Crow, and now mass incarceration. She describes how,

deliberately and strategically, the [elite] planter class extended special privileges to poor whites in an effort to drive a wedge between them and black slaves. White settlers were allowed greater access to Native American lands, white servants were allowed to police slaves through slave patrols and militias, and barriers were created so that free labor would not be placed in competition with slave labor. These measures effectively eliminated the risk of future alliances between black slaves and poor whites. Poor whites suddenly had a direct, personal stake in the existence of a race-based system of slavery. Their own plight had not improved much, but at least they were not slaves. Once the planter elite split the labor force, poor whites responded to the logic of their situation and sought ways to expand their racially privileged position. (Alexander, *The New Jim Crow*, 25)

And W.E.B. Du Bois's *Black Reconstruction in America* stands as the quintessential articulation of this phenomenon:

The theory of laboring class unity rests upon the assumption that laborers, despite internal jealousies, will unite because of their opposition to exploitation by the capitalists. . . . This would throw white and black labor into one class, and precipitate a united fight for higher wage and better working conditions. . . . [T]his failed to work . . . because the theory of race was supplemented by a carefully planned and slowly evolved method, which drove such a wedge between the white and the black workers that there probably are not today in the world two groups of workers with practically identical interests who hate and fear each other so deeply and persistently and who are kept so far apart that neither sees anything of common interest. (W.E.B. Du Bois, *Black Reconstruction in America* [New York: Meridian, 1935], 700)

46. Du Bois elaborates:

It must be remembered that the white group of laborers, while they received a low wage, were compensated in part by a sort of public and psychological wage. They were given public deference and titles of courtesy because they were white. They were admitted freely with all classes of white people to public functions, public parks, and the best schools. The police were drawn from their ranks, and the courts, dependent upon their votes, treated them with such leniency as to encourage lawlessness. Their vote selected public officials, and while this had small effect upon the economic situation, it had great effect upon their personal treatment and the deference shown to them. (ibid., 700–701)

47. David Roediger, *The Wages of Whiteness: Race and the Making of the American Working Class* (New York: Verso, 1991), 13.

48. Beckett, *Making Crime Pay*, 87.

49. Ibid.

50. Ibid.; emphasis added.

51. Ross, "The Rhetorical Tapestry of Race," 6.

52. Du Bois said that such race-based class divisions "ruined democracy." The "resulting color caste founded and retained by capitalism was adopted, forwarded and approved by white labor, and resulted in subordination of colored labor to white profits the world over. Thus the majority of the world's laborers, by the insistence of white labor, became the basis of a system of industry which ruined democracy": Du Bois, *Black Reconstruction*, 26.

More recently, the political theorist Wendy Brown argued that neoliberalism and neoconservatism of the sort I am describing "work symbiotically to produce a subject relatively indifferent to veracity and accountability in government and to political freedom and equality among the citizenry": Wendy Brown, "American Nightmare: Neoliberalism, Neoconservatism, and De-Democratization," *Political Theory* 34, no. 6 (2006): 690.

53. The Italian sociologist Maurizio Ambrosini has used the phrase *utili invasori* (useful invaders) to describe this process. See also Calavita, *Immigrants at the Margins*, 48–74; Benjamin Fleury-Steiner and Jamie Longazel, "Neoliberalism, Community Development, and Anti-immigrant Backlash in Hazleton, Pennsylvania," in *Taking Local Control: Immigration Policy Activism in U.S. Cities and States*, ed. Monica W. Varsanyi (Stanford, CA: Stanford University Press, 2010), 157–172.

54. It is therefore important to contextualize immigration to new destinations rather than understand it as a sudden, unexpected occurrence. The meatpacking industry, which (as we will see) played a significant role in Hazleton, is a good example of this. As part of a neoliberal "survival strategy," this previously urban and unionized industry that originally employed primarily White workers has come to rely on less expensive rural, nonunionized Latina/o immigrant labor: see Stephanie E. Tanger, "Enforcing Corporate Responsibility for Violations of Workplace Immigration Laws: The Case of Meatpacking," *Harvard Latino Law Review* 59 (2006): 59–89.

55. As Winant writes:

Nowhere is this new framework of the white "politics of difference" more clearly on display than in the reaction to affirmative action policies of all sorts (in hiring, university admissions, federal contracting, etc.). Assaults on these policies . . . are currently at hysterical levels. These attacks are clearly designed to effect ideological shifts, rather than to shift resources in any meaningful way. They represent whiteness as disadvantage, something which has few precedents in US racial history. . . . This imaginary white disadvantage—for which there is almost no evidence at the empirical level—has achieved widespread popular credence, and provides the cultural and political "glue" that holds together a wide variety of reactionary racial politics. (Winant, "Behind Blue Eyes," 5)

Indeed, one recent study found that Whites consider bias against Whites a more significant problem than bias against Blacks: see Michael I. Norton and Samuel R. Sommers, "Whites See Racism as a Zero-Sum Game that They Are Now Losing," *Perspectives on Psychological Science* 6, no. 3 (2011): 215–218. We also commonly see an example of this in the immigration debate when legal action favorable to immigrants is dismissed as "amnesty" while policies such as mass deportation that disaffect immigrants and their families receive uncritical praise as efforts to "secure our borders."

56. See, e.g., Engel, "The Oven Bird's Song"; Jonathan Goldberg-Hiller and Neal Milner, "Rights as Excess: Understanding the Politics of Special Rights," *Law and Social Inquiry* 28, no. 4 (2003): 1075–1118; Jeffery Dudas, "In the Name of Equal Rights: 'Special' Rights and the Politics of Resentment in Post–Civil Rights America," *Law and Society Review* 39, no. 4 (2005) : 723–757; Jeffery Dudas, *The Cultivation of Resentment: Treaty Rights and the New Right* (Stanford, CA: Stanford University Press, 2008).

CHAPTER 1

1. Personal interview with W. Kevin O'Donnell, president of CAN DO, December 3, 2009, Hazleton, PA. In contrast to other interviews and in accordance with accepted research protocols, I use O'Donnell's real name because of his status as a public figure (i.e., the head of Hazleton's primary economic development group).

2. Community Area New Development Organization (CAN DO), *The CAN DO Story: A Case History of Successful Community Industrial Development* (Hazleton, PA: CAN DO, 1974). In the introduction of the chapter, I intentionally draw mostly from CAN DO's organizational recollection of these historical events.

3. CAN DO, *The CAN DO Story*, 7.

4. Quoted from CAN DO, *Vision, Determination, Drive: The CAN DO 50th Anniversary*, DVD, on file with the author.

5. Randy Stoecker, "The CDC Model of Urban Redevelopment: A Critique and an Alternative." *Journal of Urban Affairs* 19, no. 1 (1997): 8. To be sure, as Stoecker continues, the basis for the CDC idea, even in the beginning, was "an acceptance of supply-side economic models and "free-market" philosophy." The point was not to counter capitalism but, rather, to "correct three market failures: 1) The inability of potential investors to see opportunities in the neighborhood; 2) profit maximization that prevented socially conscious investing; 3) social/legal restrictions on investment such as zoning laws." In the case of Hazleton, as Dan Rose argues in his thorough analysis of CAN DO's history, these early local campaigns tended to overemphasize the grassroots nature of the movement, neglecting the extent to which it was led by elites: see Dan Rose, *Energy Transi-*

tion and the Local Community: A Theory of Society Applied to Hazleton, Pennsylvania (Philadelphia: University of Pennsylvania Press, 1981).

In line with the nuances that both Stoecker and Rose present, I should therefore note that as I analyze CAN DO's changing prerogatives, my intent is not to idealize the "good old days" of community economic development or to argue that Hazleton's economy only recently became "elite-led." Serious problems with local democracy and economic inequality are readily apparent in each of these eras (as they were in prior eras, as well). My goal instead is to show how neoliberalism and the structural and cultural changes that accompany it *exacerbate* and *deepen* already existing problems. In other words, I do not dispute that free-market policies were favored at the time of CAN DO's founding or that this embrace had undesirable social effects. More simply, I draw attention to the market fetishism and de-democratization that many scholars argue have been ratcheted up in the contemporary era: see, e.g., Susan George, "A Short History of Neo-liberalism: Twenty Years of Elite Economics and Emerging Opportunities for Structural Change," paper presented at the Conference on Economic Sovereignty in a Globalising World, March 24–26, 1999, available at http://www.globalexchange.org/campaigns/econ101/neoliberalism.html, accessed January 4, 2011.

6. CAN DO, *Upon the Shoulders of Giants: The CAN DO Story.* (Hazleton, PA: CAN DO, 1991), 3.

7. CAN DO, *The CAN DO Story*, 12.

8. Rose, *Energy Transition and the Local Community*, 132.

9. Ibid.

10. CAN DO, *The CAN DO Story*, 14.

11. It is important to note that the land CAN DO purchased is outside Hazleton city limits. The factories on the land, however, became and remained the primary employers of Hazleton residents. This fact is relevant to my later discussion of tax breaks offered to corporations operating in these parks. Although the tax money would not have gone to the city of Hazleton per se, the more important point is that by not having a city's primary employers contributing to the local tax base, budget troubles are to be expected.

12. Concisely, I understand neoliberalism as "a structural force that affect's people's life-chances and as an ideology of governance that shapes subjectivities": Tejaswini Ganti, "Neoliberalism," *Annual Review of Anthropology* 43 (2014): 90.

David Harvey provides a more detailed definition:

> Neoliberalism is in the first instance a theory of political economic practices that proposes that human well-being can best be advanced by liberating individual entrepreneurial freedoms and skills within an institutional framework characterized by strong private property rights, free markets and free trade. The role of the state is to create and preserve an institutional framework appropriate to such practices. The state has to guarantee, for example, the quality and integrity of money. It must also set up those military, defense, police and legal structures and functions required to secure private property rights and to guarantee, by force if need be, the proper functioning of markets. Furthermore, if markets do not exist (in areas such as land, water, education, health care, social security, or environmental pollution) then they must be created, by state action if necessary. But beyond these tasks the state should not venture. State interventions in markets (once created) must be kept to a bare minimum because,

according to the theory, the state cannot possibly possess enough information to second-guess market signals (prices) and because powerful interest groups will inevitably distort and bias state interventions (particularly in democracies) for their own benefit. (David Harvey, *A Brief History of Neoliberalism* [New York: Oxford University Press, 2005], 2)

13. See, e.g., Adam Tickell and Jamie Peck "Making Global Rules: Globalization or Neoliberalization?" in *Remaking the Global Economy: Economic-Geographical Perspectives*, ed. Jamie Peck and Henry Wai-Chung Yeung (Thousand Oaks, CA: Sage, 2003), 163–177.

14. Susan E. Clarke, "Neighborhood Policy Options: The Reagan Agenda." *Journal of the American Planning Association* 50, no. 4 (1984): 493–501.

15. The term "roll back" is used here to describe the "pattern of deregulation and dismantlement" common to this era: see Jamie Peck and Adam Tickell, "Neoliberalizing Space," *Antipode* 34, no. 3 (2002): 34.

16. Jason Hackworth, *The Neoliberal City: Governance, Ideology, and Development in American Urbanism* (Ithaca, NY: Cornell University Press, 2007), 17.

17. Stoecker, "The CDC Model of Urban Redevelopment," 8; see also David Harvey, *The Urbanization of Capital: Studies in the History and Theory of Capitalist Urbanization* (Baltimore: Johns Hopkins University Press, 1985).

18. This phrase was coined in Arthur J. Rolnick and Melvin L. Burstein, "Congress Should End the Economic War among the States," *Federal Reserve Bank of Minneapolis Annual Report*, January 1994, available at http://www.minneapolisfed.org/publications_papers/pub_display.cfm?id=672, accessed July 29, 2015.

19. See, e.g., Kevin R. Cox and Andrew Mair, "Locality and Community in the Politics of Local Economic Development." *Annals of the Association of American Geographers* 78, no.2 (1988): 307–325; Greg LeRoy, *The Great American Jobs Scam: Corporate Tax Dodging and the Myth of Job Creation* (San Francisco: Berrett-Koehler, 2005).

20. See, e.g., Kathe Newman and Phillip Ashton, "Neoliberal Urban Policy and New Paths of Neighborhood Change in the American Inner City," *Environment and Planning* 36, no. 7 (2004): 1151–1172. Robert Fisher summarizes these developments:

> Beginning around 1980 CDCs found government support drastically cut. The new . . . CDCs that developed in the privatization campaigns of the Reagan years were forced into becoming much more businesslike than their predecessors. . . . The Community Services Administration and the Office of Neighborhood Development were dismantled. Other sources of federal funds were dramatically cut back. The bottom line for CDCs, as with seemingly everything else in the decade, was economic success. . . . [T]he new CDCs became less like community organizations and more like small businesses and investment projects, evaluated on their ability to be economically successful. (Robert Fisher, *Let the People Decide: Neighborhood Organizing in America*, updated ed. [New York: Twayne, 1994], 181)

21. "Wright: CAN DO Must Change Its Thinking," May 16, 1985, CAN DO Archive, book 7. Much of this chapter relies on the CAN DO Archive, which is maintained by the organization and located at its headquarters in downtown Hazleton. (See Appendix A for more information about this source.)

22. "Industrial Competition Tough, CAN DO Official Says," January 18, 1985, CAN DO Archive, book 7.

23. "Wright."

24. "CAN DO Hires Public Relations Firm," August 14, 1985, CAN DO Archive, book 7.

25. "Industrial Competition Tough, CAN DO Official Says," January 18, 1985. This particular report mentioned "seven steps to establish and maintain a program to market the local community *to make it attractive to the industrial prospect*: budget for aggressive marketing, conduct research studies determining what industries to pursue, prepare impressive brochures, offer gimmicks along with brochures, establish advertising program[s], follow-up inquiries, include testimonials in advertising material" (emphasis added).

"CAN DO Sprucing Up Way of Luring Industry," March 15, 1985, CAN DO Archive, book 7. The report states:

> CAN DO, the area's industrial development organization, is looking into sprucing up its approach to attracting industry and the tools used to do it. . . . [T]he organization's board of directors voted to form a marketing committee to analyze and identify the current assets of the area, because competition for attracting industry is becoming more and more competitive. "When CAN DO began, there were few organizations like it," said Gary Lamont, the Chairman of CAN DO's new long-range planning committee. "But now, we are starting to lose the competitive edge we once had. We have to identify what assets and liabilities we can match with the outside, to see what we have and don't have. We have to aggressively market the tools we have, and develop new ones—like new shell buildings and incubators. . . . The effort to refine the tools used by CAN DO to attract industry is also underway. O'Donnell said CAN DO is working with the local chapter of a national transportation fraternity . . . to update its transportation guide. . . . Attorney Conrad Falvello, chairman of the public relations committee is working on new folders and literature which will be distributed to industries that express an interest in locating in the area. . . . [T]he design of a two-leaf folder which will contain information about the area is being developed.

26. "CAN DO Hires Public Relations Firm"; "CAN DO Ad Begins New Campaign," November 13, 1985 (such advertisements, it was noted, "are accessible to important people in the industrial field"), and "Industrial Groups Have New Brochure," February 1, 1986, CAN DO Archive, book 7.

27. "CAN DO Reshapes Image," January 15, 1986, CAN DO Archive, book 7.

28. "Area Needs Economic Aid to Grow, Panel Told," September 9, 1986, CAN DO Archive, book 8. See also U.S. House of Representatives, "Field Hearing before the Subcommittee on Housing and Community Development of the Committee on Banking, Finance and Urban Affairs," September 8, 1986, Hazleton, PA. Grossman also pointed out that "the concept of utilizing federal funds . . . through community development block grants . . . [is] extremely important in helping to mold the quality of life in a region like this. . . . We could not have survived in Northeastern Pennsylvania without UDAG [Urban Development Action Grants], community development [block grants], [the] Appalachian Commission, EDA [the Economic Development Administration], and some of the other programs."

29. Ibid.

30. Ibid. At the time of the hearing, O'Donnell was the executive vice-president of CAN DO. He also noted at the hearing that "the investment that the federal government has made in Greater Hazleton through [the community development block grant] program has been multiplied many times over through the additional taxes that have been paid by both the companies and the employees who have benefited either directly or indirectly by projects funded by this program. Therefore, it is CAN DO's hope that this program will not only be maintained but expanded so that our's [sic] and similar organizations will be able to continue the work of creating jobs and expanding the tax base in the Greater Hazleton Area."

31. "CAN DO Building Seen as Downtown Catalyst," September 8, 1989, CAN DO Archive, book 10; "New Building Should Impress Prospects," November 23, 1990, CAN DO Archive, book 11; "CAN DO Tour Shows Casey State Funding in Action," October 24, 1990, CAN DO Archive, book 11.

32. Jim Dino, "Dodging Mines: Economic Developers Must Downplay Past to Secure Future," *Standard-Speaker*, December 16, 2007.

33. For example, one such photograph features four men in business suits rowing a canoe: accessed November 2011 from http://www.hazletoncando.com and on file with the author.

34. CAN DO, "What Vision, Drive and a Community CAN DO," n.d., available at http://www.hazletoncando.com/doc_details/87-demographic-and-workforce-statistics-information?tmpl=component, accessed March 18, 2015.

35. CAN DO, *Upon the Shoulders of Giants*, 5.

36. Janet E. Kodras, "Restructuring the State: Devolution, Privatization, and the Geographic Redistribution of Power and Capacity in Governance," in *State Devolution in America: Implications for a Diverse Society*, ed. Lynn A. Staeheli, Janet E. Kodras, and Colin R. Flint (Thousand Oaks, CA: Sage, 1997), 79–96.

37. Local Economic Revitalization Tax Assistance Act (LERTA), Pa. Stat. Ann. Tit. 72 §4722 et seq. "LERTA is a tax incentive program in which a business or industry forgoes paying property taxes for a time, but eventually works its way up to paying the full tax within a 10-year period": "CAN DO Deserves Help to Reel in Big Fish," January 4, 1998, CAN DO Archive, book 17.

38. "Major Retailer Gets Tax Breaks from Everyone," January 16, 1998, CAN DO Archive, book 17.

39. "Hazleton Misses the Target: Major Retailer Going to New York Instead," March 4, 1998, CAN DO Archive, book 17.

40. "CAN DO to Lobby State for Tax-Free Business Zones," September 15, 1998, CAN DO Archive, book 17. See Keystone Opportunity Zone, Keystone Opportunity Expansion Zone and Keystone Opportunity Improvement Zone Act, October 6, 1998, P.L. 705, no. 92 Cl. 72.

41. Stuart Butler, "The Conceptual Evolution of Enterprise Zones," in *Enterprise Zones*, ed. Roy E. Green. (Newbury Park, CA: Sage, 1991), 27. For an in-depth account of the Reagan administration's efforts to spread this policy innovation across the United States, see Karen Mossberger, *The Politics of Ideas and the Spread of Enterprise Zones* (Washington, DC: Georgetown University Press, 2000).

By this point, the so-called "roll-back" policies of the 1980s designed to eliminate government involvement had been replaced by "roll-out" policies that involved "purposeful *construction and consolidation* of neoliberalized state form": Peck and Tickell, "Neoliberalizing Space," 384. Jamie Peck and Adam Tickell elaborate: "No longer concerned narrowly with the mobilization and extension of markets (and market logics), neoliberalism is increasingly associated with the political foregrounding of new modes of "social" and penal policy making, concerned specifically with the aggressive reregulation, disciplining, and containment of those marginalized or dispossessed by the neoliberalization of the 1980s": Peck and Tickell, "Neoliberalizing Space," 389.

42. David Argall, "A Policy Analysis of the First Six Years of Pennsylvania's Keystone Opportunity Zone Program, 1998 to 2004: Enlightened Economic Development or Corporate Welfare?" (PhD diss., Pennsylvania State University, Harrisburg, 2006), 81, 83–84.

43. There are variations within the legislation. However, the Pennsylvania Department of Community and Economic Development provides the following description of the program:

> Binding ordinances and resolutions are passed granting the waiver, abatement or exemption of certain state and local taxes. Depending on the situation, *the tax burden maybe reduced to zero* through exemptions, deductions, abatements and credits for the following:
>
> State Taxes: Corporate Net Income Taxes, Capital Stock Foreign Franchise Tax, Personal Income Tax, Sales Use Tax, Bank Shares and Trust Company Shares Tax, Alternative Bank and Trust Company Shares Tax, Mutual Thrift Institutions Tax, Insurance Premiums Tax.
>
> Local Taxes: Earned Income/Net Profits Tax, Business Gross Receipts, Business Occupancy, Business Privilege and Mercantile Taxes, Local Real Property Tax, Sales and Use Tax. (see http://www.newpa.com/business/expansion-relocation/keystone-opportunity-zones, accessed February 27, 2014; emphasis added)

44. "School Board Backs CAN DO Effort for Opportunity Zones," December 9, 1998, CANDO Archive, book 17.

45. The letter, dated February 20, 2001, and on file with the author, reads:

> Please accept this letter as my support and endorsement to the City of Hazleton in their efforts to create a Keystone Opportunity Expansion Zone. The 129.4 acres proposed by [the] City, along with the KOEZ benefits, hopefully, will help bolster job creation opportunities and economic development within the City and the region. The City has lost employment opportunities for too long due to the lack of financial resources or tax abatement programs that the KOEZ offers. My staff and I have been in contact with several developers who have indicated the advantages of their relocating primarily due to the KOEZ. The approval of this application could more than likely prove to be a viable benefit for economic development. Thank you for your consideration of the City of Hazleton's Application.

46. Personal interview with O'Donnell. His full remark was, "Northeast Pennsylvania fit very well into [the KOZ criteria] because of the past coal industry and because

of our mine lands and stuff like that. A lot of the land that we own or owned fit into that category of not brownfield but, as we say, *gray*field. Also, it fit into the criteria of unemployment, because the high unemployment of this area was part of the criteria."

47. Argall, "A Policy Analysis of the First Six Years of Pennsylvania's Keystone Opportunity Zone Program." Notably, according to Argall, the five counties awarded the most KOZ acreage all suffered from high unemployment rates. Conversely, the seven Pennsylvania counties that did not participate in the KOZ program were locales with the state's lowest unemployment rates.

48. Arthur J. Rolnick, "Congress Should End the Economic War among the States Testimony," Federal Reserve Bank of Minneapolis, October 10, 2007, available at https://www.minneapolisfed.org/publications/special-studies/economic-bidding-wars/rolnick-testimony, accessed July 30, 2014.

49. The Hazleton Area School District's business manager computed this figure and made it public in 2003: see L. A. Tarone, "Pennsylvania's Keystone Opportunity Zone Program and Its Sister the Keystone Opportunity Expansion Zone Program Cost the Hazleton Area School District $978,587 in Lost Tax Revenue during the Last School Year," *Standard-Speaker,* October 20, 2003. To give this figure some context, an informant told me in 2009 that the school district's annual budget was approximately $20 million, with 92 percent of the funds committed to salary and benefits.

50. In addition to Cargill, recent arrivals to CAN DO industrial parks include, among many others, an Office Max distribution center, an Amazon.com fulfillment center, and an AutoZone distribution center.

51. The observation I make here is in reference to these types of industries generally, not to any specific employer. For example, a report by the journalist Eric Schlosser provides a damning critique of the conditions at meatpacking plants across the United States:

> According to the Bureau of Labor Statistics, meatpacking is the nation's most dangerous occupation. In 1999, more than one-quarter of America's nearly 150,000 meatpacking workers suffered a job-related injury or illness. The meatpacking industry not only has the highest injury rate, but also has by far the highest rate of serious injury—more than five times the national average, as measured in lost workdays. If you accept the official figures, about 40,000 meatpacking workers are injured on the job every year. But the actual number is most likely higher. The meatpacking industry has a well-documented history of discouraging injury reports, falsifying injury data, and putting injured workers back on the job quickly to minimize the reporting of lost workdays. Over the past four years, I've met scores of meatpacking workers in Nebraska, Colorado, and Texas who tell stories of being injured and then discarded by their employers. . . . Many now rely on public assistance for their food, shelter, and medical care. Each new year throws more injured workers on the dole, forcing taxpayers to subsidize the meatpacking industry's poor safety record. No government statistics can measure the true amount of pain and suffering in the nation's meatpacking communities today. (Eric Schlosser, "The Chain Never Stops," *Mother Jones,* July–August 2001, available at http://www.motherjones.com/politics/2001/07/dangerous-meatpacking-jobs-eric-schlosser, accessed December 22, 2014).

See also Human Rights Watch, "Blood, Sweat, and Fear: Workers' Rights in U.S. Meat and Poultry Plants," January 24, 2005, available at https://www.hrw.org/report/2005/01/24/blood-sweat-and-fear/workers-rights-us-meat-and-poultry-plants, accessed August 4, 2015.

For a similarly powerful account of life as a temporary worker in a modern warehouse, see Gabriel Thompson, "The Workers Who Bring You Black Friday: My Life as a Temp in California's Inland Empire, the Belly of the Online Shopping Beast," *The Nation*, December 16, 2013, available at http://www.thenation.com/article/holiday-crush/, accessed July 30, 2015.

52. Again, this is in reference to these types of industries more generally, not to any specific employer; see, e.g., Stephanie E. Tanger, "Enforcing Corporate Responsibility for Violations of Workplace Immigration Laws: The Case of Meatpacking," *Harvard Latino Law Review* 59 (2006): 59–89.

53. "Meat Plant to Hire 700: Excel Starts Construction on Location near Hazleton," April 19, 2001, CAN DO Archive, book 19.

54. Of course, "White" and "Hispanic or Latino" are not mutually exclusive census categories. According to the 2000 census, 4.84 percent of Hazleton's population identified as being of "Hispanic or Latino origin (of any race)."

55. Estimates of the number of employees who work at Cargill vary from 800 (see, e.g., http://www.hazletonchamber.org, accessed August 2011) to 1,300 (a number people consistently gave me when I was in the field). Dan Sheehan and Jose Cardenas report that, "according to city officials, the plant's work force of nearly 1,000 is 70 percent Latino, but attempts to verify those numbers with Cargill officials were rebuffed without explanation": Dan Sheehan and Jose Cardenas, "New Culture in Old Coal Town," *Morning Call*, July 25, 2005. Regardless, even the lowest estimates would make Cargill the largest employer in any of the Hazleton area industrial parks and one of the area's largest employers of Latina/o migrants: see, e.g., "Ethnic Changes in Northeastern Pennsylvania: With Special Emphasis on Recent History within the City of Hazleton," Joint Urban Studies Center, July 2006, available at http://www.institutepa.org/pdf/research/diversity0906.pdf, accessed July 29, 2015.

56. See "Ethnic Changes in Northeastern Pennsylvania."

57. I did not systematically study this, although it is something I heard repeatedly while in the field: see also ibid., 7. For instance, one woman told me the story of how she initially immigrated to New Jersey but later moved to Hazleton "because of the economy; the rent is cheaper here. . . . Another thing is there is a lot of companies here, and they offer a job [and] the opportunity to raise your kids in a different way. After me came four families and one of my friends. She came to live here because of me. . . . Now three of her cousins came. So everybody is bringing someone": personal interview, July 2009. See also Tom Long, "Waves of Hispanic Immigrants Changing Face of NEPA," *Times Leader*, August 14, 2005.

58. David G. Savage and Nicole Gaouette, "Judge Rejects Hazleton Law on Immigrants," *Los Angeles Times*, July 27, 2007, available at http://articles.latimes.com/2007/jul/27/nation/na-hazleton27, accessed August 10, 2015.

59. Mia Light, "Luzerne County Has the Fastest-Growing Hispanic Population in the Nation," *Standard-Speaker*, September 16, 2009.

60. About 69 percent of Hazleton residents identified as "White" in the 2010 census: see http://factfinder.census.gov/faces/tableservices/jsf/pages/productview.xhtml?src=bkmk, accessed December 21, 2014.

61. These data come from the Pennsylvania Department of Labor and Industry and are on file with the author.

62. Quotation from field notes, on file with the author. When officials subsequently renewed the KOZ status of some companies, there was likewise very little fanfare. For an exception, see Sam Galski, "CAN DO Criticized on Tax Breaks for Mericle," *Citizen's Voice*, October 2, 2009.

To be sure, however, in speaking to local residents, I did hear plenty of murmurs about these links. But as we will see, citizens became *politically active* around the issue of undocumented immigration and not around economic development. Thus, my thesis here is not that local residents ignorantly overlooked the class component of this situation. Rather, it is that prevailing ideologies nudged the public conversation along a particular trajectory and molded it in particular ways.

63. See, e.g., David Theo Goldberg, *The Threat of Race: Reflections on Racial Neoliberalism* (Oxford: Blackwell, 2009); Lisa Duggan, *The Twilight of Equality? Neoliberalism, Cultural Politics, and the Attack on Democracy* (Boston: Beacon, 2003); Henry A. Giroux, "The Terror of Neoliberalism: Rethinking the Significance of Cultural Politics," *College Literature* 32, no. 1 (2005): 1–19; Judith Goode, "Faith-Based Organizations in Philadelphia: Neoliberal Ideology and the Decline of Political Activism," *Urban Anthropology* 35, nos. 2–3 (2006): 203–236; Dana-Ain Davis, "Narrating the Mute: Racializing and Racism in a Neoliberal Moment," *Souls* 9, no. 4 (2007): 346–360; Wendy Brown, "American Nightmare: Neoliberalism, Neoconservatism, and De-Democratization," *Political Theory* 34, no. 6 (2006): 690–714.

64. Giroux, "The Terror of Neoliberalism," 10.

65. "School Board Backs CAN DO Effort for Opportunity Zones."

66. L. A. Tarone, "Hazle Allows CAN DO to Include Township in Opportunity Zone Quest," *Standard-Speaker*, November 18, 1998; emphasis added.

67. "School Board Backs CAN DO Effort for Opportunity Zones"

68. Personal interview with O'Donnell.

69. Compare Cox and Mair, "Locality and Community in the Politics of Local Economic Development"; Naomi Klein, *The Shock Doctrine: The Rise of Disaster Capitalism* (New York: Picador, 2008).

70. One economic activist I spoke with was present when CAN DO proposed KOZ to the Hazleton Area School Board. The activist noted, "Instead of saying, 'Look at the jobs we're bringing in here—these big buildings are the size of nine or ten football fields strung together, and [we're] not really going to get much back from them when it comes to wages, taxes.... [I]t's not going to happen.'... Instead of doing something that would help the community to get out of its downward spiral, [CAN DO] came to [the school board] and asked [the board to sacrifice a significant amount of money]."

71. Tarone, "Hazle Allows CAN DO to Include Township in Opportunity Zone Quest."

72. For example, CAN DO's 2008 annual report to the community briefly acknowledged the challenges associated with the national economic crisis, yet it also boasted that, "despite tougher economic times, Greater Hazleton continues to see economic growth and has had a highly successful stretch over the past five years . . . , evidenced by the number of companies that have located in Humboldt Industrial Park during that period": CAN DO, "Meeting the Challenge: CAN DO 2008 Annual Report to the Community," on file with the author.

73. Specifically, 12.8 percent of Hazleton residents were living below the poverty line in 2010: see Andrew Staub, "Census: County Demographic Changed Greatly in Last Decade," *Standard-Speaker,* December 15, 2010.

74. CAN DO, "Meeting the Challenge"

75. This is a heading from CAN DO's 2012 annual report to the community, which is on file with the author. This report also summarizes the findings of a study commissioned by CAN DO under the heading "Companies in CAN DO's Industrial Parks Generate Millions of Dollars for the Local Economy." Notably, the report mentions only positive findings and presents most of the data in terms of totals (i.e., "Jobs Created in CAN DO's Parks," "Total Estimated Compensation," "Annual Real Estate Taxes Generated"), arguably making it easy to lose sight of the economic hardships many endure and of nuances such as the increasing reliance on contingent labor.

In a comparable example, when I asked him about the increase in warehousing and distribution centers, O'Donnell focused on the sophistication of the technology within such centers:

> Unfortunately, as hard as we try, we would much prefer manufacturing over warehousing and distribution any day of the week, although I must say that the new warehousing and distribution is not like warehouses from the past. These places are so sophisticated that you need a college education or a technical degree to really be able to maintain the sophisticated computerized retrieval systems and the information technology that goes into these, to know what product you have there and where it is and everything else. So what we're seeing is . . . these companies—they're boxes and they store a lot of things in them, but behind that the operations has to be people who know how to run these sophisticated operations. (personal interview with O'Donnell)

76. "Meat Plant Eyes up to 700 Jobs for Hazleton," April 19, 2001, CAN DO Archive, book 19; "New Jobs for Area . . . Excel-lent," April 19, 2001, CAN DO Archive, book 19 (the Cargill plant was originally named for a subsidiary for the company, Excel—hence the play on words.); "EXCELerated into Production: Meat-Processing Plant in Humboldt to Employ 500 in 6 to 8 Months," March 10, 2002, CAN DO Archive, book 19.

77. For more on Cargill's reputation, see Corporate Research Project, "Cargill: Corporate Rap Sheet," available at http://www.corp-research.org/cargill, accessed March 6, 2015. A detailed investigative piece written by Tarone in 2003 is an exception to this trend. He noted that there was already evidence that "several towns [had] . . . hung out a 'not welcome' sign when Excel came knocking. In some markets, critics ran television ads, urging locals to resist relocation efforts." Elsewhere, "a high school guidance counselor went door to door seeking signatures on petitions against the plant": L. A. Tarone "Has CAN DO Lowered Its Standards?" *Standard-Speaker,* August 14, 2003.

78. In late 2012, as an example of Hazleton's continued economic troubles, Mayor Joseph Yanuzzi declared that the city had reached its "fiscal cliff" and began considering proposals to drastically increase tax rates, furlough city employees, and sell or lease its water assets: Sam Galski, "Hazleton Mayor Warns of City's 'Fiscal Cliff,'" *Citizen's Voice,* December 5, 2012.

79. "Resident Wants HASD to Request KOZ Audit," February 21, 2006, CAN DO Archive, book 21.

80. "CAN DO Will Push with Business Park," January 20, 1992, CAN DO Archive, book 12.

81. Personal interview with an economic activist, December 9, 2009.

82. Author's ethnographic field notes, December 2009.

83. Personal interview with O'Donnell.

84. One report suggested that businesses on Wyoming Street, a corridor featuring mostly Latino-owned establishments, saw business drop 20–50 percent after passage of the IIRA: see Ellen Barry, "City's Immigration Law Turns Back Clock," *Los Angeles Times*, November 9, 2006. Another report quoted Mayor Barletta as saying, "I see illegal immigrants picking up and leaving—some Mexican restaurants say business is off 75 percent.... The message is out there": Michael Powell and Michelle García, "Pa. City Put Illegal Immigrants on Notice," *Washington Post*, August 22, 2006.

85. Personal interview with O'Donnell.

86. Duggan, *The Twilight of Equality*, xiv.

87. For an in-depth discussion of this phenomenon, see Patrick J. Carr and Maria J. Kefalas, *Hollowing Out the Middle: The Rural Brain Drain and What It Means for America* (Boston: Beacon, 2009).

88. For example, the percentage of residents older than 65 declined from 22 percent in the 2000 census to 16 percent in the 2010 census. Meanwhile, Hazleton's population experienced population increases in the following categories: age 0–4 (5 percent in 2000, 7 percent in 2010); age 5–17 (16 percent in 2000, 18 percent in 2010); age 18–64 (56 percent in 2000, 58 percent in 2010).

89. Hundreds of parishioners, for example, now attend a Spanish-language Catholic mass at St. Gabriel's, a church originally built to serve Irish Catholics. The report also notes that as of 2006, Hazleton had about fifty-three Latina/o-owned businesses: see "Ethnic Changes in Northeastern Pennsylvania," 14.

90. Duggan, *The Twilight of Equality*, xiv. Ganti similarly summarizes Harvey's conception of neoliberalism as a "class-based project that seeks to restore the power of economic elites": Ganti, "Neoliberalism," 94. See also David Harvey, *A Brief History of Neoliberalism*.

91. Kitty Calavita, *Immigrants at the Margins: Law, Race, and Exclusion in Southern Europe* (New York: Cambridge University Press, 2005), 165.

CHAPTER 2

1. See the untitled article by James Conmy, *Standard-Speaker*, July 9, 2007, accessed from the Newsbank database and on file with the author.

2. Alan Gregory, "Victim's Family Wonders Why He Was Target," *Standard-Speaker*, May 17, 2006.

3. Ibid.

4. Alan Gregory, "Mourners Remember Victim with Candles, Flowers," *Standard-Speaker*, October 22, 2005.

5. Tom Ragan, "Police Identify Acquaintance of Victim as Chief Suspect," *Standard-Speaker*, October 22, 2005.

6. Some crimes that occurred in temporal proximity to Kichline's murder came up in press coverage of the case, and I mention them in my analysis. Crimes that occurred

during the week of the Calderon murder include, but are not necessarily limited to, "an 18-year-old city man report[ly] being assaulted . . . by three Hispanic teenagers," a "strong-arm robbery" wherein "two of the [suspects] brandished semi-automatic handguns and demanded money from the victims," and a "a gunman riding in a sport-utility vehicle [allegedly firing] a handgun at a man and a woman walking along Diamond Avenue": see "Hazleton Police Said an 18-Year-Old City Man Reported Being Assaulted Just after Midnight Early Friday," *Standard-Speaker*, October 24, 2005; "Hazleton Police Are Investigating a Strong-Arm Robbery That Happened near the Intersection of Alter and Eighth Streets in the Pre-dawn Hours Sunday, *Standard-Speaker*, October 24, 2005; "A Gunman Riding in a Sport Utility Vehicle Fired a Handgun at a Man and Woman Walking along Diamond Avenue in Hazleton Late Wednesday," *Standard-Speaker*, October 21, 2005. Each of these articles was accessed from the Newsbank database and is on file with the author.

7. See, e.g., Steven Mocarsky, "Expert Says Many Members of Highly Dangerous Gang in Hazleton Are Illegal Immigrants," *Times Leader*, March 22, 2007.

8. Mark Fishman, "Crime Waves as Ideology," *Social Problems* 25, no. 5 (1978): 25. Fishman acknowledges that the crime itself is what triggers initial media attention. However, after the crime occurs, the focus shifts from "'the problem' to 'what is being done about the problem.' . . . It is clear that officials with a stake in 'doing something' about crime, have power over crime waves. Whether or not they inspire crime waves, they can attempt to redirect the focus of coverage of a crime wave already being reported. . . . [N]ews of the problem becomes news of how the system is working to remedy the situation. Authorities may also use their newsmaking powers to stop certain crime themes from becoming crime waves." Applied here, officials may choose to downplay a case such as the murder of Julio Calderon if hyping it promises to bring few political rewards. In contrast, a crime such as the murder of Derek Kichline, which fits neatly into the narrative of "dangerous outsiders" invading "Small Town, USA," may very well be played up because it represents an opportunity to advocate a particular policy response—namely, a willingness to get tough on crime and on "illegal immigrants" who supposedly burden the city.

9. Tom Ragan, "Police Identify Acquaintance of Victim as Chief Suspect," *Standard-Speaker*, October 22, 2005.

10. Ibid.

11. Ibid.

12. In the report, the mayor also told the press that "police will continue with saturation patrols, foot patrols, and bike patrols": ibid. It is also worth noting that officials controversially did not cover the body of the homicide victim for nearly three hours after the shooting. To explain this decision, the police chief said, "I understand why the family and friends of the victim were upset and I would have liked to see the body covered up, but to me it's important to preserve the crime scene of a homicide and any possible trace evidence. . . . To me, the importance and strength of a future prosecution outweighs the need to cover the body": ibid.

13. Kent Jackson, "Cops: Men in Country Illegally, Dealt Drugs," *Standard-Speaker*, May 17, 2006.

14. See, e.g., Joseph Nevins, *Operation Gatekeeper: The Rise of the Illegal Alien and the Making of the U.S.-Mexico Boundary* (New York: Routledge, 2002); Sarah Hill, "Purity and Danger on the U.S.-Mexico Border, 1991–1994," *South Atlantic Quarterly*

105, no. 4 (2006): 777–799; Deborah M. Weissman, "The Politics of Narrative: Law and the Representation of Mexican Criminality," *Fordham International Law Journal* 38 (2015): 141–204.

15. Jackson, "Cops"; emphasis added.

16. Kent Jackson, "Police Plan to Continue Intensive Patrols," *Standard-Speaker*, May 17, 2006.

17. Jackson, "Cops." This quotation refers to the plural "Romeros" because as the investigation commenced, Joan's brother also faced charges relating to the case.

18. Kent Jackson, "Ferdinand: Time to Seal Off the Border," *Standard-Speaker*, May 17, 2006.

19. Ibid; emphasis added.

20. Ibid.

21. Jackson, "Police Plan to Continue Intensive Patrols."

22. Ibid.

23. Ibid.

24. Ibid; emphasis added.

25. Alan Gregory, "Homicide Suspect Turned Self In," *Standard-Speaker*, October 25, 2005.

26. Ibid.

27. Kent Jackson and Alan Gregory, "Police, Feds Hit Local Drug Targets," *Standard-Speaker*, May 19, 2006.

28. Ibid.

29. Ibid.

30. Ibid.

31. "The suspects seized Thursday were arraigned before a federal magistrate in Scranton and detained at the Lackawanna County prison pending further court action. According to the indictment, three people now in federal custody are Carmen Rodriguez-Mendez, AKA Joselyn; Guery Smith-Baldaque, AKA Big Daddy[; and] Raynes Morel": ibid.

32. Kelly Monitz, "Wyoming Street Business Owners Went to Hazleton Mayor Lou Barletta Last Week to Talk about Community Perceptions Following a Fatal Shooting Downtown," *Standard-Speaker*, November 17, 2005.

33. Ibid.

34. Ibid.

35. Shawn M. Kelly, "Alleged Killer Slipped through System," *Standard-Speaker*, May 25, 2006.

36. This comment was made at the *Lozano* trial (emphasis added). The full exchange between Attorney Witold "Vic" Walczak from the American Civil Liberties Union (ACLU) and Mayor Lou Barletta went this way:

> WALCZAK: And I think as you said, Kichline was kind of the straw that broke the camel's back that made you decide to take some kind of action?
> BARLETTA: That is how I would describe that incident, yes.
> WALCZAK: Let's talk about—a little bit about how we got to these ordinances. I believe you told me that you're not very [I]nternet savvy?
> BARLETTA: That's correct.
> WALCZAK: But you have a friend who is?

BARLETTA: Many.

WALCZAK: At least you have one friend who is [I]nternet savvy, and we don't need to mention his name here, but you went on the [I]nternet with this friend sometime after the Kichline murder?

BARLETTA: Correct.

WALCZAK: And you were looking for anything, anywhere in the United States where a city had passed an ordinance to deal with illegal immigration?

BARLETTA: I was trying to find something that we could do to protect ourselves in the form of an ordinance that we might be able to use in the City of Hazleton.

WALCZAK: So you were looking for something that a city could do?

BARLETTA: That's correct.

WALCZAK: In a municipality?

BARLETTA: That's correct.

WALCZAK: But you found only one thing?

BARLETTA: That's correct.

WALCZAK: [You] found an ordinance from San Bernardino, California?

BARLETTA: That's correct.

WALCZAK: In fact, it wasn't really an ordinance. It had been introduced in San Bernardino?

BARLETTA: It had not passed, and I believe there was an effort at the time to have a referendum to get it on the ballot, and that is where that ordinance was. (*Lozano v. Hazleton*, trial transcripts, doc. 210, 81–82, on file with the author)

37. Heidi Beirich wrote:

In 2005, Turner had created, and then led, a nativist group called Save Our State. The group was remarkable for its failure to disassociate itself from the neo-Nazi skinheads who often joined its rallies—something that virtually all other nativist groups, worried about bad publicity, worked hard to do. Save Our State's electronic bulletin board, too, was remarkable for the racist vitriol that frequently appeared there. It was in that forum that Turner made one of his more controversial remarks, amounting to a defense of white separatism. "I can make the argument that just because one believes in white separatism that that does not make them a racist. . . . I can make the argument that someone who proclaims to be a white nationalist isn't necessarily a white supremacist. I don't think that standing up for your 'kind' or 'your race' makes you a bad person." (Heidi Beirich, "FAIR: The Action Arm," *Southern Poverty Law Center Intelligence Report*, February 2009; see also Southern Poverty Law Center, "The Groups: A Listing," n.d., available at https://www.splcenter.org/fighting-hate/intelligence-report/2015/groups-listing, accessed October 29, 2015)

38. Miriam Jordan, "In Immigrant Fight, Grass-Roots Groups Boost Their Clout," *Wall Street Journal*, September 28, 2006.

39. The City Council debates over the ordinance were not all one-sided. Plenty of residents and experts testified in opposition. I explore some of that opposition in Chapter 3. Here, my focus is exclusively on city officials' testimony.

40. See Karla Mari McKanders, "Welcome to Hazleton! 'Illegal' Immigrants Beware: Local Immigration Ordinances and What the Federal Government Must Do about It," *Loyola University Chicago Law Journal* 39, no. 1 (2007): 10.

41. Kent Jackson, "Testimony Contentious at Times," *Standard-Speaker*, March 14, 2007.

42. Harold Garfinkel, "Conditions of Successful Degradation Ceremonies," *American Journal of Sociology* 6, no. 5 (1956): 420–424. Elsewhere, I expand on the theoretical relevance of Garfinkel's concept to this case: see Jamie Longazel, "Moral Panic as Racial Degradation Ceremony: Racial Stratification and the Local-Level Backlash against Latina/o Immigrants." *Punishment and Society* 15, no. 1 (2013): 96–119.

43. Garfinkel, "Conditions of Successful Degradation Ceremonies," 422.

44. Jonathan Xavier Inda, *Targeting Immigrants: Government, Technology, and Ethics* (Malden, MA: Blackwell, 2006), 110.

45. Garfinkel, "Conditions of Successful Degradation Ceremonies," 423.

46. The "nuisance of illegal immigration" is a phrase that appears in the text of the IIRA (see Appendix B). To quote Garfinkel at length on the role of certainty in the social process of degradation:

> If the denunciation is to take effect, the scheme must not be one in which the witness is allowed to elect the preferred. Rather, the alternatives must be such that the preferred is morally required. Matters must be so arranged that the validity of his choice, its justification, is maintained by the fact that he makes it. The scheme of alternatives must be such as to place constraints upon his making a selection "for a purpose." Nor will the denunciation succeed if the witness is free to look beyond the fact that he makes the selection for evidence that the correct alternative has been chosen, as, for example, by the test of empirical consequences of the choice. The alternatives must be such that, in "choosing," he takes it for granted and beyond any motive for doubt that not choosing can mean only preference for its opposite. (Garfinkel, "Conditions of Successful Degradation Ceremonies," 423)

47. Hazleton City Council, meeting transcript, June 15, 2006, on file with the author.

48. Ibid. Granted, Yanuzzi may have been referring to a violation of immigration law being "criminal." Even so, this oversimplification would be a mischaracterization. The American Civil Liberties Union's Immigrants' Rights Project provides a useful explanation regarding whether violating federal immigration law constitutes a crime:

> The act of being present in the United States in violation of the immigration laws is not, standing alone, a crime. While federal immigration law does criminalize some actions that may be related to undocumented presence in the United States, undocumented presence alone is not a violation of federal criminal law. Thus, many believe that the term "illegal alien," which may suggest a criminal violation, is inaccurate or misleading.
>
> Entering the United States without being inspected and admitted, i.e., illegal entry, is a misdemeanor or can be a felony, depending on the circumstances. 8 U.S.C. § 1325. But many undocumented immigrants do not enter the United States illegally. They enter legally but overstay, work without authorization, drop out of school or violate the conditions of their visas in some other way. Current

estimates are that approximately 45% of undocumented immigrants did not enter illegally. [On this point, the ACLU cites Pew Hispanic Center, "Modes of Entry for the Unauthorized Migrant Population," fact sheet, May 22, 2006, available at http://www.pewhispanic.org/files/2011/10/19.pdf, accessed December 22, 2014.]

Undocumented presence in the United States is only criminally punishable if it occurs after an individual was previously formally removed from the United States and then returned without permission. 8 U.S.C. § 1326 (any individual previously "deported or removed" who "enters, attempts to enter, or is at any time found in" the United States without authorization may be punished by imprisonment up to two years). Mere undocumented presence in the United States alone, however, in the absence of a previous removal order and unauthorized reentry, is not a crime under federal law. ("Issue Brief: Criminalizing Undocumented Immigrants," available at https://www.aclu.org/files/assets/FINAL_criminalizing_undocumented_immigrants_issue_brief_PUBLIC_VERSION.pdf, accessed February 27, 2015)

49. Hazleton City Council, meeting transcript, June 15, 2006.

50. Ibid.

51. See the untitled article by Wade Malcolm, *Standard-Speaker*, July 9, 2007, accessed from the Newsbank database and on file with the author.

52. Garfinkel writes, "The unique, never recurring character of the event or perpetrator should be lost. Similarly, any sense of accident, coincidence, indeterminism, chance, or monetary occurrence must not merely be minimized. Ideally, such measures should be inconceivable; at least they should be made false": Garfinkel, "Conditions of Successful Degradation Ceremonies," 422.

53. *Lozano v. Hazleton*, trial testimony, doc. 211, 212.

54. See *Lozano v. Hazleton*, "Plaintiffs' Post-trial Proposed Findings of Fact and Brief," 18, available at http://www.clearinghouse.net/chDocs/public/IM-PA-0001-0026.pdf, accessed July 31, 2015.

55. Matthew Lee and Ramiro Martinez conclude in their review of the literature on the relationship between immigration and crime that "recent research has become substantially more sophisticated in terms of analytical methods, including multivariate modeling and statistically grounded mapping techniques. But the conclusion remains largely the same. Contrary to the predictions of classic criminological theories and popular stereotypes, immigration generally does not increase crime and often suppresses it": Matthew T. Lee and Ramiro Martinez Jr., "Immigration Reduces Crime: An Emerging Scholarly Consensus" *Sociology of Crime, Law and Deviance* 13 (2009): 3. See also Walter A. Ewing, Daniel Martínez, and Rubén G. Rumbaut. "The Criminalization of Immigration in the United States," *American Immigration Council* (July 2015) available at http://immigrationpolicy.org/sites/default/files/docs/the_criminalization_of_immigration_in_the_united_states_final.pdf, accessed July 31, 2015; John Hagan and Alberto Palloni, "Sociological Criminology and the Mythology of Hispanic Immigrant Crime, *Social Problems* 46 (1999): 617–632; Charis E. Kubrin, Marjorie S. Zatz, and Ramiro Martínez, *Punishing Immigrants: Policy, Politics, and Injustice* (New York: New York University Press, 2012); Amy L. Nielsen, Matthew T. Lee, and Ramiro Martínez Jr., "Integrating Race, Place, and Motive in Social Disorganization Theory: Lessons from a Comparison of Black and Latino Homicide Types in Two Immigrant Destination Cities, *Criminology*

43 (2005): 837–872; Graham C. Ousey and Charis E. Kubrin, "Exploring the Connection between Immigration and Violent Crime Rates in U.S. Cities, 1980–2000," *Social Problems* 56, no. 3 (2009): 447–473; Lesley Williams Reid et al., "The Immigration-Crime Relationship: Evidence across US Metropolitan Areas," *Social Science Research* 34 (2005): 757–780; Robert J. Sampson, "Rethinking Immigration and Crime," *Contexts* 7., no. 1 (2008): 28–33; Robert J. Sampson, Jeffery D. Morenoff, and Stephen Raudenbush, "Social Autonomy of Racial and Ethnic Disparities in Violence," *American Journal of Public Health* 95 (2005): 224–232.

56. These figures are from "Plaintiffs' Post-trial Proposed Findings of Fact and Brief." The brief describes how plaintiff attorneys worked with city officials in the process of collecting these statistics:

> In discovery, Plaintiffs requested Hazleton to produce all pertinent crime statistics. . . . The Police Department does not keep information on the immigration status of those arrested and does not keep copies of the federal detainers, which evidence an undocumented alien being transferred to federal custody. In response to Plaintiff's discovery requests, Police Chief Robert Ferdinand searched for police records for crimes involving undocumented persons for a period spanning from 2001 to 2006. The Hazleton Police Department keeps its police reports on the "Alert" computer system. The Alert system has several informational fields, but there is no field for immigration status. To obtain information on crimes allegedly committed by illegal aliens, Chief Ferdinand (1) conducted a computer search of terms such as "illegal alien," "illegal immigrant," ICE and (2) instructed his narcotics detectives to identify individuals they believed to be illegal aliens. Chief Ferdinand's initial document search returned twenty-one incident investigation reports. Five of those reports did not reflect crimes allegedly committed by undocumented aliens. After an additional search, Chief Ferdinand produced nine Daily Information Sheets and one additional Incident Investigation Report. Of those ten additional documents, four were duplicates of incidents reflected in other reports. One of the additional ten did not evidence a crime by an undocumented person. In total, the City was able to produce only 21 documents, which it believes reflect crimes committed by undocumented persons. The City does not know whether any of the 21 crimes resulted in a conviction of an illegal immigrant from 2001 to 2006. (ibid., 19–20)

Nevertheless, it is important to acknowledge that there was some disagreement about the crime information presented in the *Lozano* trial. Countering the numbers I present here, the defendant insisted that crimes committed by undocumented immigrants were, in fact, a serious problem in Hazleton. However, my reading is that these claims suffer from several shortcomings and in some cases clearly rely on racialized, taken-for-granted assumptions.

For example, the defendant asserted that undocumented immigrants brought "new" types of crime with them into Hazleton. "Crime committed by illegal immigrants is a problem because the types of crimes committed by illegal immigrants now includes narcotics, gang activity, violent activity, carrying weapons, using weapons, [and] large fights between gang members, all of which Hazleton did not see in the past": *Lozano v. Hazleton,*

"Defendant City of Hazleton's Proposed Findings of Fact and Legal Brief," 12, available at http://www.clearinghouse.net/chDocs/public/IM-PA-0001-0025.pdf, accessed July 31, 2015. In his testimony, Ferdinand compared the use of weapons and gang activity to memories of when he "was young in high school." He said, "The way to resolve a difference would be two guys squaring off after school and punching it out. Now we're talking about these guys don't have the honor or the courage to fight one on one. They are talking about utilizing weapons against each other and having a whole crew of their buddies jump in there, too. . . . This is completely different from what we have seen years ago. . . . This is truly something that we have not seen before. I don't care what the numbers say. I'm telling you that the reality is that this is the trend now, this type of activity, this kind of violent crime": *Lozano v. Hazleton*, trial transcripts, doc. 214, 104–105.

Mirroring the Latino Threat Narrative, this statement seems to imply that it is *understood* and can *go without saying* that there is something inherently different about the immigrants who recently arrived in the city, regardless of what the numbers say. Note also how the anecdotal evidence in Ferdinand's testimony treats other "lawbreaking [as] unintelligible": Lisa Marie Cacho, *Social Death: Racialized Rightlessness and the Criminalization of the Unprotected* (New York: New York University Press, 2012), 38. In other words, even if we were to concede that it is understandable for officials to be expressing concern with crime—particularly, violent crime—the vision they offer of the crime problem and the solutions they propose to alleviate it (i.e., the IIRA) pay almost no attention to the *vast majority of offenders*, particularly those who are longtime residents. The (presumably White) youth who Ferdinand recalls "punching it out" is one example of this. The way Ferdinand told the story, they are not "criminals" committing assault but, rather, "honorable" youths demonstrating "courage." In another example, the defendant claims "illegal immigrants have been found dealing all types of drugs but particularly cocaine, crack cocaine and heroin": "Defendant City of Hazleton's Proposed Findings of Fact and Legal Brief," 12. Here a connection between immigration status and criminality is implied, yet the statement gives no information about who else police have found selling such drugs. Conceptions of "us" and "them," in other words, convert problems such as Hazleton's "drug problem" into an "illegal immigration problem." The City of Hazleton also provided a list of individual crimes that it "[believed] involved" undocumented immigrants that covered more than two typed pages: see "Defendant City of Hazleton's Proposed Findings of Fact and Legal Brief," 13–16. While presenting that information in this manner makes criminality among undocumented immigrants appear commonplace, it is important to point out that a comparable list of crimes allegedly committed by people who are not undocumented immigrants would have been *substantially longer*. For example, whereas undocumented immigrants accounted for 21 arrests between 2000 and 2006, the Hazleton police made more than *400 times* as many *total* arrests during that period (i.e., there were 8,571 arrests from 2001 to 2006).

57. René Flores used the Uniform Crime Reports and population data to assess crime rates over time in Hazleton. He found that "despite the media's increased focus on crime, both the property and violent crime rates [had] remained relatively stable since 1999": René D. Flores, "Living in the Eye of the Storm: How Did Hazleton's Restrictive Immigration Ordinance Affect Local Interethnic Relations?" *American Behavioral Scientist* 58, no. 13 (2014): 1749.

58. According to the defendant, "In 2006, the Hazleton Police Department Narcot-

ics Division made thirty arrests and ten of the arrests were of illegal immigrants." If both of these numbers are correct, there was, it seems, an increase in arrests for drug-related crimes among undocumented immigrants *in 2006*. However, these numbers also imply that *zero* undocumented immigrants were arrested for drug-related crimes between 2001 and 2005.

59. "Plaintiffs' Post-Trial Proposed Findings of Fact and Brief," 21.

60. The quote is from an interview Barletta conducted with CNN. It is available at https://www.youtube.com/watch?v=A84qJGOvfpM, accessed December 21, 2014.

61. The plaintiffs elaborate, "Detective Christopher Orozco heads the Police Department's Street Crimes Task Force. Orozco has been on Hazleton's police force for nine years. The Street Crimes Task Force was recently created to deals [*sic*] with all street crime issues, including gang activity. During Orozco's tenure, the Police Department has only arrested five alleged gang members": "Plaintiffs' Proposed Findings of Fact and Legal Brief," 24.

62. Hazleton's legal team provided similar numbers: "In 2000 there were very few crimes involving illegal immigrants; however, in 2005 there were five documented arrests involving illegal immigrants and in 2006 there were nineteen documented arrests involving illegal immigrants": "Defendant City of Hazleton's Post-Trial Findings of Fact and Legal Brief," 12. In other words, they seem to suggest a total of about twenty-four arrests of undocumented immigrants in Hazleton over the 2000–2006 time period (plus whatever the exact number of similar arrests is in 2000–2004). This number is very close to the plaintiffs' claim that undocumented immigrants accounted for just twenty-one of all arrestees in Hazleton during these years.

63. Hazleton's specific claim in the *Lozano* case was that more than "half of the 2006 overtime budget of the Hazleton Police Department was spent investigating the Derek Kichline murder, which involved illegal immigrants": "Defendant City of Hazleton's Post-Trial Finding of Fact and Legal Brief," 7.

64. This is from an earlier version of the ordinance, Illegal Immigration Relief Act Ordinance 2006-10, sec. 2, available at http://www.clearinghouse.net/chDocs/public/IM-PA-0001-0003.pdf, accessed August 10, 2015. The Findings and Declaration of Purpose were slightly edited in the more recent version of the law (see Appendix B). It now reads "that unlawful employment, the harboring of illegal aliens in dwelling units in the City of Hazleton, and crime committed by illegal aliens harm the health, safety and welfare of authorized U.S. workers and legal residents in the City of Hazleton. Illegal immigration leads to higher crime rates, subjects our hospitals to fiscal hardship and legal residents to substandard quality of care, contributes to other burdens on public services, increasing their cost and diminishing their availability to legal residents, and diminishes our overall quality of life."

65. *Lozano v. Hazleton*, trial transcripts, doc. 209, 189.

66. Lou Barletta, "An Open Letter from Mayor Lou Barletta"; emphasis added. The letter has since been taken off the city's website. However, it is available at http://lawprofessors.typepad.com/immigration/2006/07/amother_local_g.html, accessed August 4, 2015. In the letter, Mayor Barletta went on to elaborate on how the English-as-official-language portion of the ordinance was a nonracist response to pressing drains on city services:

The final part of this ordinance makes English the official language of Hazleton. All city documents will only be available in English. Those applying for a permit would have to speak English. While our emergency services will never be denied to anyone because of a language barrier, every other aspect of city business will be conducted only in English. Let me be clear, this ordinance is intended to make Hazleton one of the most difficult places in the U.S. for illegal immigrants.

This measure is not racist because it does not target one particular race. The Illegal Immigration Relief Act is intended to deter and punish any illegal immigration in the City of Hazleton. Requiring the use of English does not target any other language; it merely states that no matter what language you prefer to speak at home, English will be spoken when you conduct business with Hazleton officials.

Illegal immigration is a drain on city resources. Every domestic incident, every traffic accident, every noise complaint, each time we send our police department, fire department or code enforcement officer to respond, it costs taxpayer dollars.

If the City of Hazleton began publishing official documents or conducting business in a second language, how would we respond when someone asks us to use a third, or fourth language?

67. The *Lozano* plaintiffs, for example, pointed to a lack of evidence to support claims that undocumented immigrants posed a significant financial expense:

Hazleton is required by law to prepare audited financial statements to reflect an accurate picture of the City's financial condition. . . . The financial statements list all materials affecting the City's financial condition. The City's 2005 audited financial statements are its most recent. There is no mention of the alleged costs associated with illegal immigration in the City's 2005 audited financial statement . . . which suggests that the cost of undocumented immigrants is not material to Hazleton's finances. There is no evidence in the record showing that "illegal aliens" significantly burden the City's finances. ("Plaintiffs' Post-trial Proposed Findings of Fact and Brief," 27)

They also reported that, in addition to not examining crime statistics, the "City Council did not review any written studies or data analyzing the effect of undocumented aliens on . . . the economy, healthcare, or education. City Council also did not commission or review any study on the expected impact or effectiveness of the ordinances": ibid., 14.

68. When I visited the Hazleton One Community Center, I asked about English as a Second Language (ESL) courses (see Chapter 4). One of the directors of the center showed me a binder that contained information about registering for such classes. Not only was every single class that the organization offered full; there was also an extensive waiting list. If anything, it appears as though Hazleton is struggling to keep up with the demand for ESL classes. On the national level, Leo Chavez writes that there is a "rapid decline in use of Spanish in the Latino second and third-plus generations, [suggesting] that concerns about a threat to the prevalence of English language are unfounded. This pattern not only is occurring among the children of Mexican and other Latino American immigrants but also is widespread among the children of most immigrant groups in the United States today. Indeed, the linguistic threat is misguided, in that the real concern

should be with the loss of a major resource, languages other than English, during a time of increasing global economic, cultural, and political relationships": Leo R. Chavez, *The Latino Threat: Constructing Immigrants, Citizens, and the Nation* (Stanford, CA: Stanford University Press, 2008), 59–60.

69. Notably, as the *Lozano* plaintiffs point out, Hazleton does not provide any funding for health care; nor did the city's primary health care provider "present to City Council any . . . costs or losses or financial statements showing the hospital's costs to provide medical services to undocumented persons": "Plaintiffs' Post-trial Proposed Findings of Fact and Brief," 30–31.

70. As a report published by the Migration Policy Institute in 2006 points out, important social contextual factors such as access to employer-sanctioned health insurance are important determinants for whether one has access to various health care options. "Recent immigrants are more likely to be uninsured. Over time, their rates of insurance improve and their incomes grow. This is partly because immigrants tend to find better-quality jobs with time, and partly because both citizens' and immigrants' incomes increase with age and greater job experience. The main reason immigrants are less insured than native-born citizens is that, despite their high rates of employment, fewer immigrants have employer-sponsored health insurance": see Leighton Ku, "Why Immigrants Lack Adequate Access to Health Care and Health Insurance," Migration Policy Institute, September 1, 2006, available at http://www.migrationpolicy.org/arti cle/why-immigrants-lack-adequate-access-health-care-and-health-insurance, accessed December 22, 2014. See also Leighton Ku and Sheetal Matani, "Left Out: Immigrants' Access to Health Care and Insurance," *Health Affairs* 20, no. 1 (2001): 247–256.

71. As another example, Mayor Barletta said in an interview, "We arrested an illegal alien for selling crack cocaine on a playground. It took our detectives five hours to determine who he was. He had five different Social Security cards." Note the simultaneous assertion that undocumented immigrants threaten community safety (i.e., selling drugs on a playground), overwhelm local institutions (i.e., burdening police), and are manipulative (i.e., having multiple Social Security cards): "Welcome to Hazleton: One Mayor's Controversial Plan to Deal with Illegal Immigration," *60 Minutes*, November 17, 2006, available at http://www.cbsnews.com/news/welcome-to-hazleton, accessed July 31, 2015.

72. Video available at http://www.youtube.com/watch?v=A84qJGOvfpM, accessed February 27, 2015.

73. Mayor Barletta has stood by similar assertions in the past. As he pointed out in the *Lozano* trial, "It is well documented that most illegal aliens do not speak English, and I believe everybody would agree with that, most illegal aliens do not speak English. That has been well reported": *Lozano v. Hazleton*, trial transcripts, doc. 210, 106. The logic of his response to Chetry's question seems to go in the opposite direction, however, implying not that undocumented people do not speak English but that *people who do not speak English are undocumented*. Either way, the number of ESL students in the Hazleton Area School District is irrelevant to a conversation about immigration status. For one, the law does not permit school districts to inquire about the documentation status of students. And because the "Hazleton Area School District is a separate legal entity from the City of Hazleton," which also educates a large portion of students who live outside of Hazleton city limits (43.8 percent), the question is well beyond Hazleton's jurisdiction: see "Plaintiffs' Post-trial Proposed Findings of Fact and Brief," 28–30.

74. U.S. Senate Committee on the Judiciary, "Comprehensive Immigration Reform: Examining the Need for a Guest Worker Program Hearing," 109th Cong., 2d sess., July 5, 2006, Philadelphia. Mayor Michael Bloomberg of New York City was also on that panel. The full exchange is worth quoting at length, as the sharp distinctions between the testimony of the two mayors sheds light on many key issues:

ARLEN SPECTER: Mayor Bloomberg, if you did not have undocumented immigrants working in New York City in hotels, in the restaurants, in the hospitals, as domestics, what would the impact be on your city's economy?

BLOOMBERG: It would be devastating for our city. We estimate there's 500,000 undocumented living in a city of 8.1 million people. A lot of them provide the elbow grease to make the traditional industries you've talked about, whether it is the tourism-related industries of transportation and food and beverage, or it's home health care, or it's providing a lot of the cleaning services and driving taxi cabs, and those kinds of things. But the truth of the matter is our undocumented go all the way up the ladder into senior people at lots of different institutions.

And it's just—without them, the city could not survive in the ways it is. We couldn't provide—we wouldn't have the tax base for those that need services, and we would not have the compassionate kinds of government that I think we've provided.

I was listening to Mayor Barletta talk about the size of Hazleton. It reminded me that New York City may have 8.1 million people, but we have communities, hundreds of them, of the same size that Hazleton, Pennsylvania, is. And our people want to be able to go out in their local communities, to parks and to schools and on the streets, and be safe. And in fact, they are safe. And we've been able to do that, and the reason we've done it is we have the world's greatest police department. . . . But that's where the tax base comes from to provide that. The immigrant community in New York City has helped us, it hasn't hurt us. It is New York City's great strength rather than a weakness.

BARLETTA: And the point I want to make today is the opposite point of view, such as big cities, how they're dealing with it. In small-town America, we have a very limited resource to provide services to people, very small amount of money. And when I see those resources being used where they shouldn't be, it's concerning, and it does affect the quality of life. Our budget, as I said, is minuscule, and we're spending the little amount that I do have chasing illegal immigrants around the city of Hazleton.

75. I point all this out while realizing that part of the IIRA outlined punishments for businesses that hire undocumented immigrants (see Appendix B). One would assume that, if anywhere, discussions of corporate exploitation or de-manufacturing might emerge around debates regarding this measure. Yet this portion of the ordinance received almost no discussion during council debates. One explanation for this might have to do with the city's lifting the ordinance from elsewhere and not formatting it to fit this particular situation. In other words, in what appears to be a strictly symbolic piece of legislation, it could be that officials understandably left out of the debate the portion

of the ordinance that does not fit neatly into their narrative. It is also worth noting that the KOZ initiative contains a provision that prohibits companies operating on KOZ parcels from "knowingly permit[ting] the labor services of an illegal alien" (see "Keystone Opportunity Zone," sec. 311).

This phenomenon of including such employer restrictions but having them drowned out by rhetoric aimed at individual immigrants follows a broader pattern in immigration law and politics. Immigration laws commonly include what appear to be "tough" employer sanctions, but in practice these sanctions, at times by design, are difficult to implement. In an analysis of the Immigration Reform and Control Act (IRCA) of 1986, for example, Kitty Calavita unpacked the requirement that employers simply act in "good faith":

> Even if they admit that they employ undocumented workers, employers will probably not be subject to fines under employer sanctions. Instead, as long as they complete the paperwork (as the vast majority do), they are labeled "compliers." . . . In 1982, a "good faith" clause was inserted into the Simpson-Mazzoli bill. This clause stipulated that if employers check workers' documents, regardless of the validity of those documents, they will be assumed to have complied with the law. . . . By the time IRCA was passed in 1986, this protection was carefully spelled out. It included a provision that the required document check, conducted in "good faith," would constitute an "affirmative defense that the person or entity has not violated (the 'knowing hire' clause)." Equally important, it released employers from responsibility for detecting fraudulent documents, stating that "a person or entity has complied with the [document check] requirement . . . [i]f the document reasonably appears on its face to be genuine." (Kitty Calavita, "U.S. Immigration and Policy Responses: The Limits of Legislation," in *Controlling Immigration: A Global Perspective*, ed. Wayne Cornelius, Takeyuki Tsuda, Phillip Martin, and James Hollifield [Stanford, CA: Stanford University Press, 2004], 71)

Immigrant workers, however, do not typically enjoy such low compliance standards. A notable example of this comes from the Supreme Court's decision in *Hoffman v. National Labor Relations Board* (535 U.S. 137 2002). In *Hoffman*, the court focused on whether an undocumented worker who was fired by his employer for being involved with a union was entitled to back pay. Writing for the majority, Chief Justice Rehnquist declared, "Awarding back pay in a case like this not only trivializes the immigration laws[;] it also condones and encourages further violations [of immigration law]." In doing so, he repeatedly referred to the plaintiff's behavior as criminal, despite no previous charge or conviction, while neglecting the illegal action taken by the plaintiff's former employer in denying his right to participate in a union. The law thus plays to anti-immigrant hostilities while providing employers with an opportunity to, as Justice Breyer states in his *Hoffman* dissent, "hire with a wink and a nod those potentially unlawful aliens whose unlawful employment . . . ultimately will lower the cost of labor law violations."

76. Garfinkel, "Conditions of Successful Degradation Ceremonies," 423.

77. Mayor Barletta testified to the Senate Judiciary Committee, "If others had done their jobs by keeping this *murderous thug* and his cohorts out of the country, out of

Hazleton, Derek Kichline may still be alive today": U.S. Senate Committee on the Judiciary, "Comprehensive Immigration Reform"; emphasis added.

78. In his testimony to the Senate, Barletta explicitly referred to the playground at which an undocumented immigrant was charged with firing a gun as "sacred ground": ibid. Compare Mary Douglas, *Purity and Danger* (London: Routledge, 1966). See also Thomas Ross, "The Rhetorical Tapestry of Race: White Innocence and Black Abstraction," *William and Mary Law Review* 32, no. 1 (1990): 1–36.

79. If it is not obvious, my point here is not that Hazleton does not deserve protection from harm, in general terms. What I am drawing attention to is the notion that such deservingness is constructed vis-à-vis a racialized "enemy," making *this particular conception of deservingness* problematic. Moreover, as should be clear by this point, this is not at all an attempt to trivialize the murder of Derek Kichline. His killing was tragic, as was the murder of Julio Calderon. I in no way dispute that. What I am arguing is that the response to his murder morphed into a debate about who belongs and who does not that has implications that extend well beyond the victim and the alleged offenders in this particular case.

80. I use "White Hazletonians" here to refer not to those who identify as White per se but, rather, to those who are *constructed as White* vis-à-vis sharply drawn contrasts to racialized outsiders. I realize that some may question my assertion that the prevailing rhetoric has made Whiteness and belonging synonymous on the grounds that "legal" Latina/o residents are often said to be included in this "accepted group." I agree that this may be the case rhetorically and, on some occasions, in practice. However, there are numerous instances here—as there are and long have been in U.S. race relations more generally—in which "legal" Latina/o residents follow all of the rules yet still find themselves subjected to discrimination in practice. Moreover, we have long seen some members of subjugated groups granted inclusion by the majority. But the fact is that such inclusion is granted on majority-defined terms, which often include the "othering" of those subordinated groups that were left behind. I discuss this in more detail in Chapter 4.

81. john a. powell, *Racing to Justice: Transforming Our Conception of Self and Other to Build an Inclusive Society* (Bloomington: Indiana University Press, 2012), 53.

82. Hazleton City Council, meeting transcript, July 13, 2006.

83. For a similar observation regarding California's Proposition 187, see Lisa Marie Cacho, "'The People of California Are Suffering': The Ideology of White Injury in the Discourse of Immigration," *Cultural Values* 4 (2000): 393.

84. Illegal Immigration Relief Act Ordinance 2006-10; all emphases are added.

85. Quoting Mayor Barletta, from Hazleton City Council, meeting transcript, June 15, 2006; emphasis added.

86. Hazleton City Council, meeting transcript, July 13, 2006; emphasis added.

87. See http://www.smalltowndefenders.com, accessed May 2011. In a clip from *CBS Evening News*, Barletta also explicitly identifies this as his persona, signing off after an explanation of the "illegal immigration problem" by saying, "I'm Lou Barletta, and I'm a small town defender": http://www.cbsnews.com/news/freespeech-lou-barletta, accessed December 21, 2014.

88. Hazleton City Council, meeting transcript, July 13, 2006. Hazleton was in fact a recipient of the National Civic League's All-American City Award in 1964. In this

respect, Hazleton is in fact an "All-American city"; I am not disputing that. Instead, I am problematizing the meanings that are being assigned to the title—specifically, how it is used here to construct difference.

89. Hazleton City Council, meeting transcript, June 15, 2006; emphasis added.

90. U.S. Senate Committee on the Judiciary, "Comprehensive Immigration Reform"; emphasis added.

91. Compare this with the theoretical assertions advanced in Steve Macek, *Urban Nightmares: The Media, the Right, and the Moral Panic over the City* (Minneapolis: University of Minnesota Press, 2006).

92. See, e.g., Joe R. Feagin, "Old Poison in New Bottles: The Deep Roots of Modern Nativism," in *Immigrants Out! The New Nativism and the Anti-immigrant Impulse in the United States*, ed. Juan F. Perea (New York: New York University Press, 1997), 13–43.

93. Nancy Cervantes, Sasha Khokha, and Bobby Murray, "Hate Unleashed: Los Angeles in the Aftermath of Proposition 187," *Chicana/o-Latina/o Law Review* 17, no. 1 (1995): 1–23; Kim Ebert and Sarah M. Ovink, "Anti-immigrant Ordinances and Discrimination in New and Established Destinations," *American Behavioral Scientist* 58, no. 13 (2014): 1784–1804; Flores, "Living in the Eye of the Storm"; Andrea Christina Nill, "Latinos and SB 1070: Demonization, Dehumanization, and Disenfranchisement," *Harvard Latino Law Review* 14 (2011): 35–66; Seline Szkupinski Quiroga, Dulce M. Medina, and Jennifer Glick, "In the Belly of the Beast: Effects of Anti-immigration Policy on Latino Community Members," *American Behavioral Scientist* 58, no. 13 (2014): 1723–1742; Rogelio Sáenz, Cecilia Menjívar, and San Juanita Edilia García, "Arizona's SB 1070: Setting Conditions for Violations of Human Rights Here and Beyond," in *Sociology and Human Rights: A Bill of Rights for the Twenty-First Century*, ed., Judith Blau and Mark Frezzo (Newbury Park, CA: Sage, 2012), 155–178.

94. One activist described the experience of Latinas/os in Hazleton by saying, "Hispanic people was afraid to live here, not only because they did not have documents, but because this ordinance opened the door to people that was born and raised here to express their opinion against the newcomers. To tell the newcomers to go back to their country; shouting down the street that they are illegals; criticize them in public places like the hospital or the supermarket or the streets because the only fault was as an immigrant you look like a Hispanic that they believe was . . . illegal." This and subsequent quotations in this section, unless noted otherwise, are from interviews with activists, ethnographic field notes, and the focus group and interviews I conducted with ordinary residents (see Appendix A).

95. There were also plenty of examples of discrimination provided in testimony and as evidence in the *Lozano* trial (see Chapter 3).

96. See Flores, "Living in the Eye of the Storm."

97. Ibid., 1751.

98. Zogby International, "Greater Hazleton Area Civic Partnership," report submitted to the Greater Hazleton Area Civic Partnership, Hazleton, PA, 2007, available at http://www.wbcitizensvoice.com/pdfs/hazletonfinalreport.pdf, accessed July 31, 2015.

99. Ali Behdad, *A Forgetful Nation: On Immigration and Cultural Identity in the United States* (Durham, NC: Duke University Press, 2005), 112.

100. Bonilla-Silva defines racial story lines "as the *socially shared tales that are fable-like and incorporate a common scheme or wording.* . . . They are often based on impersonal generic arguments with little narrative content—they are the ideological 'of course'

racial narratives. In story lines characters are likely to be underdeveloped and are usually social types (e.g., the 'black man' in statements such as 'My best friend lost a job to a black man')": Eduardo Bonilla-Silva, *Racism without Racists: Color-Blind Racism and the Persistence of Racial Inequality in the United States*, 2d ed. (Lanham, MD: Rowman and Littlefield, 76). Here is an example of a "story line" from my data:

> I think [Hazleton] was a quiet town. I think people that lived here worked; they contributed to the community. They took care of the town. They took care of their neighbors. Since the Hispanic population came, that has just gone straight downhill. I hate to be like that, but it's frustrating. It's really frustrating. I don't like it. I can't stand it. They don't take care of their homes; they don't upkeep the property. They have garbage all over. There's comings and goings all hours—day and night, constantly. [There's] loud music playing; parties going on; people screaming and yelling; kids running around. It's just chaos. And then as fast as they move in, they're gone. They move out in the middle of the night, and nobody sees them again. And the house is just left—it's a mess. . . . It just seems to be part of that culture, and they refuse to change to live in our community.

Similarly but with some subtle differences, Bonilla-Silva defines *racial testimonies* as "*accounts in which the narrator is a central participant in the story or is close to the characters in the story. Testimonies provide the aura of authenticity and emotionality that only "firsthand" narrative can furnish. . . . Though seemingly involving more detail and personal investment than story lines . . . many of the testimonies whites tell still serve rhetorical functions with regard to racial issues, such as saving face, signifying nonracialism, or bolstering their arguments on controversial racial matters*": ibid., 76–77. Here is an example of racial testimony from my data:

> [Hazleton] is a lot more dangerous [than it used to be]. My father is 95 years old, and he's already been targeted with people stealing from his property, and his children . . . all fear for him a lot because he refuses to move out of the home. He lives by himself. . . . He's had property already stolen from him. He contracted out some work to a guy named Carlos, and it was within two weeks after this guy did part of the work and never came back and finished it that [my father's] lawnmower was stolen. Although we don't have proof that it was [Carlos], we sort of think he was the guy that took the lawnmower. He was contracted to do some cleaning up in the yard . . . , and all of that was done and put in a big pile in the backyard, and [Carlos] said, "I'll be right back with my truck," and [he] never came back. He had the money—my father paid him, and that was it. And within two weeks, [the new lawnmower was stolen from my father's] shed.

101. Interestingly, I found this "harmonious era" to be unidentifiable; residents from various generations had very similar fond remembrances of the "Hazleton of old." This is consistent with research on memory and nostalgia. Scholars note that people do not necessarily draw on what actually happened. Rather, they draw on an "available past": Michael Schudson, "The Present in the Past versus the Past in the Present," *Communication* 11 (1989): 105–112. The past, in this way, often becomes little more than a "resource used for meaning": Anthony Cohen, *The Symbolic Construction of Community* (New York: Tavistock, 1985), 99.

102. It is interesting also to note that while ordinary residents' discourse shared with official rhetoric the tendency to define "us" as "not them," there were variations in the way this was accomplished that suggest the construction of White identity is not purely a top-down process. In my interviews and focus groups, for example, ordinary residents spoke more about their neighbors, their co-workers, and the people they encounter while shopping than they did about immigration status.

Gary Alan Fine and Bill Ellis devote a chapter of *The Global Grapevine* to Hazleton and draw parallel conclusions. They find that fear of the immigrant "other" materializes from below in the form of rumors. Many of the rumors they discovered circulating through Hazleton while the city's demographics changed similarly depicted Latinas/os as people who commit crime or thanklessly take from people. One such rumor is what they call the "grapevine rumor," which happens to have appeared in other contexts where "the presence of outsiders has provoked concern." The rumor goes something like this: "My great aunt . . . told me a story about the Puerto Ricans that live on Wyoming Street in Hazleton. She said that her friend went to drive through the street but the entire street got blocked by Puerto Ricans. She said they demanded that the driver pay five dollars in order to pass. Eventually police showed up and the crowd disappeared": Gary Alan Fine and Bill Ellis, *The Global Grapevine* (New York: Oxford University Press, 2010), 99.

103. For example, one resident called CAN DO a "necessary evil." Others suggested that the group has intentionally kept wages down and has long failed to bring high-quality jobs into the region. It was also a pattern for respondents to begin their commentary with racial testimony / story lines, only to shift to economic concerns, such as the rise of temporary employment and the lack of professional opportunities for young people, later in the conversation. The mere existence of such economic concerns, in my opinion, is a reason to be optimistic about the type of changes I advocate in the Conclusion. However, what seems to be missing in the current political climate is acceptance of an antiracist discourse and *mobilization* around economic issues.

104. See, e.g., Chavez, *The Latino Threat Narrative*, 21–43. See also Cybelle Fox, *Three Worlds of Relief: Race, Immigration, and the American Welfare State from the Progressive Era to the New Deal* (Princeton, NJ: Princeton University Press (2012); Khalil Gibran Muhammad, *The Condemnation of Blackness: Race, Crime, and the Making of Modern Urban America*, Cambridge, MA: Harvard University Press (2011).

105. Photo on file with the author. See also http://www.npr.org/2013/04/14/177186174/in-hazleton-a-mixed-welcome-for-citys-immigrants, accessed August 11, 2015.

106. See, e.g., http://www.alipac.us/f12/hazletons-all-legals-served-sign-40708/, accessed August 11, 2015.

107. This is a quote from a focus group participant in the Zogby study: Zogby International, "Greater Hazleton Area Civic Partnership," 2007

108. Lou Barletta received 94.4 percent of the vote in the Republican primary and 63 percent of the vote in the Democratic primary as a write-in candidate: see L. A. Tarone, "Write On: Barletta Knocks Marsicano off Ballot," *Standard-Speaker*, May 16, 2007.

109. Representatives from Barletta's office have commented that "the phone hasn't stopped ringing," and the mayor has commonly boasted about the abundance of letters and e-mails his office receives from "literally every state in the union." His being invited to speak in front of Congress with nationally recognizable figures also speaks to this

visibility, as does his numerous appearances on national television and at other venues where he addresses the issue of undocumented immigration: see, e.g., Kelly Monitz, "Mayor Still Getting Fan Mail, Notoriety," *Standard-Speaker*, March 18, 2007.

110. David Engel's insightful conclusion of his classic study of the reaction to personal injury lawsuits in a small, changing community puts such reactions into context quite well:

> Local residents who denounced the assertion of personal injury claims and somewhat irrationally lamented the rise in "litigiousness" of personal injury plaintiffs were, in this sense, participating in a more broadly based ceremony of regret that the realities of contemporary American society could no longer be averted from their community if it were to survive. Their denunciations bore little relationship to the frequency with which personal injury lawsuits were actually filed, for the local ecology of conflict resolution still suppressed most such cases long before they got to court, and personal injury litigation remained rare and aberrational. Rather, the denunciation of personal injury litigation in Sander County was significant mainly as one aspect of a symbolic effort by members of the community to preserve a sense of meaning and coherence in the face of social changes that they found threatening and confusing. It was in this sense a solution—albeit a partial and unsatisfying one—to a problem basic to the human condition, the problem of living in a world that has lost the simplicity and innocence it is thought once to have had. The outcry against personal injury litigation was part of a broader effort by some residents of Sander County to exclude from their moral universe what they could not exclude from the physical boundaries of their community and to recall and reaffirm an untainted world that existed nowhere but in their imaginations. (David Engel, "The Oven Bird's Song: Insiders, Outsiders, and Personal Injuries in an American Community," *Law and Society Review* 18, no. 4 [1984]: 580–581)

111. As powell writes, "In describing whiteness, we are describing not just what whites and the racial other get from current arrangements but also the ways that those arrangements determine how our very being is constituted. One can imagine giving up one's things—a car or a house—but not one's being, with its sense of identity and all of its deeply ingrained association": powell, *Racing to Justice*, 100.

CHAPTER 3

1. Of course, these were not the only people who protested the IIRA or who confronted the backlash I describe here. They were in my estimation, however, the IIRA's most visible opponents. In addition to their various testimonies explained in this chapter, many of which are part of the public record (e.g., testimony at City Council meetings and in the *Lozano* trial), local news sources commonly turn to these leaders for comments about issues facing Hazleton's Latina/o community. For these reasons and with their permission, I have used the real names of these activists. Consistent with research protocol, I do not disclose the names of all other interviewees quoted in this chapter.

2. Unless otherwise noted, all quotes in this and the next section are from interviews with Lopez, Arias, and Arroyo. With the exception of some bracketed words or phrases

inserted for clarification, all quotes in this chapter appear in their original form and may therefore include grammatical errors.

3. Hazleton City Council, meeting transcript, July 13, 2006, on file with the author.

4. This is a phrase Ruth Frankenburg used to describe a "discursive repertoire" on race that transcends color-blindness by emphasizing racial *difference*—not difference in the "essentialist" sense that asserted biological inferiority but, rather, difference "radically redefined." Difference here, in other words, "signals autonomy of culture, values, aesthetic standards, and so on," and "inequality [here] refers not to ascribed characteristics but to the social structure": see Ruth Frankenburg, *White Women, Race Matters: The Social Construction of Whiteness* (Minneapolis: University of Minnesota Press, 1988), 14–15.

5. Ian Haney López, *Dog Whistle Politics: How Coded Racial Appeals Have Reinvented Racism and Wrecked the Middle Class* (New York: Oxford University Press, 2014), 36–37.

6. Ibid. Haney López provides an example of research on public opinion of the death penalty that is relevant to the ideas presented in this chapter:

> We can start by noting two striking facts about the death penalty: first, blacks are about 12 percent of the population but roughly 43 percent of those on death row; second, support for the death penalty varies among whites if they are first told that capital punishment "is unfair because most of the people who are executed are African Americans"—it shoots up. One might expect that informing whites that capital punishment is racially unfair would produce a drop in support. But on the contrary, when so informed in a recent study, the number of whites favoring the death penalty surged by 18 percent, while among those who claimed to "strongly favor" the death penalty, support leaped a precipitous 44 percent.
>
> What explained this shocking increase in support? This was not because whites affirmatively favored discriminating against minorities, and piled on once they understood that the death penalty did just that. Rather, it seemed that whites were so sure that the death penalty was fair, that when told the opposite, they reacted angrily by reiterating and even increasing their support for the challenged practice. Resentful at the implication of bias, instead of reconsidering, many whites doubled-down on championing capital punishment. (ibid., 35–36, citing Mark Peffley and Jon Hurwitz, "Persuasion and Resistance: Race and the Death Penalty in America," *American Journal of Political Science* 51, no. 4 [2007])

7. I borrow these concepts from Thomas Ross ("The Rhetorical Tapestry of Race: White Innocence and Black Abstraction," *William and Mary Law Review* 32, no. 1 [1990]: 1–36), with slight modification, given the subject matter: I replace "black abstraction" with "Latina/o abstraction." My analysis also differs from Ross's slightly in that he examined how these rhetorical tools were used *as* law (i.e., studying judicial opinions), whereas I consider their use in debates *around* law (i.e., in legal mobilizations). For a more in-depth theoretical discussion of this point, see Jamie Longazel, "Rhetorical Barriers to Mobilizing for Immigrant Rights: White Innocence and Latina/o Abstraction," *Law and Social Inquiry* 39, no. 3 (2014): 580–600.

8. I say "almost" here because what I describe in Chapter 4 provides an exception.

9. Hazleton City Council, meeting transcript, July 13, 2006.

10. Specifically, she said:

It says that undocumented immigrants are draining funds from the city. I would like to know from where, because these people don't get services from anywhere. When their houses get cold, they don't get oil. They may get food from somewhere if they're hungry. They don't get prenatal care when someone is pregnant; they have to pay for that. So they're not draining funds from the city. They're not littering the city. Crime is not committed by undocumented people in Hazleton. It's committed by criminals. They mere fact that someone is undocumented does not turn anyone into a criminal. (ibid.)

11. Ibid.

12. Ibid.

13. Although they were technically two different entities, many people refer to HALA and HALT interchangeably.

14. Ibid.

15. Ibid. If it is not obvious, Lopez's comments here reflect a desire for Latinas/os in Hazleton to retain their culture, as opposed to being completely absorbed into the culture of the majority. The Zogby International study found that this comment particularly agitated many local residents: "There was great resentment by a majority of participants for the many stated comments from Latino community leaders for having no interest in assimilating into the community" (Zogby International, "Greater Hazleton Area Civic Partnership," report submitted to the Greater Hazleton Area Civic Partnership, Hazleton, PA, 2007).

Arroyo also testified at this meeting. He drew attention to the population boost Hazleton had received and the rise in the number of Latina/o-owned small businesses, which, he noted, grew from four to seventy over a period of just a few years: "That's $8 million every month. Where does that money go? Yes, some of it goes out of the country, we all know that. But the majority of it is spent here—in supermarkets, at car lots, buying clothes. . . . [I]t's economics": Hazleton City Council, meeting transcript, July 13, 2006.

16. Ibid.

17. Ross, "The Rhetorical Tapestry of Race," 2.

18. Ross traces these rhetorical patterns back to slavery. He shows how in the nineteenth century judges denied the brutality of slavery by "placing the black outside of the community of humans" and depicted White slaveholders confronting abolition as "victims" whom the law unjustly compelled to give up their cherished way of life: Ross, "The Rhetorical Tapestry of Race," 8.

Ross also elaborates on the concept of Black abstraction, writing, "The power of black abstraction is that it obscures the humanness of black persons. We can more easily think of black persons as not fully human so long as we do not see them in a familiar social context. . . . The great power of black abstraction is its power to blunt the possible empathetic response": ibid., 6.

19. Hazleton City Council, meeting transcript, July 13, 2006. See also http://www .clearinghouse.net/chDocs/public/IM-PA-0001-0004.pdf, accessed August 5, 2015.

Two other examples illustrate this rhetorical pattern. First, after prosecutors dropped charges against Joan Romero and Pedro Cabrera for the murder of Derek Kichline, Vic Walczak, the ACLU attorney, commented, "This dismissal of charges adds to the long list of discredited claims Barletta has made in the course of demonizing undocumented immigrants for allegedly destroying Hazleton." Barletta replied by accusing Walczak of making such comments out of self-interest (e.g., as a "public relations spectacle"). "I find it repulsive that [he] would defend men who participated in the brutal murder of a resident in my city," Barletta said. "Derek Kichline's family and friends will never see justice for his death. The fact that the ACLU celebrates this and turns it into a public relations spectacle is disgusting and Mr. Walczak should be ashamed of himself": see the untitled article by Wade Malcolm, *Standard-Speaker*, July 9, 2007, accessed from the Newsbank database and in my possession. Second, during the City Council debates on June 15, 2006, one Hazleton resident commented:

> My issue is that my parents and my aunts have been here twenty to thirty years, and it's very hard for them to learn English. I wish that some of the papers that you want to put out be in Spanish, because it is hard for them to read in English. I feel that if you try and make this all English, it's going to cause a lot of problems. I feel that you should be able to print some of this stuff for them in Spanish and give them a chance. My mother can't read in English, so I have to translate, but she can read Spanish, so it is difficult for her—and my grandmother who has been here for sixty years. So my family sent me down to speak for them, and they feel that you should reconsider [the English-only portion of the IIRA].

In response, Barletta said that English was chosen as the "official language" because it "is the language of the Constitution, it's the language of the Declaration of Independence, it's the language that the president speaks, it's the language that the Congress speaks, and it's the language that the Supreme Court hears arguments in." Rather than addressing the challenge this constituent's family confronts, he went on to talk about the challenges that *he* faces as mayor of a multilingual city. "It's hard for me as the mayor to have a community that's separated by language, by a language barrier, where neighbors no longer talk to neighbors because they can't speak the language": Hazleton City Council, meeting transcript, June 15, 2006.

20. Michael McCann, *Rights at Work: Pay Equity Reform and the Politics of Legal Mobilization* (Chicago: University of Chicago Press, 1994).

21. You can see this in Arias's response to a question I asked her about the lawsuit:

> We knew from the beginning that what [Mayor Barletta] was doing was unfair and that he was violating people's rights, civil rights. Everyone, no matter whether you are documented or undocumented, you have a right to have a roof over your head. . . . The way this thing was written [is] that you would go to jail even if you sold a can of soda to someone. That is illegal. . . That is illegal right there. They say illegal is illegal. I don't know the meaning of that, but this is illegal: to deny someone a glass of water, a bottle of water. You cannot sell a bottle of water to someone because he is undocumented? He has a gray and green dollar bill and he is paying for it, so it should be legal.

22. A summary of the litigation is available at https://www.aclu.org/immigrants-rights/anti-immigrant-ordinances-hazleton-pa, accessed August 3, 2015.

23. Namely, Carlos Fuentes, Humberto Hernandez, Rosa Lechuga, Jose Lechuga, Brenda Lee Mieles, Casa Dominicana of Hazleton Inc., the Hazleton Hispanic Business

Association, the Pennsylvania Statewide Latino Coalition, and a group of undocumented immigrants whose identity was protected.

24. *Lozano v. Hazleton*, trial transcripts, doc. 208, 81.

25. In addition to defending Hazleton, Kobach—who as of February 2015 was the secretary of state of Kansas—played a significant role in drafting two subsequent punitive, high-profile state-level immigration measures: Arizona's SB 1070 and Alabama's HB 56. He has also been an outspoken advocate of "self-deportation"—an immigration enforcement strategy based on the idea of making life so difficult for undocumented immigrants that they choose to leave the country on their own. See, e.g., Suzy Khimm, "Kris Kobach, Nativist Son," *Mother Jones*, March–April 2012.

26. *Lozano v. Hazleton*, trial transcripts, doc. 208, 24.

27. Ibid., 23.

28. Ibid., 26–27.

29. Ibid., 28.

30. Ibid., doc. 209, 64.

31. Ibid., 15–16.

32. With the exception that they contain overt racism, these letters also interestingly mirror the rhetorical themes I have been describing. They rely on stereotypes to present Latinas/os narrowly as "lawless" and "lazy," they dismiss as excessive and misguided any claims Latinas/os have made about being harmed, and they groan that Hazleton and the nation more generally are being "overrun" by Latinas/os. One of the letters reads:

> We think [you] and your cohort, that bold, brazen Anna Arias, should spend some time on a few streets in town before defending your (Latin community). . . . Then ask why people are afraid to go out. It is time to teach your people honesty, morality, respect for property, et cetera. Another thing, these young girls having one baby after another without husbands. Must we keep them from the cradle to the grave? The well will soon run dry. Young, able-bodied men sitting on the porches. Give something back in return, cut grass, shovel snow, et cetera. Oh, yes, all have their gold jewelry and cell phones. Who is paying for all that? We think you and Anna had better think twice before you speak. Where were you Friday P.M. when Pine Street playground was once again a scene of trouble? Never see you two show your faces. Signed disgusted citizens. (ibid., 7–8)

Another letter, titled "Will America Become the United States of Mexico?" read, in part, "European-Americans are being dispossessed of their own nation. We are under invasion by millions of unskilled Mexicans who threaten to bankrupt us. . . . The consequences which this immigration disaster holds for our children [are] horrendous. Coloreds will take political control of more states, along with both houses of Congress and the presidency. Whites will quickly be stripped of their rights with our wealth confiscated for redistribution to non-whites as is taking place in South Africa": ibid. 5–6.

33. Ibid., 14.

34. Eduardo Bonilla-Silva refers to this rhetorical pattern as *minimization of racism*:

> This frame allows whites to accept facts such as the racially motivated murder of James Byrd Jr. in Jasper, Texas, the brutal police attack on Rodney King . . . [the rights violation that sparked] the 2005 lawsuit by black workers alleging that Tyson Foods maintained a "Whites Only" bathroom in one of their Ala-

bama plants, the neglect and slow response by government officials toward a mostly black population during Hurricane Katrina, and many other cases and still accuse minorities of being "hypersensitive," of using race as an "excuse," or of "playing the infamous race card." More significantly, this frame also involves regarding discrimination exclusively as all-out racist behavior, which, given the way "new racism" practices operate in post–Civil Rights America, eliminates the bulk of racially motivated actions by individual whites and institutions by fiat. (Eduardo Bonilla-Silva, *Racism without Racists: Color-Blind Racism and the Persistence of Racial Inequality in America* [Lanham, MD: Rowman and Littlefield, 2006], 29–30)

35. But this can also be read in the context of the law's more general unwillingness to take racial harm as it manifests in institutional and other forms seriously, conceptualizing it instead only narrowly in terms of overt instances of discrimination. Haney López explains:

On one side, the Court upholds even the most egregious instances of discrimination. *McCleskey v. Kemp* held that even though Georgia sentenced to death blacks who murdered whites at twenty-two times the rate it mandated death for blacks who kill blacks, there was no Constitutional harm absent the identification of a particular biased actor. On the other, the Court wields the Constitution to strike down almost every effort to ameliorate racism's legacy. Thus, *Richmond v. Croson* told us that, when the former capitol of the Confederacy adopted an affirmative action program to steer some of its construction dollars to minority owned firms, this was impermissible discrimination—even when, without the program, less than two-thirds of one percent of those dollars went to minorities in a city over fifty percent African American. (Ian Haney López, "Race and Colorblindness after *Hernandez* and *Brown*," *Chicano-Latino Law Review* 25 [2005]: 69–70)

36. *Lozano v. Hazleton*, trial transcripts, doc. 209, 205–206.

37. Regarding the issue of the federal government's authority to regulate immigration, he added, "Whatever frustrations officials of the City of Hazleton may feel about the current state of immigration enforcement, the nature of the political system in the United States prohibits the city from enacting ordinances that disrupt a carefully drawn federal statutory scheme." Judge Munley's full opinion is available at https://www.aclu.org/files/pdfs/immigrants/hazleton_decision.pdf, accessed August 3, 2015. For an analysis of the decision, see Doris Marie Provine, "Justice as Told by Judges: The Case of Litigation over Local Anti-immigrant Legislation," *Studies in Social Justice* 3, no. 2 (2009): 231–245.

After Judge Munley issued his ruling, the defendant appealed, and the decision was upheld by the U.S. Court of Appeals for the Third Circuit. That decision was also appealed and, in turn, was remanded by the U.S. Supreme Court in light of recent decisions on a pair of Arizona laws. Upon reconsideration, the Third Circuit reaffirmed the unconstitutionality of the IIRA, and the Supreme Court has since decided not to hear an appeal of that decision: see, e.g., Kent Jackson, "Supreme Court Refusal Ends City's Illegal Immigration Case," *Standard-Speaker*, March 4, 2014.

38. Damon Laabs, "Ruling Pleases Latino Residents," *Standard-Speaker*, July 27, 2007.

39. Ibid.

40. Referring to a controversy within the case regarding Judge Munley's decision to allow plaintiffs who were unauthorized immigrants to conceal their identities, Barletta, as congressman, similarly wrote on his webpage, "The judge allowed the identities of the accusers to be kept secret from the city and its attorneys, and he excused them from showing up to provide testimony in open court—all because they were illegal aliens and could have faced deportation. In essence, the federal judge in the case gave the illegal aliens more rights than an American citizen would have in a U.S. court of law": see "Background on Hazleton's Illegal Immigration Relief Act," available at http://loubarletta.com/immigration/background-on-hazletons-illegal-immigration-relief-act, accessed August 5, 2015. The question also arose as to whether these plaintiffs would be able to provide testimony via closed-circuit television. To this, Mayor Barletta responded, "[Judge Munley has] already tied our hands behind our backs by not knowing their identities. Now they want him to blindfold us": quoted in L. A. Tarone, "Lou Barletta Will Be Called by Plaintiffs Monday," *Standard-Speaker*, March 9, 2007.

41. L. A. Tarone, "Barletta Team Vows Appeal," *Standard-Speaker*, July 27, 2007.

42. Ibid.

43. Lou Barletta, "Rally In Support of Mayor Lou Barletta," Hazleton, PA, June 3, 2007. A transcript of the speech is on file with the author.

44. Tarone, "Barletta Team Vows Appeal."

45. Ibid.

46. So that this book matches the historical record of what transpired in Hazleton, I use the real names of organizations. However, I avoid associating any names with quotes to protect the identity of individuals, particularly those who participated in my research. It is also important to note that my interpretation of events in this section is simply a description of a broader mobilization. Although VOP played a prominent role in this mobilization, I by no means intend to imply that the quotes included here represent the views of that organization or its members. Nor should the reader infer that the activists I quote in this section are members of VOP. Indeed, the group's rallies featured several unaffiliated speakers, including some from across the United States, and because they were public events, plenty of non-members attended, including many people who do not live in the Hazleton area. One organizer conveyed to me that the group had no control over who was in the crowd (and accordingly, we may assume, over these attendees' actions). In short, what follows is not meant to be a commentary on the character of any specific individuals or on the practices and perspectives of any particular groups. Rather, my intent is simply to illustrate how the rhetorical patterns I have identified and the broader ideologies of which they are a part are evident in multiple venues and persist, albeit with slight modifications, through various stages of public debate.

47. Unless noted otherwise, quotations in the remainder of this chapter are from interviews with activists who mobilized in favor of the IIRA, post-*Lozano*, or from statements made at rallies hosted by VOP (which, again, in each case, are not necessarily statements made *by* members of VOP). Again, with the exception of some bracketed words or phrases inserted for clarification, all quotes appear in their original form and may therefore include grammatical errors.

48. I removed irrelevant details of this encounter from the quote to protect the identity of the respondent.

49. One organizer reflected on the outside support VOP received by saying, "We

expected to get townies, but we knew . . . this was a big subject when, like I said, there was New York, Maine, Florida, and, like, Texas people drove up from. . . . And on our guestbook on the website, we had, you could even see that, there was people from all over the country writing things to the mayor, writing things to us, showing their support. So this was really a moment."

50. See, e.g., Patricia Ewick and Susan S. Silbey, *The Common Place of Law: Stories from Everyday Life* (Chicago: University of Chicago Press, 1998).

51. For example, in his analysis of how white innocence and black abstraction were used by nineteenth-century judges, Ross quotes Justice Bradley's decision in *The Civil Rights Cases* (1883), which deemed unconstitutional the first two sections of the Civil Rights Act of 1875 written to protect Blacks from discrimination amid reconstruction:

> When a man emerges from slavery, and by the aid of beneficent legislation has shaken off the inseparable concomitants of that state, there must be some stage in the process of this elevation when he takes the rank of mere citizen, and ceases to be the *special favorite of the laws,* and when his rights as a citizen, or a man, are to be protected in the ordinary modes by which other men's rights are protected. (Ross, "The Rhetorical Tapestry of Race," 13; emphasis added)

Here, the convergence of black abstraction and a discourse on "special rights" is clear. The claim that Blacks are being treated as "special favorites of the laws," Ross notes, "is coherent only in the abstract . . . [because] this special treatment was the product of the reality of pervasive oppression of blacks by whites": ibid., 13.

It is also interesting, but perhaps not surprising, that these patterns mirror findings from scholars who have studied the Tea Party. For example, Theda Skocpol and Vanessa Williamson found that Tea Partiers possess a similar selective ambivalence when it comes to government, writing, "At the grassroots, Tea Partiers want government to get out of the way of business. Yet at the same time, virtually all want government to police immigrants. And the numerous social conservatives in Tea Party ranks want authorities to enforce their conception of traditional moral norms. More telling still, almost all Tea Partiers favor generous social benefits for Americans who "earn" them; yet in an era of rising federal deficits, they are very concerned about being stuck with the tax tab to pay for "unearned" entitlements handed to unworthy categories of people": Theda Skocpol and Vanessa Williamson, *The Tea Party and the Remaking of Republican Conservatism* (New York: Oxford University Press, 2012), 56. See also Carol J. Greenhouse, Barbara Yngvesson, and David Engel, *Law and Community in Three American Towns* (Ithaca, NY: Cornell University Press, 1994), 150); Jonathan Goldberg-Hiller and Neal Milner, "Rights as Excess: Understanding the Politics of Special Rights." *Law and Social Inquiry* 28, no. 4 (2003): 1075–1118.

52. Kevin R. Johnson and Joanna E. Cuevas Ingram, "Anatomy of a Modern-Day Lynching: The Relationship between Hate Crimes against Latina/os and the Debate over Immigration Reform," *North Carolina Law Review* 91 (2013): 1613–1656. Relying on trial testimony and other sources, Johnson and Ingram recount the event:

> One Saturday night in July 2008, a group of Shenandoah Valley High School football players beat Ramirez to death on the streets of that small town.
>
> Early in the evening, the teens spent several hours drinking malt liquor near a creek in Shenandoah. They later were asked to leave a neighborhood Polish American block party when one of the teens got into an argument and had to be

physically restrained by his friends. At trial, testimony showed that the youth had previously frequently voiced their displeasure with the growing number of Latina/os in Shenandoah. They said things like, "Get them out of here," or "[I]t's not good for our [t]own." One of the boys was known to wear a "Border Patrol" t-shirt and drove around town blasting "The White Man Marches On"—a white supremacist song that glorifies violence against minorities.

After getting thrown out of the block party, the group walked through a park and ran into Luis Ramirez, who was with . . . a white woman. One of the teens told [the woman] it was too late for her to be out. Ramirez responded in Spanish. The teen yelled back: "This is Shenandoah. This is America. Go back to Mexico." Another called Ramirez a "Spic." Still another youth told Ramirez to "[g]et the fuck out of here."

The teens ran after Ramirez. One of the football players started fighting with Ramirez, throwing him to the ground. Another teen repeatedly punched Ramirez in the face, calling him a "fucking Spic." While Ramirez was on the ground, the four teens kicked him repeatedly. One of the teens later stated that "[e]verybody else was kicking him in the upper part, in his head and his chest and his upper body."

A friend of Ramirez arrived and the beating ended. While the group began to walk away, a teen screamed, "Fucking Mexican." One of the teens threw a few more punches at Ramirez. Another said, "Fuck you Spic." Another teen chimed in defensively, "This isn't racial."

As Ramirez lay motionless, one of the teens kicked [him] in the head. A loud "crack" could be heard. The kick to Ramirez's head caused him to go into convulsions. As the teens fled, one of them yelled, "Tell your fucking Mexican friends to get the fuck out of Shenandoah or you're going to be fucking laying next to him." Two days later, Luis Ramirez died. (ibid., 1630–1632)

See also María Pabón López, "An Essay Examining the Murder of Luis Ramirez and the Emergence of Hate Crimes against Latino Immigrants in the United States," *Arizona State Law Journal* 44, no. 155 (2012): 155–173.

53. See, e.g., Kelly Monitz, "Verdict Angers, Frightens Latino Community" *Standard-Speaker*, May 7, 2009.

54. See, e.g., MALDEF, "Latino Hate Crime Death Deserves Justice," available at http://maldef.org/immigration/public_policy/shenandoah, accessed August 3, 2015.

55. See, e.g., Ed Pilkington, "Pennsylvania's Police Accused of Cover-Up in Immigrant's Murder," *The Guardian*, December 16, 2009.

56. See, e.g., "Men Convicted of Hate Crime Sentenced to Nine Years in Prison," CNN, available at http://www.cnn.com/2011/CRIME/02/23/pennsylvania.hate.crime, accessed August 3, 2015.

57. Richard Delgado summarizes the oft-forgotten history of Whites' lynching Latinas/os in the United States. Historians have reported

597 lynchings [of Latinas/os] or slightly more—most of them dating to the same period when black lynching ran rampant, Reconstruction and the years immediately following it. Moreover, the reasons that motivated the lynchings were similar for the two groups—acting "uppity," taking away jobs, making advances toward a white woman, cheating at cards, practicing "witchcraft," and refusing

to leave land that Anglos coveted—with one exception. Mexicans were lynched for acting "too Mexican"—speaking Spanish too loudly or reminding Anglos too defiantly of their Mexicanness. Even Mexican women, often belonging to lower economic classes, were lynched, often for sexual offenses such as resisting an Anglo's advances too forcefully.

Lest one think that physical brutality and harassment of Latinos ended with Reconstruction and the years immediately following it, a similar but less deadly form of violence took place during World War II, when U.S. servicemen in Los Angeles attacked young Mexican American men who loitered on street corners wearing distinctive "Zoot suits," gold watch chains, and slicked-back hair. Although the violence amounted to beatings, forcible undressings, and other forms of nonlethal humiliation, the attacks went on for several days without official intervention. As with the earlier wave of lynching, the World War II–era attacks targeted Mexican youths who displayed their identity too proudly and openly. The numbers of African Americans lynched during the period in question were, of course, higher—around 3400 to 5000. But the Latino group in the United States was much smaller then (and the Mexican American group smaller still), so that the rate of lynching for the two groups was similar. As with blacks, Latino lynching went on with the knowledge and, in some cases, active participation of Anglo law enforcement authorities, especially the Texas Rangers, some of whom seemed to harbor a special animus toward persons of Mexican descent. (Richard Delgado, "The Law of the Noose: A History of Latino Lynching," *Harvard Civil Rights–Civil Liberties Law Review* 44 [2009]: 299–300)

Drawing on insights from Américo Paredes's novel *With His Pistol in His Hand* (Austin: University of Texas Press, 1958), Lisa Marie Cacho makes a compelling observation about such rhetorical inversions. Historically, she writes, "the white man 'projected' his own actions onto racialized others.... A pro–[Proposition] 187 activist was quoted in the *Los Angeles Times* as saying, 'I have no intention of being the object of "conquest," peaceful or otherwise, by Latinos, Asians, blacks, Arabs or any other group of individuals who have claimed my country.' Historically, the United States has 'conquered' other racialized groups, yet [this activist] inverted the victim-perpetrator relationship, claiming that she was in danger of being 'conquered by people of color'": Lisa Marie Cacho ("'The People of California' Are Suffering': The Ideology of White Injury in the Discourse of Immigration." *Cultural Values* 4 (2000): 396.

Johnson and Ingram likewise list characteristics that Ramirez's murder shares with past lynchings. They write:

The episode surrounding the killing of Luis Ramirez sounds eerily reminiscent of the violence directed at African Americans in the South during the height of Jim Crow. During that era, violence was used to maintain the subordination of Blacks, and sympathetic state court juries refused to punish the white perpetrators of the violence. Local police sought to protect the white perpetrators of brutality. The similarities do not end there. The federal civil rights prosecution brought by the U.S. government resembled the prosecutions brought to combat violence against African Americans and civil rights workers in the South in the 1950s and 1960s. The aim was to remedy the problem of all-white juries reflexively acquitting white defendants accused of violence in state courts. Nor does it appear to be mere coincidence that the tragic killing of Luis Ramirez came at a time of a prolonged, heated national debate over immigration—and a rapid proliferation of state and local immigration enforcement legislation passed after considerable acrimony in the region as well as the nation. National agitation about immigration, and frequent allegations about the destruction of U.S. society by immigrants, including in nearby Hazleton, almost unquestionably influenced the young men who told Luis Ramirez to "go back to Mexico" before kicking him to death. (Johnson and Ingram, "Anatomy of a Modern-Day Lynching," 1634–1635)

58. The mobilization I describe in this section bears many similarities to the sociolegal scholar Jeffery Dudas's study of Native American treaty rights. He argues that "special rights" politics "[inflate] the resentment that activists feel" so that they perceive "their efforts as defenses not only of their own interests but also of the equal rights of all Americans." This has the effect, he adds, of making otherwise local claims "intelligible to a wider audience," expanding "the "scope of the conflict" to include new actors": Jeffery Dudas, *The Cultivation of Resentment: Treaty Rights and the New Right* (Stanford, CA: Stanford University Press, 2008), 3.

59. To the dismay of the group's founder, the Southern Poverty Law Center designated ALIPAC a "hate group" in 2014: see http://www.alipac.us/f8/open-letter-southern-poverty-law-center-william-gheen-301890, accessed August 4, 2015. The group attracted attention recently when its president issued a call on an online message board for Americans to send "used underwear" to detained undocumented immigrants: see, e.g., Esther Yu-Hsi Lee, "Group Asks Americans to Send Dirty Underwear to Undocumented Immigrants" *Think Progress*, June 26, 2014, available at http://thinkprogress.org/immigration/2014/06/26/3453174/alipac-dirty-underwear-to-undocumented, accessed August 4, 2015.

60. Others evoked the theme of "immigrants as agents of contagion," as well. One activist attributed the spread of the H1N1 virus, which many commonly referred to as "swine flu" when it was spreading in 2009, to Mexican immigrants, calling it "Mexican pig flu."

61. I quote the text of this sign and others exactly as they appeared at videotaped rallies. Factcheck.org traced the source of a widely circulated chain e-mail that included this exact claim, finding it "more bogus than believable." The figure, the report notes, appears to be linked to a transcript from an episode of *Lou Dobbs Tonight* that aired on October 29, 2006. In the episode, Robert Rector of the conservative Heritage Foundation stated, "Well, assuming that we have about 11 million immigrants in the U.S., the net cost or the total cost of services and benefits provided to them, education, welfare, general social services would be about $90 billion a year, and they would pay very little in taxes. It's important to remember that at least half of illegal immigrants are high school dropouts": see http://www.factcheck.org/2009/04/cost-of-illegal-immigrants, accessed December 21, 2014.

62. The Southern Poverty Law Center reported on the faulty assumptions underlying an estimate that undocumented immigrants commit 2,200 homicides per year in the United States. The figure was reported from a crude estimate made by Mack Johnson, a contributor to *Human Events*, a publication that describes itself as "the nation's

leading conservative voice since [it was] established in 1944": see http://humanevents
.com/about-human-events, accessed August 3, 2015. Johnson's estimate was over-inflated because he based it on the faulty assumption that undocumented immigrants would commit homicide at the same rates in the United States as in their country of origin. A protestor held this particular sign at a 2008 rally, implying that the statistic was (approximately) from the period of 2001 to 2008. Thus, it suggested that undocumented immigrants commit about 6,000 homicides per year against U.S. citizens (i.e., 48,000 divided by 8). This represents *almost three times as many homicides as Johnson's already inflated estimate*: see Sonia Scherr, "Fox Uses Dubious Stats to Demonize Undocumented Immigrants," *Hatewatch*, May 6, 2010, available at http://www.splcenter .org/blog/2010/05/06/fox-uses-dubious-murder-stats-to-demonize-undocumented-immigrants, accessed December 22, 2014.

63. This and other videos are on file with the author.

64. Compare Dudas, who notes how staunch opposition to "special rights" leads activists to develop a "counter-subversive mentality": Dudas, *The Cultivation of Resentment*, 10.

65. I should point out participants did not entirely ignore Latina/o victimization at these rallies. However, consistent with broader patterns, its acknowledgment seemed to be contingent on whether a particular case aligned with the views advocated at the rally. For example, in a speech one activist demanded justice for the killing of two Latino border patrol agents. Compare this with the discussion of "Rightwing Affirmative Action" in Haney López, *Dog Whistle Politics*, 137–145.

66. Tracie Mauriello, "Rally Backs Hazleton Mayor," *Pittsburg Post-Gazette,* June 3, 2007. To be sure, as with any social movement, there were internal disagreements on many of these issues. Here, for example, one activist I spoke with emphasized that a public apology for what happened to Arroyo was issued. The same is true on the issue of hate groups attending VOP rallies. Some participants took no issue with this, brushing their presence aside as insignificant. Others, however, were intentional about creating distance from such groups. Regardless, I should emphasize again that my focus is not on individual actors or particular organizational beliefs but on broader narratives and specific rhetorical patterns.

67. What is more, when Ramirez's grieving fiancée showed up at the rally with two other women, holding a Mexican flag, the crowd shouted nativist and sexist taunts at and about her: "Why did she come here to try to wreck everything?"; "She's a criminal. She committed a crime!"; "Why don't you go to Mexico if it's so good?"; "Why don't you spread your legs for another Mexican?" The crowd then chanted that she, too, should "go home!"

68. These developments are all according to an activist I interviewed.

69. For a review and analysis of the doctrinal implications of *Lozano* and other legal decisions involving state and local legislation, see Juliet P. Stumpf, "States of Confusion: The Rise of State and Local Power Over Immigration" *North Carolina Law Review* 86 (2008): 1557–1618.

70. This term is from Ian Haney López, who writes, "Colorblindness is a form of racial jujitsu. It co-opts the moral force of the civil rights movement, deploying that power to attack racial remediation and simultaneously defend embedded racism. It defends racial injustice directly, for instance by insisting that massive racial disparities are not racism. It also does so indirectly, and perhaps ultimately more powerfully, by providing cover for racial stereotypes expressed in cultural and behavioral terms, for

example through the imagery of minorities as criminals": Ian Haney López, "Post-racial Racism: Racial Stratification and Mass Incarceration in the Age of Obama," *California Law Review* 98, no. 3 (2010): 1064.

71. Goldberg-Hiller and Milner, "Rights as Excess," 1079. Indeed, it is a common historical occurrence for the majority to assert itself most forcefully in moments when resistance against racism is elevated: see, e.g., Michael J. Klarman, "How *Brown* Changed Race Relations: The Backlash Thesis," *Journal of American History* 81, no. 1 (1994): 81–118.

72. As Michael McCann writes, "In this view, legal discourses, logics, and language—the raw material processed by legal consciousness—may not rigidly determine what subjects think, but they do shape the capacity for understanding social reality, imagining options, and choosing among them": Michael McCann, "On Legal Rights Consciousness: A Challenging Analytical Tradition," in *The New Civil Rights Research: A Constitutive Approach*, ed. Benjamin Fleury-Steiner and Laura Beth Nielsen (Burlington, UK: Ashgate, 2006), xiv. See also, generally, Benjamin Fleury-Steiner and Laura Beth Nielsen, *The New Civil Rights Research: A Constitutive Approach* (Burlington, UK: Ashgate), 2006.

CHAPTER 4

1. Sergio and Juan are pseudonyms.

2. This quote is from a CPH brochure advertising the first anniversary celebration. The brochure is on file with the author.

3. Unless noted otherwise, quotes in this chapter are from interviews or participant observations I conducted with members of CPH. With the exception of some bracketed words or phrases inserted for clarification, all quotes appear in their original form and may therefore include grammatical errors.

4. According to the program distributed at the first anniversary celebration, truancy rates have gone down since CPH began working in the schools. The program is on file with the author.

5. At the time of the first anniversary celebration (June 7, 2009), according to the event program, "every Friday 12 parents from the community receive computer literacy courses in the office."

6. For more on the accomplishments of CPH and its predecessor, the Hazleton Integration Project, see Chris Echegaray and Susan Eaton, "We Are from Hazleton: A Baseball Celebrity Helps Bring His Divided Pennsylvania Hometown Together," *One Nation Indivisible*, 2013, available at http://www.onenationindivisible.org/wp-content/uploads/2013/06/ONIstoryNo.10-hazelton_Final.pdf, accessed May 26, 2014.

7. In the second half of the chapter, I also draw on newspaper reports.

8. See, e.g., Fredrick C. Harris, *The Price of the Ticket: Barack Obama and the Rise and Decline of Black Politics* (New York: Oxford University Press, 2012), 100–136.

9. Amanda Christman, "Guardian Angels May Land Here" *Standard-Speaker*, June 16, 2008; Amanda Christman, "Hazleton May Soon Have Guardian Angels Watching," *Standard-Speaker*, June 22, 2008.

10. One of my interviewees discussed how the group, at the time it was first emerging, had an internal debate around this question and struggled "to come to a conclusion." Some were interested in approaching the mayor for support in developing a community

group and to increase communication between city officials and recent immigrants. Others, including this particular activist, were hesitant to do so, feeling that Mayor Barletta "needs to know what the community thinks." Those who took this position felt that if they approached the mayor, the "first thing [they] should say is that we disagree with him" and preferred turning to the community first and then presenting the community's sentiments to Barletta. In short, it is important to keep in mind that, as is typically the case, there are within-group variations in terms of preference for particular strategies.

Regardless of whether what I describe in the chapter is the result of strategic messaging or activists' actual attitudes, however, I want to be clear that my primary goal is to explore activists' rhetoric and actions *as they relate* to the prevailing discourse to illustrate the power of dominant narratives. Consistent with earlier chapters, I have no interest here in scrutinizing the sentiments or attitudes of individuals or of organizations. I instead aim my critique at the political climate and the field of possibilities it offers those who are working for social justice. From this perspective, if activists consciously agree not to talk about race as a way to make the best of this social and political climate, this is an indication that the prevailing narrative is exerting its power by pushing them into a particular discursive zone. If, however, this is not strategy and activists believe in the appropriateness of "post-racial" rhetoric, then that, too, points to the hegemonic power of color-blindness.

I also want to point out that I am cognizant of making this argument from a position of privilege as a White scholar. Accordingly, I want to be clear that my intent is especially not to criticize activists of color who opted for an approach that has limitations. I realize that for many, these decisions (which, as a White person, I am not forced to make) are a question of survival—especially in a climate of hostility—and that, in addition to appreciating the progress that has been made, we can also understand decision making of this sort as an exhibition of agency. What I am critical of is the *existence of such limitations*. My larger goal is to expose them, to chart them, and to get us thinking about ways to get around them.

11. Ian Haney López, *Dog Whistle Politics: How Coded Racial Appeals Have Reinvented Racism and Wrecked the Middle Class* (New York: Oxford University Press, 2014), 196–197.

12. Compare, e.g., Dana Cloud, "Hegemony or Concordance? The Rhetoric of Tokenism in 'Oprah' Winfrey's Rags-to-Riches Biography," *Critical Studies in Mass Communication* 13, no. 2 (1996): 115–137.

13. An observation I made from my interview data is that, at times, these activists would use phrases such as "immigrants" or "newcomers" to draw attention to the specific problems Latina/o immigrants in Hazleton confront, only to quickly retract those words and replace them later in their dialogue with more generic terms, such as "community." At other times, I noticed interviewees following race-cognizant assertions with defensive statements (e.g., "What our group says all the time is we don't want special attention; we don't want special consideration"). Ian Haney López refers to this as "post-racialism." He presents a comparable example in his analysis of how President Barack Obama has discussed issues of race. He writes, "To avoid . . . imbroglios, [President Obama] adopts a post-racial strategy of avoiding race insofar as possible, and of quickly denying the salience of race on those few occasions when either race cannot be avoided or he slips and inadvertently ventures into the forbidden zone": Haney López, *Dog Whistle Politics*, 196–197.

14. Leo Chavez, *The Latino Threat: Constructing Immigrants, Citizens, and the Nation* (Stanford, CA: Stanford University Press, 2008), 2.

15. To be clear, I am making a distinction here between the actual reduction of crime and the political contestation of immigrant criminalization.

16. See Mychal Denzel Smith, "Three Ways to Fight Racism in 2014," *The Nation*, January 3, 2014, available at http://www.thenation.com/blog/177772/three-ways-fight-racism-2014, accessed December 22, 2014. Smith's full comment, in which he calls for "putting respectability politics on the shelf where they belong," reads as follows:

> At the ugliest times, the politics of respectability—the idea that individuals can defeat systems of oppression by modifying their behavior and/or presentation to be more "acceptable" or "deserving"—reared its head and diverted our attention from real people's pain and suffering. Children were being shot dead in the streets, and we were debating whether their pants sagged too low. Their schools were being closed, and we talked about whether they had good father figures in their home. They were stopped, frisked and beaten by police, and we somehow managed to chastise them for littering. This is the current state of discussion about racism: one that places the onus on those who are oppressed to comport themselves according to the rules that oppress them rather than eliminating the system. The problem is that there is no escape. You can do everything "right," obey all of the rules, be exemplary in every way, and racism still does its work. Respectability politics are not rooted in fact or reality, only in a false notion of individualism that upholds structural oppression.

17. See, e.g., Chris Hine, "Joe Maddon Crusades to Save His Hometown," *Chicago Tribune*, February 6, 2015, available at http://www.chicagotribune.com/sports/baseball/cubs/ct-joe-maddon-hazleton-cubs-spt-0208-20150207-story.html#page=1, accessed August 13, 2015.

18. While I was in the field, multiple people told me about instances in which as bilinguals they confronted backlash for speaking Spanish in public.

19. When asked about CPH, one pro-IIRA activist responded:

> It's Hispanic [Parent Teacher Association] PTA, that's what it is. . . . I think anybody in this country and here legally needs to support the other people who are here legally, and anybody who comes illegally, they need to be shut out. No services, no help, no funding, no nothing. And if you have Hispanic legal citizens or legal immigrants who are here, why are they supporting the people who are of the same ethnic background who are doing things that are wrong and criminal? They need to stop supporting the bad people who are coming here just to suck off the system and to cause a ruckus. They need to support American citizens like the rest of us, and then maybe they will be bridging some gaps. They are so worried about their ethnicity. They are not worried about being American.

Another pro-IIRA activist, when asked about CPH's strategy to "bridge the gap," responded:

> If you are illegal, there is no gap. You don't belong in this country, period. What gap is there? If you are a legal citizen, no problem. First of all, our schools are

overrun. Our kids don't get the right education because of it. The PSSA [Pennsylvania System of School Assessment] scores are so low that the state might step in next year and take over the school. Well, [it] wasn't like that when I went to school. Yeah, you had maybe a Latino, a Hispanic. So what? One or two. But you didn't have the school overrun.

You can't put a Band-Aid on a problem that needs stitches, if you know what I'm saying. If these people are illegal, there is no gap. You want to come to the United States of America? You want to be part of our society? You need to adapt to our society, not us to your society. End of story. . . . They are not even illegal; they are invaders. They are invading our country. They have no right here, [and] they need to get out. You will see our economy pick back up because we ain't spending trillions and trillions and trillions of dollars on them. It will be spent on the American people, and the American people will go back and start buying again.

20. As this book goes to press, Maddon is the manager of the Chicago Cubs.

21. Jill Whalen, "Maddon 'HIP' to Change in Hazleton," *Standard-Speaker*, September 20, 2011.

22. ESPN, "Joe Maddon's Hazleton," *Outside the Lines*, February 19, 2012 (video available at http://vimeo.com/38722340, accessed June 17, 2014); transcript available at http://tv.ark.com/transcript/outside_the_lines/3366/ESPN/Sunday_February_19_2012/599213, accessed December 22, 2014).

23. Whalen, "Maddon 'HIP' to Change in Hazleton."

24. Echegaray and Eaton, "We Are from Hazleton," 1.

25. Ibid.

26. Echegaray and Eaton, "We Are from Hazleton," 2.

27. Since the formation of HIP, CPH has retained its own identity. For example, the organization maintains an office at the Hazleton One Community Center. Yet for the most part, my understanding is that the two groups are inextricably linked.

28. For example, a local news report described the 2012 event this way:

An air of excitement filled the Lincoln Ballroom on Friday as Genetti Best Western Inn & Suites hosted Tampa Bay Rays Manager Joe Maddon and a group of Major League Baseball players and sports personalities for a celebrity dinner and sports memorabilia auction for charity. Maddon, a Hazleton native, brought the stars to the Hazle Township venue for the event, which will benefit his Hazleton Integration Project.

More than 600 people paid $50 per ticket to have dinner with . . . sports personalities and bid on memorabilia that included autographed jerseys from MLB stars. . . . Before dinner, guests had the opportunity to meet the stars, talk with them, get autographs and pose for photos. (Mia Light, "Stars Come Out to Support Maddon Effort," *Standard-Speaker*, December 15, 2012)

29. For example, the group received $450,000 from the city's share of the state's gambling proceeds to be used toward establishing the community center: see Kent Jackson, "Gambling Pay Off: Hazleton-Area Projects get $2M in Gaming Proceeds," *Standard-Speaker*, March 21, 2013. On its website as of December 2014, HIP listed as "partners" the Cal Ripken Sr. Foundation, the Tampa Bay Rays, the STAR Alliance, the Creative

Coalition, and WWE: see http://www.hazletonintegrationproject.com/about/partners, accessed December 22, 2014.

30. See Jill Whalen, "Community Center Has a Lot to Offer," *Standard-Speaker*, June 16, 2013.

31. See http://www.hazletonintegrationproject.com/about/mission, accessed December 22, 2014.

32. Echegaray and Eaton, "We Are from Hazleton," 3.

33. To be sure, this term has a number of meanings and applications. What I offer here is an analysis of a particular version of multiculturalism that is not necessarily applicable to all practices that use such terminology.

34. Mia Light, "Maddon's Vision for Community Center Is Now a Reality," *Standard-Speaker*, June 18, 2013.

35. ESPN, "Joe Maddon's Hazleton."

36. Light, "Maddon's Vision for Community Center Is Now a Reality."

37. Mia Light, "Stars Out for Fundraiser," *Standard-Speaker*, December 17, 2011.

38. Ibid.

39. As is obviously implied by the name, a focus on children is also central to CPH's approach.

40. Light, "Maddon's Vision for Community Center Is Now a Reality."

41. To reemphasize, many original members of CPH remained in the mix as HIP formed. Thus, while we can understand HIP as a new initiative with a fresh approach on one hand, one might also think of it as an "updated" version of CPH, on the other.

42. To cite just a couple of examples of Maddon's local popularity: When his Rays faced the local Philadelphia Phillies in the 2008 World Series, Rays fan displays seemed equally if not more prevalent throughout the city. Hazleton's high school baseball field also bears Maddon's name.

43. See, e.g., "For Joe Maddon, It All Started at Home," *Chicago Sun Times*, December 8, 2014, available at http://chicagosuntimes.com/sports/for-joe-maddon-it-all-started-at-home, accessed December 22, 2014. As another example, when the Chicago Cubs introduced him as their new manager, Maddon ended his press conference by offering to buy a round of drinks for all in attendance. After putting the microphone down, he picked it back up again to specify, "That's a shot *and* a beer. That's the Hazleton way": see https://www.youtube.com/watch?v=kn0QfA4f9cM, accessed December 22, 2014.

44. One example of this is the overwhelming popularity of the annual fundraising event. As a HIP executive said, "If we had 1,000 tickets available we could have sold 1,000. . . . Part of the reason is because of the celebrities that are here, and the other part is the number of people who stand behind the cause": quoted in Light, "Stars Out for Fundraiser."

45. To give another example, in addition to the opening of the community center, HIP recently hosted a "Unity Walk." An advertisement for the event read, "The Board of Directors of the Hazleton Integration Project will hold the first Unity Walk . . . 'Walk as One.' The purpose of the 1.1 mile walk that begins and ends at The Hazleton One Community Center, is to gather as many people together as possible to display their solidarity with the idea that Hazleton will be a stronger community when everyone works together. We are inviting individuals, families, corporate and business participation. Tee Shirts will be available for sale through preorder in advance of the walk":

see http://hazletonpacoc.weblinkconnect.com/events/eventdetail.aspx?EventID=88, accessed March 3, 2014.

46. The sports journalist Dave Zirin has written extensively about this issue: see, e.g., Dave Zirin, *Welcome to the Terrordome: The Pain, Politics, and Promise of Sports* (Chicago: Haymarket, 2007).

47. Cloud, "Hegemony or Concordance?" 116.

48. The same point I made about CPH regarding strategizing holds true for HIP. I am not at all suggesting that the group is naive. In fact, there are plenty of reasons to believe that here, too, these are well-thought-out, strategic initiatives carried forward by a group that is trying to make do with the circumstances they confront. Again, however, the extent to which these actions are strategic is not my concern; my intent is to shed light on the power of prevailing narratives by documenting how they limit what is discursively and politically possible.

49. Judith Goode, "Let's Get Our Act Together: How Racial Discourses Disrupt Neighborhood Activism," in *The New Poverty Studies: The Ethnography of Power, Politics, and Impoverished People in the United States*, ed. Judith Goode and Jeff Maskovsky (New York: New York University Press, 2001), 376.

In fieldwork observations of similar multicultural programs, Goode elaborates:

> [An administrator] often stated unlimited faith in such folklore-based programs to solve local problems: "People will eat each other's food and enjoy each other's culture and tensions will melt away. They will know how to understand each other." Soon initiatives titled "Hands across X" and "Building Bridges in Y" dotted the neighborhood landscape. Avoiding race and power, such festivals limited culture to aesthetic domains. They avoided confronting those cultural stereotypes connected to moral conflict zones of family structures and work ethics. Demonstrating the desire for consuming exotic commodities, one workshop sponsor urged the audience to approach multicultural situations "as if you are going into a museum looking for treasures." Another spoke of "the adrenalin rush I get when I hear other languages on the street and see the crafts in store windows." (ibid.)

Goode continues by offering a critique of these programs: "These remedies totally ignored (1) the material structures of inequality produced by late capitalism; (2) the ideological structures of institutionalized racism, which conflate race and class; and (3) the contradictions between the ideology of white privilege/superiority and the poverty and downward mobility of poor whites."

50. Ibid., 374–375.

51. Eduardo Bonilla-Silva, *Racism without Racists: Color-Blind Racism and the Persistence of Racial Inequality in America* (Lanham, MD: Rowman and Littlefield, 2006), 28.

52. Ibid. Bonilla-Silva notes that *naturalization* is a common frame in contemporary racial discourse:

> *Naturalization* is a frame that allows whites to explain away racial phenomena by suggesting they are natural occurrences. For example, whites can claim "segregation" is natural because people from all backgrounds "gravitate toward likeness." Or that their taste for whiteness in friends and partners is just "the way things are." Although the above statements can be interpreted as "racist"

and as contradicting the colorblind logic, they are actually used to reinforce the myth of nonracialism. How? By suggesting these preferences are almost biologically driven and typical of all groups in society, preferences for primary associations with members of one's race are rationalized as nonracial because "*they* (racial minorities) do it too."

53. Charles M. Payne, "'The Whole United States Is Southern!' *Brown v. Board* and the Mystification of Race," *Journal of American History* 91, no. 3 (2004): 87. Payne's discussion of the legacy of the "Confederate Paradigm" is also relevant to the concepts of innocence and abstraction discussed in Chapter 3 and to the notion of the ideology of white injury: "Southern elites have always preferred discussions about race in which they are presented as the aggrieved party, whether that means bearing the burden of having to civilize and support blacks in the 19th century or having to put up with reverse discrimination in the 20th. The states' rights argument is another version of this. When he stood in the schoolhouse door, George Wallace was trying to frame the issue in terms of his rights being trampled by central authority, not in terms of his doing anything to black people."

54. See, e.g., Joe R. Feagin, *Racist America: Roots, Current Realities, and Future Reparations* (New York: Routledge, 2010).

55. In addition to those listed, Latinas/os in the United States continue to suffer from inequality in various other institutional realms. To name a few, the rate of Latina/o unemployment is consistently higher than the rate of White unemployment, the criminal justice system disproportionately incarcerates Latina/os, and Latinas/os "receive lower-quality health care, suffer worse health outcomes, and have higher rates of certain illnesses": see Vanessa Cárdenas and Sophia Kerby, "The State of Latinos" in the United States," Center for American Progress, August 8, 2012, available at https://www.americanprogress.org/issues/race/report/2012/08/08/11984/the-state-of-latinos-in-the-united-states, accessed May 26, 2014.

56. See, e.g., Victor Rios, *Punished: Policing the Lives of Black and Latino Boys* (New York: New York University Press, 2011).

57. See, e.g., Patricia Gándara and Frances Contreras, *The Latino Education Crisis: The Consequences of Failed Social Policies* (Cambridge, MA: Harvard University Press, 2009). The authors point out that "low-income and minority students are less likely to gain access to college preparatory, honors, and Advanced Placement classes than other students, and they are more likely than nonminority students to be placed in the low, non-college-bound track, independent of the actual academic achievement": ibid., 31.

58. I received this information from an informant who is active in political circles and describes himself as "very familiar" with Hazleton politics. Again, this is not to say that activists are unaware of these disparities. Indeed, many who have worked with CPH and HIP have made *significant* efforts to get a Latino candidate elected and I have observed that they are very conscientious of the importance of doing so. The problem I am describing is therefore not their lack of motivation or unawareness but *the challenge of articulating such concerns in this ideological context.*

59. I received the numbers about teachers from a Freedom of Information Act request on September 18, 2013. Regarding students, in 2006, according to the Joint Urban Studies Center, 10 percent of the students enrolled at Hazleton Area High School identified as Hispanic. By 2012, that number had increased to 36 percent and many I have spoken with suspect that these numbers continue to grow: see http://www.public

schoolreview.com/school_ov/school_id/69441. To offer a comparison point, nationally in 2011–2012, 8 percent of public school teachers and 5 percent of private school teachers identified as Hispanic (compared with about 16 percent of the total U.S. population): see "Characteristics of Public and Private Elementary and Secondary School Teachers in the United States: Results from the 2011–2012 Schools and Staffing Survey," National Center for Education Statistics, 2013, available at http://nces.ed.gov/pubs2013/2013314 .pdf, accessed March 18, 2015.

I should also note again that CPH members in particular are intimately familiar with this; indeed, this seems to be part of what motivated them to get involved with the local schools in the first place. The challenge, however, lies in getting specific problems like this into the public discourse.

60. Author's ethnographic field notes. To paint a fuller picture of the event, I should note that, like members of CPH, there were other local elites who were wearing formal attire.

61. Author's ethnographic field notes, June 2009.

62. See Kent Jackson, "Tensions Fading as Law Plods through Courts," *Standard-Speaker* February 3, 2013.

63. Light, "Stars Out for Fundraiser."

64. See http://barletta.house.gov/media-center/opinion-editorials/the-day-immigration-reform-died-roll-call. It is worth noting that despite the prevalence of national political rhetoric suggesting that the Obama administration has been particularly lenient with undocumented immigrants, the administration has overseen a record number of deportations, including approximately 240,000 classified as noncriminal and 198,000 classified as criminal in fiscal year 2013: see Ana Gonzalez-Barrera and Jens Manuel Krogstad, "U.S. Deportations of Immigrants Reach Record High in 2013," Pew Research Center, October 2, 2014, available at http://www.pewresearch.org/fact-tank/2014/10/02/u-s-deportations-of-immigrants-reach-record-high-in-2013, accessed March 4, 2015.

65. The full quote is "Let's not take on any more water on this sinking ship. Let's patch the holes. Then we'll decide what do we do with all this water that's here": Trip Gabriel, "New Attitude on Immigration Skips an Old Coal Town," *New York Times,* March 31, 2013. Again, for more on the pervasive and problematic nature of the "IMMIGRATION AS DANGEROUS WATERS" metaphor, see Otto Santa Ana, *Brown Tide Rising: Metaphors of Latinos in Contemporary American Public Discourse* (Austin: University of Texas Press, 2002), 72–73.

66. "Every year, the anti-immigrant group FAIR holds an event called 'Hold Their Feet to the Fire,' which invites radio hosts to broadcast from Washington, DC, and interview lawmakers and conservative activists": see Miranda Blue, "Rep. Lou Barletta Says There's Nothing More Dangerous Than Immigration Reform, Ties It to 9/11," April 10, 2014, available at http://www.rightwingwatch.org/content/rep-lou-barletta-says-theres-nothing-more-dangerous-immigration-reform-ties-it-911, accessed December 22, 2014.

Here is the full exchange between Lou Barletta and Secure Freedom Radio's Frank Gaffney:

GAFFNEY: To the extent that the president is, at best, selectively enforcing the law and in some cases rewriting the law or ignoring it altogether, do you agree with those who describe this as a constitutional crisis?

BARLETTA: Oh, there's no question about it. This has been a slippery slope that this administration has taken, that the president has taken, walking over the Constitution and taking us down a path that, quite frankly, I don't know if we've ever been this far down a road before, on a road to where we're now electing a dictator who will try to pick and choose what laws and challenging Congress to try to stop me. And there may not be anything more dangerous than what he's doing, to give amnesty to millions of people. We know for a fact that there are people who have come here illegally who want to harm America. (ibid.)

67. The full quote—which, importantly, followed a discussion of immigration—was "We have a president that's taken this to a new level. And it's put us in a real position where he's just absolutely ignoring the Constitution and ignoring the laws and ignoring the checks and balances. You know, the problem is, you know, what do you do for those that say impeach him for breaking the laws or bypassing the laws? You know, could that pass in the House? It probably could. Is the majority of the American people in favor of impeaching the president? I'm not sure." For analysis and audio, see Sean Sullivan, "GOP Congressman Says House 'Probably' Has Votes to Impeach Obama," *Washington Post*, July 17, 2014, available at http://www.washingtonpost.com/blogs/post-politics/wp/2014/06/17/gop-congressman-says-house-probably-has-votes-to-impeach-obama, accessed December 22, 2014.

68. See "U.S. Rep. Lou Barletta Unveils Bill Cutting Federal Funds for 'Sanctuary Cities,'" May 31, 2011, available at http://barletta.house.gov/media-center/press-releases/us-rep-lou-barletta-unveils-bill-cutting-federal-funds-for-sanctuary, accessed August 3, 2015.

As Barletta told another radio host, Lars Larson, at the Hold Their Feet to the Fire rally:

In the case of immigration—illegal immigration—you have mayors who declare themselves sanctuary cities, who are not going to enforce immigration laws. Nothing happens to them. We continue to send federal dollars to mayors who are above the law. And then you have a mayor, such as myself in Hazleton, who gets sued for wanting to enforce the laws. And there's something wrong with the direction this country's been going when we begin to reward people who want to tear down our laws and make us a Third World country where we get to pick and choose what we want to do. (Miranda Blue, "Rep. Lou Barletta: Sanctuary Cities Making U.S. 'A Third-World Country,'" available at http://www.rightwingwatch.org/content/rep-lou-barletta-sanctuary-cities-making-us-third-world-country, accessed December 22, 2014)

69. For a discussion of Hazleton's persistence in defending the IIRA, see Sam Galski, "Immigration Act Appeal Imminent," *Standard-Speaker*, August 29, 2013. More recently, the editorial board of the *Citizen's Voice* noted:

It's true that Barletta won himself three terms in Congress by capitalizing on national publicity for the city ordinance. . . . But while the former mayor is firmly ensconced in a seat now made safely Republican by redistricting, his constituents in Hazleton are facing a $2.3 million legal bill from the city's quixotic bid to enforce the unconstitutional ordinance through the federal courts. . . .

The possibility that Hazleton could be stuck with those fees was well-known throughout the legal campaign, but Barletta and his supporters waved off the consequences. . . . Perhaps the residents of Hazleton will have to consider that $2.3 million an involuntary contribution to his campaign war chest. ("An Expensive Lesson in Hazleton," *Citizen's Voice*, March 8, 2015)

For a discussion of the economic costs of the IIRA and similar legislation across the United States, see also American Civil Liberties Union, "Anti-immigrant Ordinances Have Real Economic and Political Costs for Cities That Enact Them, 2013, available at http://www.migrante.com.mx/pdf/antimig.pdf, accessed December 22, 2014.

70. ESPN, "Joe Maddon's Hazleton."

71. As has been the case throughout the book, my intent here, too, in considering these questions is not to speculate on the motives of individual politicians such as Congressman Barletta or Mayor Yanuzzi. My focus remains on narratives. Although political actors influence and are influenced by this context, what I am describing is ultimately not about individual perceptions or intent but rather an ideology that is woven into the cultural fabric of the United States.

I also acknowledge that White-Latina/o relations in Hazleton are still in their infancy. Whereas much of the book to this point has had an empirical basis, in this section I am drawing on prior theorizing and lessons from other contexts in order to discern the direction in which Hazleton may be heading with regard to issues of racial and economic inequality in light of what we have seen.

72. Derrick A. Bell Jr., "*Brown v. Board of Education* and the Interest-Convergence Dilemma," *Harvard Law Review* 93 (1980): 523.

73. Goode notes how some multicultural programs unsurprisingly repel working-class whites because instead of providing an explanation for downward economic mobility, they are "based on the assumption that once "processed" through a workshop, the individual's behaviors and attitudes will be transformed." Here, too, "rooting out the racism of poor and working-class whites appeals to state professionals because it displaces the responsibility for racism from institutions of power onto individuals and requires no structural change": Goode, "Let's Get Our Act Together," 385–386.

74. See, e.g., Mary L. Dudziak, "*Brown* as a Cold War Case," *Journal of American History* 91 (2004): 32–42.

75. Lester Spence, *Stare in the Darkness: The Limits of Hip-Hop and Black Politics* (Minneapolis: University of Minnesota Press, 2011), 15.

76. See, e.g., discussions of "tokenism" such as Cloud, "Hegemony or Concordance?" and historical studies of instances where previously subordinated immigrant groups embraced the opportunity to "become White" on the condition that they participate in the continued subordination of Blacks: Noel Ignatiev, *How the Irish Became White* (New York: Routledge, 1995). Some scholars have flagged the latter as a concern in the context of racial formations among Latinas/os in the United States: see e.g., Daniel A. Rochmes and G. A. Elmer Griffin, "The Cactus That Must Not Be Mistaken for a Pillow: White Racial Formation among Latinos," *Souls* 8, no. 2 (2006): 77–91.

77. Frederick C. Harris, "The Rise of Respectability Politics," Winter 2014, available at http://www.dissentmagazine.org/article/the-rise-of-respectability-politics, accessed March 4, 2015, accessed March 4, 2015.

78. Ibid.

79. Ibid. Cacho makes a similar point in her analysis of how the media constructs Black-Latina/o conflict. She writes about how stories of Latina/o immigrants who work hard and do not complain support neoliberalism in that "these stories erase the workings of global capital by exaggerating the importance of personal qualities such as ambition and motivation. In this narrative, Latina/o immigrants function as the 'model minority' of the working poor, putting family first, working hard, and doing whatever it takes to get ahead, while impoverished African American young men are depicted as wayward, unmotivated drifters waiting for the U.S. government to solve their problems or refusing to take advantage of the many opportunities available to them": Lisa Marie Cacho, *Social Death: Racialized Rightlessness and the Criminalization of the Unprotected* (New York: New York University Press, 2012), 133–134.

80. For example, the community center's kitchen has been named the "Giant" kitchen in order to acknowledge a gift from Giant Supermarkets: see http://www.hazleton integrationproject.com/news/53-giant-supermarket-helps-make-giant-kitchen-possible, accessed December 22, 2014.

81. See "Cargill Supports Hazleton Integration Project," *Standard-Speaker* March 8, 2014.

82. See, e.g., Mona Atia, "'A Way to Paradise': Pious Neoliberalism, Islam, and Faith-Based Development," *Annals of the Association of American Geographers* 102, no. 4 (2012): 808–827; Judith Goode, "Faith-Based Organizations in Philadelphia: Neoliberal Ideology and the Decline of Political Activism," *Urban Anthropology* 35, nos. 2–3 (2006): 203–236.

83. See "Cargill Supports Hazleton Integration Project."

84. For example, a "KOZ Sample Saving Analysis" posted on the CAN DO website informs potential firms that they can expect to save approximately $462,194 in their first year under KOZ: see http://hazletoncando.com/tax-free-koz, accessed April 8, 2015.

85. According to U.S. Bureau of Labor Statistics, Pennsylvania's average hourly meatpacking wage in 2014 was $13 per hour. According to the Massachusetts Institute of Technology's Living Wage Calculator, this is well below the amount "an individual must earn to support their family, if they are the sole provider and are working full time," unless the individual lives alone. The calculator estimates the wage required to support one adult and one child at $20.48: see http://livingwage.mit.edu/counties/42079, accessed August 3, 2015.

86. As a U.S. Bureau of Labor Statistics report issued in 2012 points out, 13.8 percent of Hispanics were considered "working poor," a figure that is "more than twice" the rate for Whites: see U.S. Bureau of Labor Statistics, "A Profile of the Working Poor, 2012," March 2014, available at http://www.bls.gov/cps/cpswp2012.pdf, accessed December 22, 2014.

87. I made this observation while in the field after hearing various firsthand and secondhand accounts.

88. Paul Kivel, "Social Service or Social Change? In *The Revolution Will Not Be Funded: Beyond the Non-profit Industrial Complex*, ed. Incite! Women of Color against Violence (Cambridge, MA: South End, 2007), 139. It is important to acknowledge, however, as Kivel does, that social service work is not a problem in and of itself. The problem, he explains, is when *social service work* consumes all of our energy to the detriment of *social change work*:

Social service work addresses the needs of individuals reeling from the personal and devastating impact of institutional systems of exploitation and violence. Social change work challenges the root causes of the exploitation and violence. . . . We need to provide services for those most in need, for those trying to survive, for those barely making it. We also need to work for social change so that we create a society in which our institutions and organizations are equitable and just, and all people are safe, adequately fed and sheltered, well educated, afforded safe and decent jobs, and empowered to participate in the decisions that affect their lives. (ibid., 129–130)

89. Ibid., 139.

90. See "Cargill Supports Hazleton Integration Project."

91. See, e.g., Brewster Kneen, *Invisible Giant: Cargill and Its Transnational Strategies*, 2d ed. (Sterling, VA: Pluto, 2002).

CONCLUSION

1. Ali Behdad, *A Forgetful Nation: On Immigration and Cultural Identity in the United States* (Durham, NC: Duke University Press, 2005), 172–173.

2. In the particular case I describe here, there is indeed a monument honoring the victims of the Lattimer Massacre, and there are groups that have worked hard to keep this event in the public memory: see, e.g., the Lattimer Archeology Project (https://lattimerarchaeology.wordpress.com) and the Lattimer Massacre Project (https://lattimermassacre.wordpress.com). What follows is by no means a criticism of their work; in fact, I have great appreciation for such efforts and see them as consistent with my argument, which is that *deep collective remembering* of this and similar events has the potential to transform community identities in ways that promote true democratic engagement.

3. I do not mean to suggest naively that an understanding of this particular event is the key to freedom or that only by reading history can we achieve liberation. Other histories—including similar stories from other locales—and other forms of engagement can and should help accomplish these ends, as well. But I do think that history—particularly revisionist history, told from the bottom up—happens to serve these purposes quite well. The Zinn Education Project is a great example of such work: see http://zinnedproject.org.

4. Stated differently, I am not retelling or rewriting this history as much as I am *repurposing* it. While I am attentive to historical facts throughout this recounting of the Lattimer Massacre (i.e., relying on credible historical sources), I do not try to engage with historical debates or make a new contribution by studying primary sources. The reason I chose to tell this particular story is that I think it enables those of us in the present to see our own circumstances through a new lens that is *otherwise not within the realm of accessible possibilities* in the de-democratized climate of color-blind neoliberalism. In this way, what I do here with history has similarities to how Lani Guinier and Gerald Torres use literature—specifically, "magical realism." The goal, they write, is to

infuse ordinary situations with an enchanted quality that distorts both physical and temporal reality. This allows the narrative to take paths that would ordinarily fall outside the range of acceptable accounts. . . . The reader sees previously familiar things in a completely new context. The change in context is critical, for it provides the foundation for radically different meanings. . . . By liberating the imagination, magical realists give voice to the possibilities of futures that are not held hostage to either the military juntas in power or the juntas' neoliberal defenders. (Lani Guinier and Gerald Torres, *The Miner's Canary: Enlisting Race, Resisting Power, Transforming Democracy* [Cambridge, MA: Harvard University Press, 2002], 22–23)

5. Paulo Freire defines prescriptive acts as "the imposition of one individual's choice upon another, transforming the consciousness of the person prescribed to into one that conforms with the prescriber's consciousness. Thus, the behavior of the oppressed is a prescribed behavior, following as it does the guidelines of the oppressor": Paulo Freire, *Pedagogy of the Oppressed* (New York: Continuum, 1989), 31.

6. Unless noted otherwise, throughout this section I paraphrase from Donald L. Miller and Richard E. Sharpless, *The Kingdom of Coal: Work, Enterprise, and Ethnic Communities in the Mine Fields* (Philadelphia: University of Pennsylvania Press, 1985), 213–240, and from Michael Novak, *The Guns of Lattimer* (New York: Basic, 1978).

7. Miller and Sharpless, *The Kingdom of Coal*, 221.

8. Novak, *The Guns of Lattimer*, 17.

9. Miller and Sharpless, *The Kingdom of Coal*, 221.

10. Ibid.

11. Novak, *The Guns of Lattimer*, 17–18.

12. See, e.g., Miller and Sharpless, *The Kingdom of Coal*, 221; Novak, *The Guns of Lattimer*, 18.

13. Novak, *The Guns of Lattimer*, 17.

14. Ibid., 17.

15. Ibid., 20.

16. Miller and Sharpless, *The Kingdom of Coal*, 222.

17. Novak, *The Guns of Lattimer*, 20.

18. Harold Aurand, "The Lattimer Massacre: Who Owns History?—An Introduction," *Pennsylvania History* 68, no. 1 (2002): 4. The Campbell Act was later ruled unconstitutional.

19. Miller and Sharpless, *Kingdom of Coal*, 222.

20. Quoted in ibid.

21. Ibid., 225. Miller and Sharpless explain in more depth:

A handful of powerful families dominated the Lehigh field. Clans such as the Markles, Coxes, Pardees, Van Wickles, and Fells owned not only mining companies but also railroads, land trusts, banks, lumber companies, powder and flour mills, ironworks, and retail establishments. They interlocked their holdings through memberships on boards of directors and convenient marriages, and they invested in each other's ventures. They built stately mansions and churches on Hazleton's highest hill, with a fine view of their surrounding collieries and mine patches. Politicians and local businessmen were in their debt; the clergy and teachers upheld their values. Thousands depended upon the soundness of their decisions for their livelihoods. They were lords of a small fiefdom they had made through their own enterprise. (ibid., 224–225)

22. Quoted in ibid., 225–226.

23. Ibid., 226–227; emphasis added.

24. Ibid., 227.

25. Ibid., 215. As Miller and Sharpless point out, other variations of this tactic included bribing striking workers to return to the mines and revoke their union membership with pay increases that were in actuality associated with a temporary rise in the cost of coal. Some families were evicted from their company-owned homes, company stores would deny many workers credit, folks who lead labor uprisings often found themselves fired or having their wages withheld, and promises about wages were often broken. Political efforts were undertaken as well. Strikers approached the U.S. House of Representatives in 1874, convincing them to investigate the tactics of the coal bosses. What the investigation uncovered was that they had in fact launched a "conspiracy against organized labor" by forming "a pool to regulate production and prices." Given the staunchly pro-business climate of the era, however, nothing was done to address what the committee found: ibid., 219.

26. Ibid., 218. As Miller and Sharpless explain in more detail, "Merchants in the anthracite towns and cities served as financial advisers on strike committees, contributed to relief funds, made their stores food distribution centers, and encouraged other individuals in their communities, including the clergy, to work on the strikers' behalf. Their efforts were based upon resentment that had developed over the years because of the domination of the economy by the independent operators": ibid., 217–218.

27. Ibid., 227.

28. Quoted in Perry K. Blatz, *Democratic Miners: Work and Labor Relations in the Anthracite Coal Industry, 1875–1952* (Albany: State University of New York Press, 1994), 137.

29. Miller and Sharpless, *The Kingdom of Coal*, 220.

30. Ibid. Fahy had also "secured an amendment of the Miner's Certificate Law of 1889 to require a candidate to answer at least twelve questions in English": Aurand, "The Lattimer Massacre," 6.

31. Fahy's quick organizing success is a testament to this. As Miller and Sharpless explain, "Fahy immediately began organizing local chapters. He decided to place each ethnic group in a separate chapter because of the somewhat different interests of each nationality and because of the prevailing settlement patterns in the mining patches. At the end of Thursday, August 19, Fahy had in one day formed six chapters representing six different ethnic groups, with a total of more than 800 members": Miller and Sharpless, *The Kingdom of Coal*, 223.

32. They now requested "a 15 per cent wage increase; the right to pay and select their own physician; the end to the company store system; and the same pay as 'Americans'": Aurand, "The Lattimer Massacre," 8.

33. Miller and Sharpless, *The Kingdom of Coal*, 224.

34. Quoted in Novak, *The Guns of Lattimer*, 69.

35. Miller and Sharpless, *The Kingdom of Coal*, 224.

36. Ibid., 229.

37. Miller and Sharpless write, "To form a posse [Martin] had to declare a state of disorder, which constituted a riot or threat to life or property": ibid.

38. Ibid.

39. Ibid.

40. Ibid., 228

41. Novak, *The Guns of Lattimer*, 112.

42. Miller and Sharpless, *The Kingdom of Coal*, 230.

43. Ibid., 231.

44. Ibid., 233.

45. Ibid.

46. Ibid., 234.

47. Ibid.

48. Novak, *The Guns of Lattimer*, 128.

49. Ibid., 128–129.

50. Miller and Sharpless, *The Kingdom of Coal*, 234.

51. Ibid.

52. George A. Turner, "The Lattimer Massacre: A Perspective from the Ethnic Community" *Pennsylvania History* 69, no. 1 (2002): 15.

53. See Kenneth C. Wolensky, "The Lattimer Massacre," Historic Pennsylvania Leaflet no. 15, Pennsylvania Historical and Museum Commission, Harrisburg, 1997, available at http://www.portal.state.pa.us/portal/server.pt/community/events/4279/lat timer_massacre/478735, accessed March 4, 2015.

54. Miller and Sharpless, *The Kingdom of Coal*, 234. "Hunkies" is an ethnic slur commonly used at the time to describe people—usually workers—of Hungarian or Slavic decent.

55. After the massacre, there was a strong collective response that was mostly nonviolent (with the exception of a ransacking of Gomer Jones's home). Various immigrant groups mourned the tragedy in solidarity. Many elites went into hiding until it seemed they were no longer at risk. Later, the state charged Martin and his deputies with homicide. However, in a classic case of disparities in criminal prosecution, the local prosecutor charged them with the killing of a single protestor, making it nearly impossible to determine with certainty who had fired the particular shot that killed this particular man. Thus, all managed to escape justice. This by no means ended the conflict between labor and capital, however. There were subsequent strikes in the region, particularly the Great Strike of 1902, which led to the creation of the U.S. Department of Labor: see, e.g., Robert A. Janosov, Joseph P. McKerns, Lance E. Metz, Robert C. Wolensky, and Joseph M. Gowaskie, *The Great Strike: Perspectives on the 1902 Anthracite Coal Strike* (Easton, PA: Canal History and Technology Press, 2002).

56. *Hazleton Daily Standard*, September 17, 1897, reprinted in Novak, *The Guns of Lattimer*, viii–ix.

57. I should clarify that I see this as a powerful example of solidarity to the extent that it deliberately subverts divide-and-conquer arrangements. The multiethnic strikers in this story, albeit with some strife along the way, managed to dodge elites' efforts to tear them apart, standing strongly in solidarity as they made economic demands. I want to be clear about distinguishing this from the tendency to over-idealize past unity among European immigrants to the point where we overlook the realities of race and racism that characterize the current historical moment. Many of the groups who confronted racial/ethnic oppression in this story no longer do, having since "become White." As Charles Gallagher observes in his study of White university students, "Many . . . now

think about themselves as whites, not as ethnics; they see themselves as individuals who are members of a racial category with its own particular set of interests": Charles A. Gallagher, "White Racial Formation: Into the Twenty-First Century," in *Critical White Studies: Looking behind the Mirror*, ed. Richard Delgado and Jean Stefancic (Philadelphia: Temple University Press, 1997), 7. Yet at the same time, he continues,

> young whites selectively resurrect their ethnicity through "immigrant tales" mainly when they feel white privilege is being contested, even though their perceived ethnic history does not necessarily concern a specific nation but rather a generalized idea of a European origin. This common, yet fuzzy, connection to the "old country" provides the historical backdrop and cultural space for the construction of white identity. . . . Past group victimization or hardship is part of the American experience; young whites, when confronted by real or perceived charges of racism, can point to the mistreatment of their older relatives when they were newly arrived immigrants in the United States. (ibid., 8)

In other words, I am cautious of the tendency among Whites to read stories such as this as evidence that European immigrants once had it "just as bad" as current immigrant groups and therefore conclude that existing racial hierarchies are built on merit alone. It is thus important to supplement stories like the one I tell here with studies of the various privileges European immigrant groups went on to receive that historically have not been made available to immigrants of color: see, e.g., Cybelle Fox, *Three Worlds of Relief: Race, Immigration, and the American Welfare State from the Progressive Era to the New Deal* (Princeton, NJ: Princeton University Press, 2012). Consistent with my argument, doing so is actually beneficial to Whites in that it represents an authentic engagement with one's roots as opposed to settling for watered-down, co-opted versions of history that are used to construct difference.

58. See, e.g., Nicholas De Genova, "Migrant Illegality and Deplorability in Everyday Life." *Annual Review of Anthropology* 31 (2002): 419–447; Mae Ngai, *Impossible Subjects: Illegal Aliens and the Making of Modern America* (Princeton, NJ: Princeton University Press, 2004); Kevin R. Johnson, "'Aliens' and the U.S. Immigration Laws: The Social and Legal Construction of Nonpersons," *University of Miami Inter-American Law Review* 28 (1996): 263–292.

59. For several examples of this idea in action, see John Gaventa, Barbara Ellen Smith, and Alex Willingham, eds., *Communities in Economic Crisis: Appalachia and the South* (Philadelphia: Temple University Press, 1990).

60. As is evident in Chapter 1, it is important that such local resistance efforts link themselves to national and international movements.

61. Women were very active in the movement for fair treatment in the anthracite coal mines. Mary Septak, known as "Big Mary," was one such leader. She was all too aware of dangerous working conditions after one of her children was killed in a mining accident. She also keenly understood the importance of unity in building workers' strength. After the massacre, she led "a band of over two hundred women . . . across the minefields," a group the press dubbed "Hungarian Amazons": Novak, *The Guns of Lattimer*, 174–177. Mother Jones also became active in the anthracite region in subsequent years, trying to reinvigorate the strike in the face of the fear the massacre evoked: ibid., 50–51.

62. Paulo Freire writes about the importance of the oppressed leading movements for collective liberation:

This . . . is the great humanistic and historical task for the oppressed: to liberate themselves and their oppressors as well. The oppressors, who oppress, exploit, and rape by virtue of their power, cannot find in this power the strength to liberate either the oppressed or themselves. Only power that springs from the weakness of the oppressed will be sufficiently strong to free both. Any attempt to "soften" the power of the oppressor in deference to the weakness of the oppressed almost always manifests itself in the form of false generosity; indeed, the attempt never goes beyond this. (Freire, *Pedagogy of the Oppressed*, 44)

63. See, e.g., David Harvey, *A Brief History of Neoliberalism* (New York: Oxford University Press, 2005).

64. Leo R. Chavez, *The Latino Threat: Constructing Immigrants, Citizens, and the Nation* (Stanford, CA: Stanford University Press, 2008), 42.

65. Thomas Ross, "The Rhetorical Tapestry of Race: White Innocence and Black Abstraction," *William and Mary Law Review* 32, no. 1 (1990): 2. The full passage reads, "Rhetoric is a magical thing. It transforms things into their opposites. Difficult choices become obvious. Change becomes continuity. Real human suffering vanishes as we conjure up the specter of righteousness. Rhetoric becomes the smooth veneer to the cracked surface of the real and hard choices in law."

66. Fabio Dasilva and Jim Faught, "Nostalgia: A Sphere and Process of Contemporary Ideology," *Qualitative Sociology* 5, no. 1 (1982): 49. These scholars add that nostalgia, in this way, is "ironically, an ahistorical defense of the status quo." Richard Aden similarly notes how nostalgia at once provides people with a "sanctuary of meaning . . . where they feel safe from oppressive cultural conditions" and also "perpetuates the hegemonic forces from which individuals seek escape" by blurring the realities of the situation: Richard C. Aden, "Nostalgic Communication as Temporary Escape: *When It Was a Game*'s Reconstruction of a Baseball/Work Community," *Western Journal of Communication* 59, no. 1 (1995): 35–36.

67. David Roediger, *Toward the Abolition of Whiteness* (London: Verso, 1994), 13. john a. powell similarly notes that "the problematic and isolated white self forms the backbone of resistance to a truly robust, inclusive America." He writes that

this self is all too easily controlled by fears—in part because it was born of fear—whether of declining property values, the "predatory" black man, the other's "culture of poverty," or any of a range of similar racialized images. Beyond these distortions, however, lies a more fundamental fear: self-annihilation. For in the context of this society's unwillingness to come to terms with its racial organization, to ask people to give up whiteness is to ask them to give up their sense of self. We cannot expect people to expose themselves to ontological death or worse. Instead, we must provide space—institutional space, political space, social space, and conceptual space—for the emergence of new relationships and a new way of being that exists beyond isolation and separation. (john a. powell, *Racing to Justice: Transforming Our Conception of Self and Other to Build an Inclusive Society* [Bloomington: Indiana University Press, 2012], xvii—xviii)

68. For example, the Poverty Initiative at the Union Theological Seminary in New York implements "reality tours"—"activities in which leaders travel to historic sites as well as sites where significant organizing from within our movement has taken place—to study social movement history and reinforce shared values. These reality tours draw on at once multiple sense perceptions and the reflective capacities of people to think and feel": Willie Baptist and Jan Rehmann, *Pedagogy of the Poor: Building a Movement to End Poverty* (New York: Teachers College Press, 2011), 168.

Participatory Action Research (PAR) is another example of this. The Highlander Research and Education Center in Tennessee is one of many entities engaging in such work as it relates to both racial and economic justice: "Participatory Action Research . . . challenges the belief that only academics or trained professionals can produce accurate information, and instead recognizes information as POWER and puts that power in the hands of people seeking to overcome problems in their daily lives. PAR is a collective process of investigation, empowerment, and action. The people most affected by the problems, sometimes with the help of "experts," investigate and analyze the issues, and ultimately act together to bring about meaningful, long-term solutions": see http://highlandercenter.org/programs/methodologies/participatory-research, accessed March 2, 2015.

69. Richard Delgado and Jean Stefancic, *Critical Race Theory: An Introduction* (New York: New York University Press, 2012), 10.

70. Despite the lure of Whiteness's "psychological wage," researchers have found that Whites who can "approximate" their experiences—that is, understand the conditions under which they, too, are oppressed (e.g., social class, gender)—can begin to "empathize with the pain of racism" and therefore join the sort of efforts I describe: see Ellen O'Brien, *Whites Confront Racism: Antiracists and Their Paths to Action* (New York: Rowman and Littlefield, 2001), xxxvii. For a compelling history of how slave "self-emancipation" similarly inspired other oppressed groups to reimagine their social position, see David Roediger, *Seizing Freedom: Slave Emancipation and Liberty for All* (London: Verso, 2014). For recent examples, see Chris Crass, *Towards Collective Liberation: Antiracist Organizing, Feminist Praxis, and Movement Building Strategy* (Oakland, CA: PM Press, 2013), 197–213.

71. See, e.g., Sara M. Evans and Harry C. Boyte, *Free Spaces: The Sources of Democratic Change in America* (Chicago: University of Chicago Press, 1986).

72. Richard Shaull, "Foreword," in Freire, *Pedagogy of the Oppressed*, 15.

73. Behdad, *A Forgetful Nation*, 174.

74. Ibid.

APPENDIX A

1. Michael Burawoy, "The Extended Case Method," *Sociological Theory* 16, no. 1 (1998): 4–33.

2. Thomas Dublin and Walter Licht, *The Face of Decline: The Pennsylvania Anthracite Region in the Twentieth Century* (Ithaca, NY: Cornell University Press, 2005).

3. Catherine Welch, "The Archeology of Business Networks: The Use of Archival Records in Case Study Research," *Journal of Strategic Management* 8, no. 2 (2000): 197–208.

4. This application is housed within the Pennsylvania Department of Community and Economic Development in Harrisburg. I accessed it in December 2009.

5. I conducted these interviews between April 2008 and December 2009.

6. Stanley Cohen defined a moral panic as what happens when a "condition, episode, person or group of persons emerges to become defined as a threat to societal values and interests; its nature is presented in a stylized and stereotypical fashion by the mass media; the moral boundaries are manned by . . . right thinking people; socially accredited experts pronounce their diagnosis and solutions; ways of coping are evolved or (more often) resorted to; the condition disappears, submerges or deteriorates and becomes more visible": see Stanley Cohen, *Folk Devils and Moral Panics: The Creation of the Mods and Rockers* (London: MacGibbon and Kee, 1972).

7. For example, many later reports mention the Kichline case only briefly to point out that it catalyzed the IIRA. Later stages of reporting on the Calderon case tended to focus on legal proceedings as opposed to the reactions of public officials.

8. I discuss a second of these themes—the patterned dismissal of resistance—in Chapter 3. For an excellent comparative piece that uses these data, as well as testimony from the lawmaking bodies of other locales that considered similar measures, see Jill Esbenshade, Benjamin Wright, Paul Cortopassi, Arthur Reed, and Jerry Flores, "The 'Law-and-Order' Foundations of Local Ordinances: A Four-Locale Study of Hazleton, PA, Escondido, CA, Farmers Branch, TX, and Prince William County, VA," in *Taking Local Control: Immigration Policy Activism in U.S. Cities and States*, ed. Monica W. Varsanyi (Stanford, CA: Stanford University Press, 2008), 255–274.

9. I requested and obtained the *Lozano* trial transcripts from the court. They are on file with the author.

10. Conducting interviews and accessing archival sources were the primary purpose of many of my trips into the field. However, I also used many of these opportunities, including subsequent trips that occurred as recently as 2013, to take ethnographic field notes as I engaged in informal conversations and participated in and observed life in this setting: see, e.g., Robert M. Emerson, Rachel I. Fretz, and Linda L. Shaw, *Writing Ethnographic Fieldnotes*, 2d ed. (Chicago: University of Chicago Press, 2007).

I should note that at times having some familiarity with the workings of the city and the local culture allowed me to navigate my research site with relative ease. Yet on other occasions, it felt as if I was entering the field with a "blank slate." Having not lived in Hazleton for quite some time (I moved away in 2001), I encountered as an ethnographer a city that was very different from the one I had encountered as a resident. In addition, the research process drove me to ask questions about Hazleton I had never asked before.

11. Eleven ordinary people participated in formal, in-depth, semi-structured focus groups or interviews in December 2009. All such participants, whom I recruited using a combination of public advertisements, snowball sampling, and personal invitations offered at random in public places and over the phone, were longtime (mostly lifelong) White residents of the Hazleton area. There were six women and five men; their mean age was 43.4; and all were retired, unemployed, or in working-class occupations.

12. See, e.g., René D. Flores, "Living in the Eye of the Storm: How Did Hazleton's Restrictive Immigration Ordinance Affect Local Interethnic Relations?" *American Behavioral Scientist* 58, no. 13 (2014): 1743–1763; Zogby International, "Greater Hazleton Area Civic Partnership," 2007; *Lozano v. Hazleton*, trial transcripts.

13. Among activists opposed to the IIRA, I interviewed seven men and five women; nine of these activists identify as Latina/o, and three identify as White. Among activists

who support the IIRA, I interviewed eight men and four women; eleven of these activists identify as White, one as Latina.

14. Compare Kristin Luker, *Abortion and the Politics of Motherhood* (Berkeley: University of California Press, 1984).

15. See, e.g., Catherine Kohler Riessman, *Narrative Analysis* (Thousand Oaks, CA: Sage, 1993). Sociolegal scholars who study legal consciousness also influenced my data collection and analysis strategy. I asked participants to tell their stories with the intent of allowing them to evoke issues of race, class, law, and immigration on their own: see, e.g., Patricia Ewick and Susan S. Silbey, *The Common Place of Law: Stories from Everyday Life* (Chicago: University of Chicago Press, 1998); Benjamin Fleury-Steiner and Laura Beth Nielsen, *The New Civil Rights Research: A Constitutive Approach* (Burlington, UK: Ashgate, 2006).

16. Anne Swidler, *Talk of Love: How Culture Matters* (Chicago: University of Chicago Press, 2001), 221.

17. According to one activist I spoke with, there were seven rallies in all.

18. I should note that the footage I have watched and downloaded contains some editing (e.g., added music). However, most speeches appear to be uninterrupted and presented in their entirety. Also, some of the rally speakers were from other parts of the state and country. I still considered these in my analysis, but given my local focus, I was careful not to allow them to carry too much weight.

Bibliography

Aden, Richard C. "Nostalgic Communication as Temporary Escape: *When It Was a Game*'s Reconstruction of a Baseball/Work Community." *Western Journal of Communication* 59, no. 1 (1995): 20–38.

Alexander, Michelle. *The New Jim Crow: Mass Incarceration in an Age of Colorblindness.* New York: New Press, 2012.

Ambrosini, Maurizio. *Itili Invasori: L'inserimento degli Immigranti nel Mercato del Lavoro.* Milan: FrancoAngeli, 1999.

American Civil Liberties Union. "Anti-immigrant Ordinances Have Real Economic and Political Costs for Cities That Enact Them," 2013. Available at http://www.migrante.com.mx/pdf/antimig.pdf. Accessed December 22, 2014.

Argall, David. "A Policy Analysis of the First Six Years of Pennsylvania's Keystone Opportunity Zone Program, 1998 to 2004: Enlightened Economic Development or Corporate Welfare?" Ph.D. diss., Pennsylvania State University, Harrisburg, 2006.

Atia, Mona. "'A Way to Paradise': Pious Neoliberalism, Islam, and Faith-Based Development." *Annals of the Association of American Geographers* 102, no. 4 (2012): 808–827.

Aurand, Harold. "The Lattimer Massacre: Who Owns History?—An Introduction." *Pennsylvania History* 68, no. 1 (2002): 5–10.

Bacon, David. *The Right to Stay Home: How U.S. Policy Drives Mexican Migration.* Boston: Beacon, 2014.

Baptist, Willie, and Jan Rehmann. *Pedagogy of the Poor: Building a Movement to End Poverty.* New York: Teachers College Press, 2011.

Barry, Ellen. "City's Immigration Law Turns Back Clock." *Los Angeles Times*, November 9, 2006.

Beckett, Katherine. *Making Crime Pay: Law and Order in Contemporary American Politics.* New York: Oxford University Press, 1997.

Behdad, Ali. *A Forgetful Nation: On Immigration and Cultural Identity in the United States.* Durham, NC: Duke University Press, 2005.

Beirich, Heidi. "FAIR: The Action Arm." *Southern Poverty Law Center Intelligence Report,* February 2009.

Bell, Derrick. *And We Are Not Saved: The Elusive Quest for Racial Justice.* New York: Basic, 1989.

———. "*Brown v. Board of Education* and the Interest Convergence Dilemma." *Harvard Law Review* 93 (1980): 518–533.

———. *Faces at the Bottom of the Well: The Persistence of Racism.* New York: Basic, 1992.

Blatz, Perry K. *Democratic Miners: Work and Labor Relations in the Anthracite Coal Industry, 1875–1952.* Albany: State University of New York Press, 1994.

Blue, Miranda. "Rep. Lou Barletta: Sanctuary Cities Making U.S. 'A Third-World Country.'" *Right Wing Watch,* April 14, 2014. Available at http://www.rightwingwatch. org/content/rep-lou-barletta-sanctuary-cities-making-us-third-world-country. Accessed December 22, 2014.

———. "Rep. Lou Barletta Says There's 'Nothing More Dangerous' than Immigration Reform, Ties It to 9/11." *Right Wing Watch,* April 10, 2014. Available at http://www .rightwingwatch.org/content/rep-lou-barletta-says-theres-nothing-more-danger ous-immigration-reform-ties-it-911. Accessed December 22, 2014.

Bonilla-Silva, Eduardo. *Racism without Racists: Color-Blind Racism and the Persistence of Racial Inequality in America.* Lanham, MD: Rowman and Littlefield, 2006.

Brown, Wendy. "American Nightmare: Neoliberalism, Neoconservatism, and De-Democratization." *Political Theory* 34, no. 6 (2006): 690–714.

Burawoy, Michael. 1998. "The Extended Case Method." *Sociological Theory* 16, no. 1 (1998): 4–33.

Butler, Stuart. "The Conceptual Evolution of Enterprise Zones." In *Enterprise Zones,* ed. Roy E. Green, 27–40. Newbury Park, CA: Sage, 1991.

Cacho, Lisa Marie. "'The People of California Are Suffering': The Ideology of White Injury in the Discourse of Immigration." *Cultural Values* 4 (2000): 389–418.

———. *Social Death: Racialized Rightlessness and the Criminalization of the Unprotected.* New York: New York University Press, 2012.

Calavita, Kitty. *Immigrants at the Margins: Law, Race, and Exclusion in Southern Europe.* New York: Cambridge University Press, 2005.

———. "The New Politics of Immigration: 'Balanced Budget Conservatism' and the Symbolism of Proposition 187." *Social Problems* 43, no. 3 (1996): 284–305.

———. "U.S. Immigration and Policy Responses: The Limits of Legislation." In *Controlling Immigration: A Global Perspective,* ed. Wayne Cornelius, Takeyuki Tsuda, Phillip Martin, and James Hollifield, 55–81. Stanford, CA: Stanford University Press, 2004.

Cárdenas, Vanessa, and Sophia Kerby. "The State of Latinos in the United States." Center for American Progress, August 8, 2012. Available at https://www.americanprogress .org/issues/race/report/2012/08/08/11984/the-state-of-latinos-in-the-united-states. Accessed May 26, 2014.

"Cargill Supports Hazleton Integration Project." *Standard-Speaker,* March 8, 2014.

Carr, Patrick J., and Maria J. Kefalas. *Hollowing Out the Middle: The Rural Brain Drain and What It Means for America.* Boston: Beacon, 2009.

Cervantes, Nancy, Sasha Khoka, and Bobby Murray. "Hate Unleashed: Los Angeles in the Aftermath of Proposition 187." *Chicana/o-Latina/o Law Review* 17, no. 1 (1995): 1–23.

Chacón, Justin Akers, and Mike Davis. *No One Is Illegal: Fighting Racism and State Violence on the U.S.-Mexico Border.* Chicago: Haymarket, 2006.

"Characteristics of Public and Private Elementary and Secondary School Teachers in the United States: Results from the 2011–2012 Schools and Staffing Survey." National Center for Educational Statistics, 2013. Available at http://nces.ed.gov/pubs2013/2013314.pdf. Accessed March 18, 2015.

Chavez, Leo R. *The Latino Threat: Constructing Immigrants, Citizens, and the Nation.* Stanford, CA: Stanford University Press, 2008.

Chishti, Muzaffar, and Claire Bergeron. "Hazleton Immigration Ordinance that Began with a Bang Goes Out with a Whimper." Migration Policy Institute, Washington, DC, March 28, 2014. Available at http://www.migrationpolicy.org/article/hazleton-immigration-ordinance-began-bang-goes out-whimper. Accessed March 18, 2015.

Chomsky, Avia. *"They Take Our Jobs!" and Twenty Other Myths about Immigration.* Boston: Beacon Press, 2007.

Christman, Amanda. "Guardian Angels May Land Here." *Standard-Speaker,* June 16, 2008.

———. "Hazleton May Soon Have Guardian Angels Watching." *Standard-Speaker,* June 22, 2008.

Clarke, Susan E. "Neighborhood Policy Options: The Reagan Agenda." *Journal of the American Planning Association* 50, no. 4 (1984): 493–501.

Cloud, Dana. "Hegemony or Concordance? The Rhetoric of Tokenism in 'Oprah' Winfrey's Rags-to-Riches Biography." *Critical Studies in Mass Communication* 13, no. 2 (1996): 115–137.

Cohen, Anthony. *The Symbolic Construction of Community.* New York: Tavistock, 1985.

Cohen, Stanley. *Folk Devils and Moral Panics: The Creation of the Mods and Rockers.* London: MacGibbon and Kee, 1972.

Community Area New Development Organization (CAN DO). *The CAN DO Story: A Case History of Successful Community Industrial Development.* Hazleton, PA: CAN DO, 1974.

———. *Upon the Shoulders of Giants: The CAN DO Story.* Hazleton, PA: CAN DO, 1991.

Corporate Research Project. "Cargill: Corporate Rap Sheet." April 9, 2014. Available at http://www.corp-research.org/cargill. Accessed March 6, 2015.

Coutin, Susan Bibler. *Nation of Emigrants: Shifting Boundaries of Citizenship in El Salvador and the United States.* Ithaca, NY: Cornell University Press, 2007.

Cox, Kevin R., and Andrew Mair. "Locality and Community in the Politics of Local Economic Development." *Annals of the Association of American Geographers* 78, no. 2 (1988): 307–325.

Crass, Chris. *Towards Collective Liberation: Anti-racist Organizing, Feminist Praxis, and Movement Building Strategy.* Oakland, CA: PM Press, 2013.

Daniels, Roger. *Coming to America: A History of Immigration and Ethnicity in American Life.* New York: HarperCollins, 2002.

Dasilva, Fabio, and Jim Faught. "Nostalgia: A Sphere and Process of Contemporary Ideology." *Qualitative Sociology* 5, no. 1 (1982): 47–61.

Davis, Dana-Ain. "Narrating the Mute: Racializing and Racism in a Neoliberal Moment." *Souls* 9, no. 4 (2007): 346–360.

De Genova, Nicholas. "Migrant 'Illegality' and Deplorability in Everyday Life." *Annual Review of Anthropology* 31 (2002): 419–447.

Delgado, Richard. "The Law of the Noose: A History of Latino Lynchings." *Harvard Civil Rights–Civil Liberties Law Review* 44 (2009): 297–312.

Delgado, Richard, and Jean Stefancic. *Critical Race Theory: An Introduction.* New York: New York University Press, 2012.

Dino, Jim. "Dodging Mines: Economic Developers Must Downplay Past to Secure Future." *Standard-Speaker,* December 16, 2007.

Donato, Katherine M., Charles Tolbert, Alfred Nucci, and Yukio Kawano. "Changing Faces, Changing Places: The Emergence of New Nonmetropolitan Immigrant Gateways." In *New Faces in New Places: The Changing Geography of American Immigration,* ed. Douglas Massey. New York: Russell Sage Foundation, 2008.

Douglas, Mary. *Purity and Danger.* London: Routledge, 1966.

Downes, Lawrence. "No More 'Illegal Immigrants.'" *New York Times,* April 4, 2013.

Dublin, Thomas, and Walter Licht. *The Face of Decline: The Pennsylvania Anthracite Region in the Twentieth Century.* Ithaca, NY: Cornell University Press, 2005.

Du Bois, W. E. B. *Black Reconstruction in America.* New York: Meridian, 1935.

Dudas, Jeffery. *The Cultivation of Resentment: Treaty Rights and the New Right.* Stanford, CA: Stanford University Press, 2008.

———. "In the Name of Equal Rights: 'Special' Rights and the Politics of Resentment in Post–Civil Rights America." *Law and Society Review* 39, no. 4 (2005): 723–757.

Dudziak, Mary. "*Brown* as a Cold War Case." *Journal of American History* 91 (2004): 32–42.

Duggan, Lisa. *The Twilight of Equality? Neoliberalism, Cultural Politics, and the Attack on Democracy.* Boston: Beacon, 2003.

Ebert, Kim, and Sarah M. Ovink. "Anti-immigrant Ordinances and Discrimination in New and Established Destinations." *American Behavioral Scientist* 58, no. 13 (2014): 1784–1804.

Echegaray, Chris, and Susan Eaton. "We Are from Hazleton: A Baseball Celebrity Helps Bring His Divided Pennsylvania Hometown Together." One Nation Indivisible, 2013. Available at http://www.onenationindivisible.org/wp-content/uploads/2013/06/ONIstoryNo.10-hazelton_Final.pdf. Accessed May 26, 2014.

Emerson, Robert M., Rachel I. Fretz, and Linda L. Shaw. *Writing Ethnographic Fieldnotes.* 2d ed. Chicago: University of Chicago Press, 2007.

Engel, David. "The Oven Bird's Song: Insiders, Outsiders, and Personal Injuries in an American Community." *Law and Society Review* 18, no. 4 (1984): 551–582.

Esbenshade, Jill, Benjamin Wright, Paul Cortopassi, Arthur Reed, and Jerry Flores. "The 'Law-and-Order' Foundations of Local Ordinances: A Four-Locale Study of Hazleton, PA, Escondido, CA, Farmers Branch, TX, and Prince William County, VA." In *Taking Local Control: Immigration Policy Activism in U.S. Cities and States,* ed. Monica W. Varsanyi, 255–274. Stanford, CA: Stanford University Press, 2008.

ESPN. "Joe Maddon's Hazleton." *Outside the Lines,* February 19, 2012. Video available at http://vimeo.com/38722340. Accessed June 17, 2014. Transcript available at http://tv.ark.com/transcript/outside_the_lines/3366/ESPN/Sunday_February_19_2012/599213. Accessed December 22, 2014.

Estrada, Leobardo F., Chris Garcia, Reynaldo Flores Macis, and Lionel Maldonado. "Chicanos in the United States: A History of Exploitation and Resistance." *Daedalus* 110, no. 2 (1981): 103–131.

"Ethnic Changes in Northeastern Pennsylvania: With Special Emphasis on Recent History within the City of Hazleton." Joint Urban Studies Center, July 2006. Available at http://www.institutepa.org/pdf/research/diversity0906.pdf. Accessed July 29, 2015.

Evans, Sara M., and Harry C. Boyte. *Free Spaces: The Sources of Democratic Change in America*. Chicago: University of Chicago Press, 1986.

Ewick, Patricia, and Susan S. Silbey. *The Common Place of Law: Stories from Everyday Life*. Chicago: University of Chicago Press, 1998.

"An Expensive Lesson in Hazleton." Editorial. *Citizen's Voice*, March 8, 2015.

Feagin, Joe R. "Old Poison in New Bottles: The Deep Roots of Modern Nativism." In *Immigrants Out! The New Nativism and the Anti-immigrant Impulse in the United States*, ed. Juan F. Perea, 13–43. New York: New York University Press, 1997.

———. *Racist America: Roots, Current Realities, and Future Reparations*. New York: Routledge, 2010.

———. *Systemic Racism: A Theory of Oppression*. New York: Routledge, 2006.

Feagin, Joe R., and Hernán Vera. *Liberation Sociology*, 2d ed. Boulder, CO: Paradigm, 2008.

Fine, Gary Alan. "The Sociology of the Local: Action and Its Publics." *Sociological Theory* 28, no. 4 (2010): 355–376.

Fine, Gary Alan, and Bill Ellis. *The Global Grapevine: Why Rumors of Terrorism, Immigration, and Trade Matter*. New York: Oxford University Press, 2010.

Fisher, Robert. *Let the People Decide: Neighborhood Organizing in America*, updated ed. New York: Twayne, 1994.

Fishman, Mark. "Crime Waves as Ideology." *Social Problems* 25, no. 5 (1978): 531–543.

Flagg, Barbara. *Was Blind, but Now I See: White Race Consciousness and the Law*. New York: New York University Press, 1997.

Fleury-Steiner, Benjamin, and Jamie Longazel. "Neoliberalism, Community Development, and Anti-immigration Backlash in Hazleton, Pennsylvania." In *Taking Local Control: Immigration Policy Activism in U.S. Cities and States*, ed. Monica W. Varsanyi, 157–172. Stanford, CA: Stanford University Press, 2010.

Fleury-Steiner, Benjamin, and Laura Beth Nielsen. *The New Civil Rights Research: A Constitutive Approach*. Burlington, UK: Ashgate, 2006.

Flores, René D. "Living in the Eye of the Storm: How Did Hazleton's Restrictive Immigration Ordinance Affect Local Interethnic Relations?" *American Behavioral Scientist* 58, no. 13 (2014): 1743–1763.

"For Joe Maddon, It All Started at Home." *Chicago Sun Times*, December 8, 2014. Available at http://chicagosuntimes.com/sports/for-joe-maddon-it-all-started-at-home. Accessed December 22, 2014.

Fox, Cybelle. *Three Worlds of Relief: Race, Immigration, and the American Welfare State from the Progressive Era to the New Deal*. Princeton, NJ: Princeton University Press, 2012.

Frankenburg, Ruth. *White Women, Race Matters: The Social Construction of Whiteness*. Minneapolis: University of Minnesota Press, 1988.

Freire, Paulo. *Pedagogy of the Oppressed*. New York: Continuum, 1989.

Gabriel, Trip. "New Attitude on Immigration Skips an Old Coal Town." *New York Times*, March 31, 2013.

Gallagher, Charles A. "White Racial Formation: Into the Twenty-First Century." In *Critical White Studies: Looking behind the Mirror*, ed. Richard Delgado and Jean Stefancic, 6–11. Philadelphia: Temple University Press, 1997.

Galski, Sam. "CAN DO Criticized on Tax Breaks for Mericle." *Citizen's Voice*, October 2, 2009.

———. "Hazleton Mayor Warns of City's 'Fiscal Cliff.'" *Citizen's Voice*, December 5, 2012.

———. "Immigration Act Appeal Imminent." *Standard-Speaker*, August 29, 2013.

———. "Maddon Envisions Community Center as Bridge to City's Cultural Divide." *Standard-Speaker*, December 1, 2012.

Gándara, Patricia, and Frances Contreras. *The Latino Education Crisis: The Consequences of Failed Social Policies*. Cambridge, MA: Harvard University Press, 2009.

Ganti, Tejaswini. "Neoliberalism." *Annual Review of Anthropology* 43 (2014): 89–104.

Garfinkel, Harold. "Conditions of Successful Degradation Ceremonies." *American Journal of Sociology* 61, no. 5 (1956): 420–424.

Gaventa, John, Barbara Ellen Smith, and Alex Willingham, eds. *Communities in Economic Crisis: Appalachia and the South*. Philadelphia: Temple University Press, 1990.

Geertz, Clifford. *The Interpretation of Cultures: Selected Essays*. New York: Basic Books, 1973.

George, Susan. "A Short History of Neo-liberalism: Twenty Years of Elite Economics and Emerging Opportunities for Structural Change." Paper presented at the Conference on Economic Sovereignty in a Globalising World, March 24–26, 1999. Available at http://www.globalexchange.org/campaigns/econ101/neoliberalism.html. Accessed January 4, 2011.

Giroux, Henry A. "The Terror of Neoliberalism: Rethinking the Significance of Cultural Politics." *College Literature* 32, no. 1 (2005): 1–19.

Goldberg, David Theo. *The Threat of Race: Reflections on Racial Neoliberalism*. Oxford: Blackwell, 2009.

Goldberg-Hiller, Jonathan, and Neal Milner. "Rights as Excess: Understanding the Politics of Special Rights." *Law and Social Inquiry* 28, no. 4 (2003): 1075–1118.

Gómez, Laura. *Manifest Destinies: The Making of the Mexican American Race*. New York: New York University Press, 2007.

Gonzalez-Barrera, Ana, and Jens Manuel Krogstad, "U.S. Deportations of Immigrants Reach Record High in 2013." Pew Research Center, October 2, 2014. Available at http://www.pewresearch.org/fact-tank/2014/10/02/u-s-deportations-of-immigrants-reach-record-high-in-2013. Accessed March 4, 2015.

Goode, Judith. "Faith-Based Organizations in Philadelphia: Neoliberal Ideology and the Decline of Political Activism." *Urban Anthropology* 35, nos. 2–3 (2006): 203–236.

———. "Let's Get Our Act Together: How Racial Discourses Disrupt Neighborhood Activism." In *The New Poverty Studies: The Ethnography of Power, Politics, and Impoverished People in the United States*, ed. Judith Goode and Jeff Maskovsky, 364–398. New York: New York University Press, 2001.

Greenhouse, Carol J., Barbara Yngvesson, and David Engel. *Law and Community in Three American Towns.* Ithaca, NY: Cornell University Press, 1994.

Gregory, Alan. "Homicide Suspect Turned Self In." *Standard-Speaker*, May 17, 2006.

———. "Mourners Remember Victim with Candles, Flowers." *Standard-Speaker*, October 22, 2005.

———. "Victim's Family Wonders Why He Was Target." *Standard-Speaker*, May 17, 2006.

Guinier, Lani, and Gerald Torres. *The Miner's Canary: Enlisting Race, Resisting Power, Transforming Democracy.* Cambridge, MA: Harvard University Press, 2002.

Hackworth, Jason. *The Neoliberal City: Governance, Ideology, and Development in American Urbanism.* Ithaca, NY: Cornell University Press, 2007.

Hagan, John, and Alberto Palloni. "Sociological Criminology and the Mythology of Hispanic Immigrant Crime." *Social Problems* 46 (1999): 617–632.

Haney López, Ian. *Dog Whistle Politics: How Coded Racial Appeals Have Reinvented Racism and Wrecked the Middle Class.* New York: Oxford University Press, 2014.

———. "Post-racial Racism: Racial Stratification and Mass Incarceration in the Age of Obama." *California Law Review* 98, no. 3 (2010): 1023–1074.

———. "Race and Colorblindness after *Hernandez* and *Brown.*" *Chicano-Latino Law Review* 25 (2005): 61–76.

Hardiman, Rita, and Bailey Jackson. "Conceptual Foundations for Social Justice Education." In *Teaching for Diversity and Social Justice*, 2d ed., ed. Maurianne Adams, Lee Anne Bell, and Pat Griffin, 35–66. New York: Routledge, 2007.

Harris, Fredrick C. *The Price of the Ticket: Barack Obama and the Rise and Decline of Black Politics.* New York: Oxford University Press, 2012.

———. "The Rise of Respectability Politics." *Dissent*, Winter 2014. Available at http://www.dissentmagazine.org/article/the-rise-of-respectability-politics. Accessed March 4, 2015.

Harvey, David. *A Brief History of Neoliberalism.* New York: Oxford University Press, 2005.

———. *The Urbanization of Capital: Studies in the History and Theory of Capitalist Urbanization.* Baltimore: Johns Hopkins University Press, 1985.

Hill, Sarah. "Purity and Danger on the U.S.-Mexico Border, 1991–1994." *South Atlantic Quarterly* 105, no. 4 (2006): 777–799.

Hine, Chris. "Joe Maddon Crusades to Save His Hometown." *Chicago Tribune*, February 6, 2015. Available at http://www.chicagotribune.com/sports/baseball/cubs/ct-joe-maddon-hazleton-cubs-spt-0208-20150207-story.html#page=1. Accessed August 13, 2015.

Human Rights Watch. "Blood, Sweat, and Fear: Workers' Rights in U.S. Meat and Poultry Plants." January 24, 2005. Available at: https://www.hrw.org/report/2005/01/24/blood-sweat-and-fear/workers-rights-us-meat-and-poultry-plants. Accessed August 4, 2015.

Ignatiev, Noel. *How the Irish Became White.* New York: Routledge, 1995.

Inda, Jonathan Xavier. *Targeting Immigrants: Government, Technology, and Ethics.* Malden, MA: Blackwell, 2006.

Jackson, Kent. "Cops: Men in Country Illegally, Dealt Drugs." *Standard-Speaker*, May 17, 2006.

———. "Ferdinand: Time to Seal Off the Border." *Standard-Speaker*, May 17, 2006.

———. "Gambling Pay Off: Hazleton-Area Projects get $2M in Gaming Proceeds." *Standard-Speaker*, June 16, 2013.

———. "Police Plan to Continue Intensive Patrols." *Standard-Speaker*, May 17, 2006.

———. "Supreme Court Refusal Ends City's Illegal Immigration Case." *Standard-Speaker*, March 4, 2014.

———. "Tensions Fading as Law Plods through Courts." *Standard-Speaker*, February 3, 2013.

———. "Testimony Contentious at Times." *Standard-Speaker*, March 14, 2007.

Jackson, Kent, and Alan Gregory. "Police, Feds Hit Local Drug Targets." *Standard-Speaker*, May 19, 2006.

Janosov, Robert A., Joseph P. McKerns, Lance E. Metz, Robert C. Wolensky, and Joseph M. Gowaskie. *The Great Strike: Perspectives on the 1902 Anthracite Coal Strike.* Easton, PA: Canal History and Technology Press, 2002.

Jensen, Leif. "New Immigrant Settlements in Rural America: Problems, Prospects, and Policies." Carsey Institute, 2006. Available at http://scholars.unh.edu/cgi/viewcontent.cgi?article=1016&context=carsey. Accessed December 22, 2014.

Johnson, Kevin R. "'Aliens' and the U.S. Immigration Laws: The Social and Legal Construction of Nonpersons." *University of Miami Inter-American Law Review* 28 (1996): 263–292.

Johnson, Kevin R., and Joanna E. Cuevas Ingram. "Anatomy of a Modern-Day Lynching: The Relationship between Hate Crimes against Latina/os and the Debate over Immigration Reform." *North Carolina Law Review* 91 (2013): 1613–1656.

Jordan, Miriam. "In Immigrant Fight, Grass-Roots Groups Boost Their Clout." *Wall Street Journal*, September 28, 2006.

Kelly, Shawn M. "Alleged Killer Slipped through System." *Standard-Speaker*, May 25, 2006.

Khimm, Suzy. "Kris Kobach, Nativist Son." *Mother Jones*, March–April 2012.

Kivel, Paul. "Social Service or Social Change?" In *The Revolution Will Not Be Funded: Beyond the Non-profit Industrial Complex*, ed. Incite! Women of Color against Violence, 129–149. Cambridge, MA: South End, 2007.

Klarman, Michael J. "How *Brown* Changed Race Relations: The Backlash Thesis." *Journal of American History* 81, no. 1 (1994): 81–118.

Klein, Naomi. *The Shock Doctrine: The Rise of Disaster Capitalism*. New York: Picador, 2008.

Kneen, Brewster. *Invisible Giant: Cargill and Its Transnational Strategies*, 2d ed. London: Pluto, 2002.

Kodras, Janet E. "Restructuring the State: Devolution, Privatization, and the Geographic Redistribution of Power and Capacity in Governance." In *State Devolution in America: Implications for a Diverse Society*, ed. Lynn A. Staeheli, Janet E. Kodras, and Colin R. Flint, 79–96. Thousand Oaks, CA: Sage, 1977.

Ku, Leighton. "Why Immigrants Lack Adequate Access to Health Care and Health Insurance." Migration Policy Institute, September 1, 2006. Available at http://www.migrationpolicy.org/article/why-immigrants-lack-adequate-access-health-care-and-health-insurance. Accessed December 22, 2014.

Ku, Leighton, and Sheetal Matani. "Left Out: Immigrants' Access to Health Care and Insurance." *Health Affairs* 20, no. 1 (2001): 247–256.

Kubrin, Charis E., Marjorie Zatz, and Ramiro Martínez. *Punishing Immigrants: Policy, Politics, and Injustice*. New York: New York University Press, 2012.

Laabs, Damon. "Ruling Pleases Latino Residents." *Standard-Speaker*, July 27, 2007.

Lee, Esther Yu-Hsi. "Group Asks Americans to Send Dirty Underwear to Undocumented Immigrants," *Think Progress*, June 26, 2014. Available at http://thinkprogress .org/immigration/2014/06/26/3453174/alipac-dirty-underwear-to-undocumented. Accessed August 4, 2015.

Lee, Matthew T., and Ramiro Martinez Jr. "Immigration Reduces Crime: An Emerging Scholarly Consensus." *Sociology of Crime, Law and Deviance* 13 (2009): 3–16.

LeRoy, Greg. *The Great American Jobs Scam: Corporate Tax Dodging and the Myth of Job Creation*. San Francisco: Berrett-Koehler, 2005.

Light, Mia. "Luzerne County Has the Fastest-Growing Hispanic Population in the Nation." *Standard-Speaker*, September 16, 2009.

———. "Maddon's Vision for Community Center Is Now a Reality." *Standard-Speaker*, June 18, 2013.

———. "Stars Come Out to Support Maddon Effort." *Standard-Speaker*, December 15, 2012.

———. "Stars Out for Fundraiser." *Standard-Speaker*, December 17, 2011.

Long, Tom. "Waves of Hispanic Immigrants Changing Face of NEPA." *Times Leader*, August 14, 2005.

Longazel, Jamie. "Moral Panic as Racial Degradation Ceremony: Racial Stratification and the Local-Level Backlash against Latina/o Immigrants." *Punishment and Society* 15, no. 1 (2013): 96–119.

———. "Rhetorical Barriers to Mobilizing for Immigrant Rights: White Innocence and Latina/o Abstraction." *Law and Social Inquiry* 39, no. 3 (2014): 580–600.

López, María Pabón. "An Essay Examining the Murder of Luis Ramirez and the Emergence of Hate Crimes against Latino Immigrants in the United States." *Arizona State Law Journal* 44, no. 155 (2012): 155–173.

Luker, Kristin. *Abortion and the Politics of Motherhood*. Berkeley: University of California Press, 1984.

Macek, Steve. *Urban Nightmares: The Media, the Right, and the Moral Panic over the City*. Minneapolis: University of Minnesota Press, 2006.

Massey, Douglas, ed. *New Faces in New Places: The Changing Geography of American Immigration*. New York: Russell Sage Foundation, 2008.

Mauriello, Tracie. "Rally Backs Hazleton Mayor." *Pittsburgh Post-Gazette*, June 3, 2007.

McCann, Michael. "On Legal Rights Consciousness: A Challenging Analytical Tradition." In *The New Civil Rights Research: A Constitutive Approach*, ed. Benjamin Fleury-Steiner and Laura Beth Nielsen, ix–xxix. Burlington, UK: Ashgate, 2006.

———. *Rights at Work: Pay Equity Reform and the Politics of Legal Mobilization*. Chicago: University of Chicago Press, 1994.

McKanders, Karla Mari. "Welcome to Hazleton! 'Illegal' Immigrants Beware: Local Immigration Ordinances and What the Federal Government Must Do about It." *Loyola University Chicago Law Journal* 39, no. 1 (2007): 3–48.

Miller, Donald L., and Richard E. Sharpless. *The Kingdom of Coal: Work, Enterprise, and*

Ethnic Communities in the Mine Fields. Philadelphia: University of Pennsylvania Press, 1985.

Mize, Ronald L., and Grace Peña Delgado. *Latino Immigrants in the United States.* Malden, MA: Polity, 2012.

Mocarsky, Steven. "Expert Says Many Members of Highly Dangerous Gang in Hazleton Are Illegal Immigrants." *Times Leader,* March 22, 2007.

Monitz, Kelly. "Mayor Still Getting Fan Mail, Notoriety." *Standard-Speaker,* March 18, 2007.

———. "Verdict Angers, Frightens Latino Community." *Standard-Speaker,* May 7, 2009.

———. "Wyoming Street Business Owners Went to Hazleton Mayor Lou Barletta Last Week to Talk about Community Perceptions Following a Fatal Shooting Downtown." *Standard-Speaker,* November 17, 2005.

Mossberger, Karen. *The Politics of Ideas and the Spread of Enterprise Zones.* Washington, DC: Georgetown University Press, 2000.

Muhammad, Khalil Gibran. *The Condemnation of Blackness: Race, Crime, and the Making of Modern Urban America.* Cambridge, MA: Harvard University Press, 2011.

"A Nation of Immigrants: A Portrait of the 40 Million, Including 11 Million Unauthorized." Pew Research Center, January 29, 2013. Available at http://www.pewhispanic .org/2013/01/29/a-nation-of-immigrants. Accessed December 22, 2014.

Nevins, Joseph. *Operation Gatekeeper: The Rise of the Illegal Alien and the Making of the U.S.-Mexico Boundary.* New York: Routledge, 2002.

Newman, Kathe, and Phillip Ashton. "Neoliberal Urban Policy and New Paths of Neighborhood Change in the American Inner City." *Environment and Planning* 36, no. 7 (2004): 1151–1172.

Ngai, Mae. *Impossible Subjects: Illegal Aliens and the Making of Modern America.* Princeton, NJ: Princeton University Press, 2004.

Nielsen, Amy L., Matthew T. Lee, and Ramiro Martinez Jr. "Integrating Race, Place, and Motive in Social Disorganization Theory: Lessons from a Comparison of Black and Latino Homicide Types in Two Immigrant Destination Cities." *Criminology* 43 (2005): 837–872.

Nill, Andrea Christina. "Latinos and SB 1070: Demonization, Dehumanization, and Disenfranchisement." *Harvard Latino Law Review* 14 (2011): 35–66.

Norton, Michael I., and Dan Ariely. "Building a Better America—One Wealth Quintile at a Time." *Perspectives on Psychological Science* 6 (2011): 9–12.

Norton, Michael I., and Samuel R. Sommers. "Whites See Racism as a Zero-Sum Game that They Are Now Losing." *Perspectives on Psychological Science* 6, no. 3 (2011): 215–218.

Novak, Michael. *The Guns of Lattimer.* New York: Basic, 1978.

O'Brien, Eileen. *Whites Confront Racism: Antiracists and Their Paths to Action.* New York: Rowman and Littlefield, 2001.

Omi, Michael, and Howard Winant. *Racial Formation in the United States: From the 1960s to the 1980s.* New York: Routledge, 1986.

Ousey, Graham C., and Charis E. Kubrin. "Exploring the Connection between Immigration and Violent Crime Rates in U.S. Cities, 1980–2000." *Social Problems* 56, no. 3 (2009): 447–473.

Paredes, Américo. *With His Pistol in His Hand: A Border Ballad and Its Hero.* Austin: University of Texas Press, 1958.

Payne, Charles M. "'The Whole United States Is Southern!' *Brown v. Board* and the Mystification of Race." *Journal of American History* 91, no. 3 (2004): 83–91.

Peck, Jamie, and Adam Tickell. "Neoliberalizing Space." *Antipode* 34, no. 3 (2002): 380–404.

Peffley, Mark, and Jon Hurwitz. "Persuasion and Resistance: Race and the Death Penalty in America." *American Journal of Political Science* 51, no. 4 (2007): 996–1012.

Pew Hispanic Center, "Modes of Entry for the Unauthorized Migrant Population." Fact sheet, May 22, 2006. Available at http://www.pewhispanic.org/files/2011/10/19.pdf. Accessed December 22, 2014.

Pilkington, Ed. "Pennsylvania's Police Accused of Cover-Up in Immigrant's Murder." *The Guardian*, December 16, 2009.

powell, john a. *Racing to Justice: Transforming Our Conception of Self and Other to Build an Inclusive Society*. Bloomington: Indiana University Press, 2012.

Powell, Michael, and Michelle García. "Pa. City Put Illegal Immigrants on Notice." *Washington Post*, August 22, 2006.

Provine, Doris Marie. "Justice as Told by Judges: The Case of Litigation over Local Anti-immigrant Legislation." *Studies in Social Justice* 3, no. 2 (2009): 231–245.

Quiroga, Seline Szkupinski, Dulce M. Medina, and Jennifer Glick. "In the Belly of the Beast: Effects of Anti-immigration Policy on Latino Community Members." *American Behavioral Scientist* 58, no. 13 (2014): 1723–1742.

Ragan, Tom. "Police Identify Acquaintance of Victim as Chief Suspect." *Standard-Speaker*, October 22, 2005.

Reid, Lesley Williams, Harold E. Weiss, Robert M. Adelman, and Charles Jaret. "The Immigration-Crime Relationship: Evidence across U.S. Metropolitan Areas." *Social Science Research* 34 (2005): 757–780.

Riessman, Catherine Kohler. *Narrative Analysis*. Thousand Oaks, CA: Sage, 1993.

Rios, Victor. *Punished: Policing the Lives of Black and Latino Boys*. New York: New York University Press, 2011.

Rochmes, Daniel A., and G. A. Elmer Griffin. "The Cactus That Must Not Be Mistaken for a Pillow: White Racial Formation among Latinos." *Souls* 8, no. 2 (2006): 77–91.

Roediger, David. *Seizing Freedom: Slave Emancipation and Liberty for All*. London: Verso, 2014.

———. *Toward the Abolition of Whiteness*. London: Verso, 1994.

———. *The Wages of Whiteness: Race and the Making of the American Working Class*. New York: Verso, 1991.

Rolnick, Arthur J. "Congress Should End the Economic War among the States Testimony." Federal Reserve Bank of Minneapolis, October 10, 2007. Available at https://www.minneapolisfed.org/publications/special-studies/economic-bidding-wars/rolnick-testimony. Accessed July 30, 2015.

Rolnick, Arthur J., and Melvin L. Burstein. "Congress Should End the Economic War among the States." Federal Reserve Bank of Minneapolis, January 1994. Available at https://minneapolisfed.org/publications/annual-reports/congress-should-end-the-economic-war-among-the-states. Accessed July 30, 2015.

Romero, Mary. "Racial Profiling and Immigration Law Enforcement: Rounding Up the Usual Suspects in the Latino Community." *Critical Sociology* 32, nos. 2–3 (2006): 447–473.

Rose, Dan. *Energy Transition and the Local Community: A Theory of Society Applied to Hazleton, Pennsylvania*. Philadelphia: University of Pennsylvania Press, 1981.

Ross, Thomas. "The Rhetorical Tapestry of Race: White Innocence and Black Abstraction." *William and Mary Law Review* 32, no. 1 (1990): 1–36.

Rubio-Goldsmith, Pat, Mary Romero, Raquel Rubio-Goldsmith, Manuel Escobedo, and Laura Khoury. "Ethno-Racial Profiling and State Violence in a Southwest Barrio." *Aztlán: A Journal of Chicano Studies* 34, no. 1 (2009): 93–123.

Sáenz, Rogelio, Cecilia Menjívar, and San Juanita Edilia García. "Arizona's SB 1070: Setting Conditions for Violations of Human Rights Here and Beyond." In *Sociology and Human Rights: A Bill of Rights for the Twenty-First Century*, ed. Judith Blau and Mark Frezzo, 155–178. Newbury Park, CA: Sage, 2012.

Safa, Helen I. "Women and Globalization: Lessons from the Dominican Republic." In *The Spaces of Neoliberalism: Land, Place and Family in Latin America*, ed. Jacquelyn Chase, 141–158. Bloomfield, CT: Kumarian, 2002.

Sampson, Robert J. "Rethinking Immigration and Crime." *Contexts* 7, no. 1 (2008): 28–33.

Sampson, Robert J., Jeffrey D. Morenoff, and Stephen Raudenbuch. "Social Autonomy of Racial and Ethnic Disparities in Violence." *American Journal of Public Health* 95 (2005): 224–232.

Santa Ana, Otto. *Brown Tide Rising: Metaphors of Latinos in Contemporary American Public Discourse*. Austin: University of Texas Press, 2002.

Savage, David G. and Nicole Gaouette, "Judge Rejects Hazleton Law on Immigrants," *Los Angeles Times*, July 27, 2007. Available at http://articles.latimes.com/2007/jul/27/nation/na-hazleton27. Accessed August 10, 2015.

Schlosser, Eric. "The Chain Never Stops." *Mother Jones*, July–August 2001. Available at http://www.motherjones.com/politics/2001/07/dangerous-meatpacking-jobs-eric-schlosser. Accessed December 22, 2014.

Schudson, Michael. "The Present in the Past versus the Past in the Present." *Communication* 11 (1989): 105–112.

Sheehan, Dan, and Jose Cardenas. "New Culture in Old Coal Town." *Morning Call*, July 25, 2005.

Skocpol, Theda, and Vanessa Williamson. *The Tea Party and the Remaking of Republican Conservatism*. New York: Oxford University Press, 2012.

Smith, Mychal Denzel. "Three Ways to Fight Racism in 2014." *The Nation*, January 3, 2014. Available at http://www.thenation.com/blog/177772/three-ways-fight-racism-2014. Accessed December 22, 2014.

Soni, Saket. "Low-Wage Nation." *The Nation*, January 20, 2014.

Soper, Spencer, and Matt Birkbeck. "Hazleton Gears Up to Keep Illegals Out." *Morning Call*, July 15, 2006.

Sosar, David P. "Water Authority for Sale: Disadvantages of Selling City Assets to Purge Budgetary Deficits." *International Journal of Humanities and Social Science* 1, no. 18 (2011): 134–142.

Spence, Lester. *Stare in the Darkness: The Limits of Hip-Hop and Black Politics*. Minneapolis: University of Minnesota Press, 2011.

Staub, Andrew. "Census: County Demographic Changed Greatly in Last Decade." *Standard-Speaker*, December 5, 2010.

Stein, Arlene. *The Stranger Next Door: The Story of a Small Community's Battle over Sex, Faith, and Civil Rights*. Boston: Beacon, 2012.

Steinbugler, Amy C., Julie E. Press, and Janice Johnson Dias. "Gender, Race, and Affirmative Action: Operationalizing Intersectionality in Survey Research." *Gender and Society* 20 (2006): 822–823.

Stoecker, Randy. "The CDC Model of Urban Redevelopment: A Critique and an Alternative." *Journal of Urban Affairs* 19, no. 1 (1997): 1–22.

Stumpf, Juliet P. "States of Confusion: The Rise of State and Local Power over Immigration." *North Carolina Law Review* 86 (2008): 1557–1618.

Sullivan, Sean. "GOP Congressman Says House 'Probably' Has Votes to Impeach Obama." *Washington Post*, June 17, 2014. Available at http://www.washingtonpost.com/blogs/post-politics/wp/2014/06/17/gop-congressman-says-house-probably-has-votes-to-impeach-obama. Accessed December 22, 2014.

Swidler, Anne. *Talk of Love: How Culture Matters*. Chicago: University of Chicago Press, 2001.

Tanger, Stephanie E. "Enforcing Corporate Responsibility for Violations of Workplace Immigration Laws: The Case of Meatpacking." *Harvard Latino Law Review* 59 (2006): 59–89.

Tarone, L. A. "Barletta Team Vows Appeal." *Standard-Speaker*, July 27, 2007.

———. "Has CAN DO Lowered Its Standards?" *Standard-Speaker*, August 14, 2004.

———. "Hazle Allows CAN DO to Include Township in Opportunity Zone Quest." *Standard-Speaker*, November 18, 1998.

———. "Lou Barletta Will Be Called by Plaintiffs Monday." *Standard-Speaker*, March 9, 2007.

———. "Pennsylvania's Keystone Opportunity Zone Program and Its Sister the Keystone Opportunity Expansion Zone Program Cost the Hazleton Area School District $978,587 in Lost Revenue during the Last School Year." *Standard-Speaker*, October 20, 2003.

———. "Write On: Barletta Knocks Marsicano off Ballot." *Standard-Speaker*, May 16, 2007.

Thompson, Gabriel. "The Workers Who Bring You Black Friday: My Life as a Temp in California's Inland Empire, the Belly of the Online Shopping Beast." *The Nation*, November 26, 2013. Available at: http://www.thenation.com/article/holiday-crush. Accessed July 30, 2015.

Tickell, Adam, and Jamie Peck. "Making Global Rules: Globalization or Neoliberalization?" In *Remaking the Global Economy: Economic-Geographical Perspectives*, ed. Jamie Peck and Henry Wai-Chung Yeung, 163–177. Thousand Oaks, CA: Sage, 2003.

Turner, George A. "The Lattimer Massacre: A Perspective from the Ethnic Community." *Pennsylvania History* 69, no. 1 (2002): 11–30.

U.S. Bureau of Labor Statistics. "A Profile of the Working Poor, 2012." March 2014. Available at http://www.bls.gov/cps/cpswp2012.pdf. Accessed December 22, 2014.

Varsanyi, Monica W. *Taking Local Control: Immigration Policy Activism in U.S. Cities and States*. Stanford, CA: Stanford University Press, 2010.

Weigt, Jill. "Compromises to Carework: The Social Organization of Mothers' Experiences in the Low-Wage Labor Market after Welfare Reform." *Social Problems* 53, no. 3 (2006): 322–351.

Weissman, Deborah M. "The Politics of Narrative: Law and the Representation of Mexican Criminality." *Fordham International Law Journal* 38 (2015): 141–204.

Welch, Catherine. "The Archeology of Business Networks: The Use of Archival Records in Case Study Research." *Journal of Strategic Management* 8, no. 2 (2000): 197–208.

Whalen, Jill. "Community Center Has a Lot to Offer." *Standard-Speaker,* June 16, 2013.

———. "Maddon 'HIP' to Change in Hazleton." *Standard-Speaker,* September 20, 2011.

Winant, Howard. "Behind Blue Eyes: Whiteness and Contemporary U.S. Racial Politics." In *Off White: Readings on Race, Power, and Society,* ed. Michelle Fine, Lois Weis, Linda C. Powell, and L. Mun Wong, 3–16. New York: Routledge, 1997.

Wolensky, Kenneth C. "The Lattimer Massacre." Historic Pennsylvania Leaflet no. 15. Pennsylvania Historical and Museum Commission, Harrisburg, 1997. Available at http://www.portal.state.pa.us/portal/server.pt/community/events/4279/lattimer_massacre/478735. Accessed March 4, 2015.

Zirin, Dave. *Welcome to the Terrordome: The Pain, Politics, and Promise of Sports.* Chicago: Haymarket, 2007.

Zogby International. "Greater Hazleton Area Civic Partnership." Report submitted to the Greater Hazleton Area Civic Partnership, Hazleton, PA, 2007.

Index

Jamie Longazel is an Assistant Professor of Sociology and a Human Rights Center Research Fellow at the University of Dayton and the co-author (with Benjamin Fleury-Steiner) of *The Pains of Mass Imprisonment*.